The Companion
to

The Companion to French Cinema

Ginette Vincendeau

BFI PUBLISHING

First published in 1996 by
Cassell
Wellington House
125 Strand
London WC2R 0BB
and the
British Film Institute
21 Stephen Street
London W1P 2LN

The British Film Institute exists to promote appreciation, enjoyment, protection and development of moving image culture in and throughout the whole of the United Kingdom. Its activities include the National Film and Television Archive; the National Film Theatre; the Museum of the Moving Image; the London Film Festival; the production and distribution of film and video; funding and support for regional activities; Library and Information Services; Stills, Posters and Designs; Research, Publishing and Education; and the monthly *Sight and Sound* magazine.

British Library Cataloguing-in-Publication Data
A catalogue record for this book is available from the British Library.

ISBN 0 304 34157 6

Cover design by Jamie Tanner
Cover still: *Indochine*
courtesy of Electric Pictures

Typesetting by Fakenham Photosetting Ltd
Fakenham, Norfolk

Printed and bound in Great Britain by Redwood Books,
Trowbridge, Wiltshire

CONTENTS

ACKNOWLEDGMENTS

The Companion to French Cinema regroups and updates all the French material I wrote for the Cassell/BFI *Encyclopedia of European Cinema* (1995), which I edited. My gratitude therefore goes in the first place to all those who made the *Encyclopedia* possible. But I especially wish to thank the following collaborators for their help with the research, checking and editing of the French material: Claire Beadle, Chris Darke, Nicky Foster, Simon Horrocks, Guy Jowett, Valerie Orpen, Richard Perkins, Markku Salmi, Carrie Tarr and David Wilson. I am also grateful to the writers who contributed to the entries on European personnel and issues included in the 'French Cinema in Europe' section: John Caughie, Chris Darke, Richard Dyer, Thomas Elsaesser, Peter Evans, Cathy Fowler, Joseph Garncarz, Sabine Gottgetreu, Simon Horrocks, Andrea Lang, Richard Taylor, and Ania Witkowska. I owe special thanks to the staff of the BFI Library, and especially David Sharp and Gillian Hartnoll, and to Sue Bobbermein, Ed Buscombe and Roma Gibson in BFI Publishing.

A work such as this inevitably relies on other sources: trade publications, data provided by embassies and film commissions, journals, filmographies, catalogues, dictionaries, monographs, etc. It is impossible to cite them all, though many appear in the bibliographical notes at the end of some entries and in the final bibliography, as well as with the statistics. May they all be thanked collectively here, including the BFI Library.

Stills were provided by BFI Stills, Posters and Designs.

Last but not least, I am most grateful to my husband Simon Caulkin, for his heroic moral, practical and professional support, as ever.

Ginette Vincendeau
London, February 1996

Ginette Vincendeau is Professor of Film Studies at the University of Warwick (UK). She is the author of numerous articles on French cinema and co-editor of *French Film, Texts and Contexts* and *20 ans de théories féministes*, and co-author of *Jean Gabin, Anatomie d'un mythe*. She is the author of the forthcoming BFI Film Classic *Pépé le Moko* and of *The Art of Spectacle: Popular French Cinema in the 1930s*.

INTRODUCTION

'If World War I enabled American cinema to ruin French cinema, World War II, together with the advent of television, enabled it to finance, that is to say ruin, all the cinemas of Europe.'

Jean-Luc Godard, *Histoire(s) du cinéma* (1989)

A year ago in 1995, Godard's typically sweeping statement seemed to have come true. France, belatedly and despite a valiant resistance, was going the way of the rest of Europe, where indigenous cinema has all but collapsed. French screens *are* increasingly dominated by American product. Yet the 1995 French box-office points to a more hopeful scenario: two comedies, Jean-Marie Poiré's *Les Anges gardiens* (starring Gérard Depardieu and Christian Clavier) and Josiane Balasko's *Gazon maudit/French Twist* (with Balasko and Victoria Abril), beat the year's American top blockbuster, *Die Hard III*. Against relentless competition (and vastly superior financial means) from Hollywood, the resilience of contemporary French cinema is to be celebrated.

Altogether, 120 films were produced or co-produced in France in 1995, ranging from monumental productions such as *Le Hussard sur le toit/The Horseman on the Roof* (directed by Jean-Paul Rappeneau, and starring Juliette Binoche) and *La Cité des enfants perdus/The City of Lost Children* (Jean-Pierre Jeunet and Marc Caro) to films by established directors – for instance Claude Chabrol (*La Cérémonie/ Judgement in Stone*), Eric Rohmer (*Les Rendez-vous de Paris*) and Bertrand Tavernier (*L'Appât/The Bait*) – to small-scale films by young auteurs. Among the latter, particularly remarkable for their combination of aesthetic value and social relevance, are *La Haine/Hate* (Mathieu Kassovitz), *En avoir ou pas* (Laetitia Masson), and *N'oublie pas que tu vas mourir* (Xavier Beauvois), all evidence of a new generation in the long tradition of French auteur cinema. It is the tradition which has produced the most famous figures of French cinema, from Abel Gance and Germaine Dulac through Jean Renoir to Agnès Varda, François Truffaut, Jean-Luc Godard, Marguerite Duras and Leos Carax, and many others, and internationally renowned 'movements' such as Poetic Realism and the New Wave, not to mention its own stars (Jeanne Moreau for example). Its success and projection of national identity stem from a combination of personal vision, aesthetic specificity and 'universal' themes. If the significance of auteur cinema lies in its cultural prestige rather than box-office success, it nevertheless has been an important category, since the 1920s, in the general economy of French film. Still at the core of the *identity* of Fench national cinema, it has been systematically supported by state cultural policy since World War II, by independent producers such as Georges de Beauregard and more recently Marin Karmitz and Claude Berri, and of course by television (especially Canal Plus). It is also at the heart of critical practice, as shown in journals such as *Cahiers du cinéma* and *Positif*, still coming out forty years after the New Wave.

But independent auteurs can only emerge where there is a solid popular base. The success of *Les Anges gardiens* and *Gazon maudit* confirms that, though undoubtedly under threat, this base is still in place after a century. As Josiane Balasko put it in a recent interview: 'There is no future for French cinema without popular cinema [...] there is no art cinema without popular cinema.' This is worth emphasizing, because it is often forgotten, outside France, that French cinema is *also* – and for its home audience, primarily – a popular cinema. It is a cinema with its own auteurs (for example Pierre Chenal, Christian-Jaque, Henri Verneuil, Claude Berri, Coline Serreau), genres (comedy, the policier, more recently the 'cinéma du look' and the heritage film), and stars: Fernandel, Jean Gabin, Brigitte Bardot, Bourvil, Martine Carol, Louis de Funès, Catherine Deneuve, Isabelle Adjani and Béatrice Dalle to name a few.

The economic viability of both auteur and popular French cinema is constantly under threat, and the trade (as it has since the 1920s) rightly talks of a state of permanent 'crisis'. But the *cultural* space occupied by French cinema in France is still enviably vital, as shown by the media attention devoted to it, from the Césars ceremony to a wide range of film journals. Critics outside (and sometimes in) France often deride the high level of public subsidy, speaking of an 'official' cinema. But this is to forget that there is also a high level of genuine popular engagement with the medium. As Balasko also said, 'Luckily, there is still a home audience for popular French film.' 1995 may have been a particularly good year, but let us hope it will be followed by many others.

The Companion to French Cinema aims to bring together, under one volume, the breadth and variety of French cinema, from the world's pioneering screening by the Lumière brothers on 28 December 1895 in Paris, to the spirited resistance against American 'invasion' in the mid-1990s. Its objective is to do so in a concise, accessible and informative manner. The desire to include a considerable amount of information in a manageable and affordable single volume, however, dictated drastic choices, both in the number of entries and in their length. Many people, genres and institutions had to be left out and every reader no doubt will regret the exclusion of some, as I do myself. *The Companion to French Cinema* thus does not claim to be exhaustive, but to provide an accurate and comprehensive picture of French cinema, including both its key figures and 'golden eras', and its popular traditions. This book does not claim to be 'impartial' either; the entries contain key factual points about a person, institution or critical concept, but also indicate areas of interest and debate, in other words not just what a person, type of film or institution did and when, but why they are interesting, famous or controversial. Extreme care has been taken to check all sources, but as no work of reference can ever be without errors, I apologize in advance for any that may have remained.

Contents

The Companion to French Cinema contains the following:

1. An historical overview of French cinema. Readers unfamiliar with French cinema are encouraged to read this first, before 'browsing' or looking up entries.
2. The core of the book is made of over 200 alphabetically arranged entries, on personnel (directors, actors, critics, musicians, producers, set designers), critical concepts (e.g. Poetic Realism, *Cinéma beur*) and institutions (e.g. Cinémathèque française).
3. A section entitled 'French cinema in Europe', which draws on material from *The Encyclopedia of European Cinema*. This includes entries on film personnel from other countries who have made a significant contribution to French cinema (such as Chantal Akerman, Luis Buñuel, Roman Polanski), and entries on pan-European issues (for instance European art cinema, Lesbian and gay cinema in Europe).
4. Two appendices:
– Appendix I: production and audience statistics in Europe.
– Appendix II: select bibliography on European and French cinema.

Conventions

Personnel entries are classified under their surname or most common name. This is followed by their date and place of birth and, as the case may be, death, as well as their real name. The country of birth/death is only mentioned if it *not* France. As a rule, biographical details such as marriage and children are indicated only if considered relevant to the work or achievement of this person.
Film titles and dates, and filmographies. On first mention, films are indicated in the entry under their original title, followed by their British release title or an English translation, when necessary; thereafter only the original title is mentioned. For space reasons, filmographies are not necessarily exhaustive. Three cases apply:
• all films, or all important films, are mentioned in the text, in which case no filmography follows;
• all other films made by the person (and not mentioned in the text) are added at the end. This is indicated by 'Other films', followed by the films in chronological order. If a complete filmography is provided, it is indicated as 'Films';
• a selection of other major films made by the person (and not men-

tioned in the text) are added at the end. This is indicated by 'Other films include', followed by the films in chronological order.

Whenever possible, the date indicated is that of the release of the film in France.

Bibliography. Some entries are followed by a single short bibliographical reference (under 'Bib') in an abbreviated form, to direct the reader to further reading. There is also a bibliography on European cinema and French cinema in appendix II.

Cross-referencing. Throughout the text, persons, institutions and concepts that have their own entry in the rest of the book are signalled by an asterisk placed after the name. Alternatively, an arrow can point to related material. Between entries, other terminologies or related persons may be signalled [e.g. 'IDHEC: see FEMIS']

THE COMPANION TO FRENCH CINEMA

FRANCE: AN HISTORICAL OVERVIEW

'Let French cinema be real cinema, let French cinema be really French.' (Louis Delluc*)

Silent cinema

Louis and Auguste Lumière's* first public (and paying) screening of films at the Grand Café in Paris on 28 December 1895 remains the reference point for the beginning of world cinema (despite the numerous inventions and experimentations leading up to that moment, including those of Max Skladanowsky among many others). The key to the historic success of the Lumière Cinematograph was its ability to project images to an audience (as opposed to Edison's single-viewer Kinetoscope), creating cinema as a *social* activity, at a time of rising popularity for a new 'image culture', notably with postcards, illustrated magazines, and world exhibitions (the Paris World Exhibition of 1900 was instrumental in promoting the new cinema).

Early French cinema was, as elsewhere, a fairground entertainment presenting novelties: short 'realist views' such as the Lumière films – *L'Arrivée d'un train en gare de La Ciotat*, *La Sortie des usines Lumière*, *Le Déjeuner de bébé* (all 1895) – comic scenes such as *L'Arroseur arrosé* (1895) and Alice Guy's* farce *La Fée aux choux/The Cabbage Fairy* (1896), inspired by contemporary cartoons and music-hall shows. It is customary to oppose the documentary impulse of the Lumières' cinema to the fiction of Georges Méliès*, who imported the tricks of his stage phantasmagorias to the screen, though the distinction now appears less clear-cut. Apart from its popular success and creative ferment, the distinctiveness of early French cinema was the business acumen of its practitioners. The Lumières promptly took their Cinematograph to all corners of the globe, fixing for posterity the term 'cinema'. While Méliès also expanded, Charles Pathé's* and Léon Gaumont's* newly created companies were extraordinarily successful at producing, distributing (switching from selling to renting in 1907) and exhibiting their films, both at home and abroad; Pathé's Gallic cockerel and Gaumont's daisy became household symbols the world over, holding sway until World War I. Films were exhibited in fairgrounds and in theatres, *cafés-concerts* and department stores, until permanent cinemas became the main sites of exhibition between 1906 (the Omnia-Pathé) and 1911. Major distribution companies such as Etablissements Aubert and AGC were also set up. In June 1916 the first centralised censorship body was instituted, for the granting of exhibition certificates, a system which formed the basis of most subsequent censorship legislation.

Pathé and Gaumont (joined from 1907 by Eclair, Eclipse, Lux and smaller companies) and Méliès (until 1911) developed a multitude of early genres: *actualités*, comic chase and trick films, *féeries*, religious scenes, historical films, erotic films, realist films, melodrama, animation (Emile Cohl*), even 'Westerns' (shot in the Camargue). Although initially it did not matter much who 'directed', emerging personalities included, after Guy and Méliès, Ferdinand Zecca, Léonce Perret, Albert Capellani and Victorin Jasset. The years preceding World War I saw the move to longer films and a rich field of detective series (*Nick Carter*), and especially comic series: *Bébé*, *Bout-de-Zan*, *Calino*, *Onésime*, *Pétronille*, etc., dominated by actors André Deed* (*Boireau*, *Cretinetti*), Max Linder* (*Max*) and 'Prince'* (*Rigadin*). Concurrently, the Film d'Art* and SCAGL (a branch of Pathé) crystallised the process of 'embourgeoisement' of the cinema, or, in historian Tom Gunning's words, its transition from the 'cinema of attractions' to the 'cinema of narrative integration', by adapting literary works (though the traditional view that all pre-1908 French cinema was 'primitive' has been challenged by Richard Abel [> BIBLIOGRAPHY]). Between 1909 and 1911 there was a move to even longer films, partly to get ahead of American competition. Like Italy and Denmark, France moved to features, with a preference for realist films (*Les Victimes de l'alcool*, 1911), including historical films and Louis Feuillade's* crime serials (*Fantômas*, 1913–14).

The rise of an increasingly organised Hollywood film industry and the outbreak of World War I dealt a fatal blow to the French world hegemony, and French cinema entered a state of crisis until the coming of sound. Whereas France had dominated the pre-1914 world market, by 1925 only seventy-three French films were shown on the French market, compared to over 500 American films. Pathé and Gaumont were dismantled in the 1920s, leading to an endemic 'atomisation' of the French film industry, though both resurfaced later in different guises. The long and arduous struggle against Hollywood had begun, although, in a now familiar phenomenon, American films – Chaplin, Keaton, Cecil B. DeMille, Griffith – also found their most enthusiastic audiences in France. A 'first wave' of passion for the cinema as an art developed with the French avant-garde*, whose interests were both formal and cultural: defining the specificity of film in theory and in practice, exploring (already) authorship, setting up film clubs, art cinemas and film journals. Louis Delluc* and Ricciotto Canudo* were the movement's first critics; Delluc (*Fièvre*, 1921), Marcel L'Herbier* (*El Dorado*, 1921), Jean Epstein* (*Cœur fidèle*, 1923), Germaine Dulac* (*La Fête espagnole*, 1920) were at the centre of its film-making experiments, though all also worked in narrative film; Abel Gance* in particular (*La Roue*, 1921–23, *Napoléon*, 1927) combined formal experiments with great popular epics. More cosmopolitan and politically motivated practitioners joined them, including René Clair*, Jean Grémillon*, Man Ray, Luis Buñuel*, Jean Vigo*, Marcel Carné*, Alberto Cavalcanti* and others. Popular genres continued to flourish, even though production had declined. These included comedies and serials (Feuillade's *Judex*, 1917), bourgeois melodramas, realist films (Jacques Feyder's* *Crainquebille*, 1923), 'modern studio spectaculars' (L'Herbier's *L'Argent*, 1929), colonial melodramas (Feyder's *L'Atlantide*, 1921) and historical epics (Raymond Bernard's* *Le Miracle des loups*, 1924), this last genre greatly influenced by the important group of Russian émigrés at the Albatros studio of Alexandre Volkoff. [> EMIGRATION AND EUROPEAN CINEMA]

Although the coming of sound signalled the end of some avant-garde practices, continuity was evident in the carrying over of some silent preoccupations into the sound era, especially realism; many avant-garde film-makers also continued or began a successful career in the 1930s (L'Herbier, Gance, Clair, Feyder, Julien Duvivier* and Jean Renoir*).

1930–1960: the classical age

The French film industry was ill-prepared for the coming of sound (although French scientists had invented sound systems as early as 1900, none had been patented) and technically the transition was anything but smooth: American and German systems were imported, short-lived methods such as multi-language versions were tried (1929–32), especially at the Paramount studios in Joinville ('Babel-on-Seine'), and the first French sound films (*L'Eau du Nil*, *Le Collier de la Reine*, 1929) were little more than silent films with sound passages. René Clair's populist *Sous les toits de Paris* (1930), on the other hand, shot for the powerful German firm Tobis at the Epinay studios near Paris, became a worldwide hit. It used sound and music imaginatively and fixed for decades to come a nostalgic vision of old Paris and its 'little people'.

French film-makers quickly adapted to the talkies, and the early 1930s saw a rapid increase in features – up to 157 in 1931, settling down eventually at 100–120 films a year, a figure which with the exception of the 1940s has been maintained to the present day. Studios around Paris (Epinay, Boulogne-Billancourt, Joinville) and in the south of France (Marseilles, Nice) invested in equipment and expertise. Many new large cinemas were built in city centres and a classification system for film exhibition was put in place in 1931. Though they occasionally clashed with conservative local censorship (town mayors had the power to ban film exhibition), the decisions of the Commission de contrôle were characterised by liberalism towards depictions of morality, adultery, etc. – contributing to the perennial 'naughty' reputation of French film outside France – and repressiveness towards political issues; criticism of major institutions was severely sanctioned (a *cause célèbre* of the decade was Jean Vigo's* *Zéro de conduite*, 1934). The booming film scene was swelled by more émigrés, from Germany and central Europe, including Fritz Lang, Anatole Litvak*, Max Ophuls* and Robert Siodmak* (provoking xenophobic and anti-semitic attacks from the right). Apart from Gaumont-Franco-Film-Aubert (GFFA) and Pathé-Natan, production was in the hands of numerous individual producers, some with shaky finances. Scandals and bankruptcies, aggravated by the recession, were common; GFFA and Pathé-Natan collapsed. Government attempts at putting the industry in order came to little, and the industry had to cope with strong competition from Hollywood (for every French film shown, there were two to three American films; distribution was now largely in US hands). However, with few exceptions, the top box-office successes of the decade were French.

The novelty of sound prompted the two most popular genres of the early 1930s: musicals and filmed theatre. Apart from Clair's films, musicals tended to be filmed operettas, often French versions of German films starring Annabella*, Albert Préjean*, Henri Garat* or Lilian Harvey, or pictures with comic singers, especially Georges Milton*, Bach, and Fernandel*, the star of the *comique troupier**. Other music-hall performers – Josephine Baker*, Mistinguett, Maurice Chevalier*, Tino Rossi and Charles Trenet – also appeared frequently in films. This was the typical fare of the '*cinéma du sam'di soir*', when people went regularly to their local flea-pit or to the new picture palaces built in city centres. Filmed theatre, based on *boulevard* comedies, showcased star performances and sparkling dialogue (by scriptwriters like Jacques Prévert*, Henri Jeanson*, Charles Spaak and Marcel Achard). These films' investment in the French language and in performance were adored by the audience and did much to shore up a specifically French cinema in the face of the Hollywood 'threat'; their genres, traditionally considered socially and aesthetically of little worth, constitute a fascinating testimony to the period. Key directors included Yves Mirande, Louis Verneuil, Pière Colombier, Marcel Pagnol* and Sacha Guitry*, and among the main stars were Raimu*, Harry Baur*, Arletty*, Jules Berry*, Louis Jouvet* and Michel Simon*.

In contrast to the light-hearted genres which dominated the box-office, the dark realist-melodramatic current in French cinema, usually referred to as Poetic Realism*, was favoured by critics. Based on realist literature or original scripts and set in working-class milieux, the films featured pessimistic narratives and night-time settings, prefiguring American *film noir*. Many great *auteurs* of the time chose this idiom: Duvivier, Feyder, Grémillon, Renoir, Jean Vigo, Pierre Chenal*, Albert Valentin*. The Poetic Realist drama was that of the male hero, best embodied by Jean Gabin*; it was also that of the Parisian *faubourgs*, beautifully recreated by Lazare Meerson* and Alexander Trauner* and lit by Curt Courant, Eugen Schüfftan, Jules Kruger and Claude Renoir, among others. Other melodramatic genres were important: classic melodramas were (re)made, such as Raymond Bernard's *Les Misérables* (1933), and new ones emerged: military or navy melodramas, high society dramas (by L'Herbier and Gance among others), and the 'Slav' melodramas associated with the Russian émigrés (stars included Danielle Darrieux*, Charles Boyer*, Pierre Richard-Willm*, Pierre Fresnay* and Pierre Blanchar*).

There is some justification in seeing Jean Renoir as the towering figure in French cinema of the 1930s, not so much because he was set apart from the rest but because he encompassed the practices of his time, making avant-garde films, comedies, popular melodramas, committed Popular Front* and poetic realist films all within one decade. His last film of the 1930s, *La Règle du jeu/Rules of the Game* (1939, for many his masterpiece, though a flop at the time), ended a decade of both great artistic achievement and vital popular cinema. Film culture was thriving; the Cinémathèque Française* was founded in 1936, popular magazines like *Pour Vous* and *Cinémonde* were read weekly by millions; Maurice Bardèche* and Robert Brasillach*, and later Georges Sadoul*, began writing film history. The Cannes* film festival was planned.

The German occupation had a paradoxical effect on French cinema. Some film-makers and actors – Renoir, Duvivier, Gabin, Michèle Morgan* – emigrated to the US, while others, like Alexander Trauner and Joseph Kosma*, went into hiding, and the industry framework changed. On the other hand, the majority of film personnel remained in France and worked relatively smoothly under the new regime, and historians have argued for an aesthetic and generic continuity between the 1930s and 1940s. Pétain's Vichy government created a new ruling body (COIC), which introduced a sounder financial framework, box-office control, a boost to short film production, and a new film school (IDHEC*). A few films (such as *Les Visiteurs du soir* and *Lumière d'été*, both 1943) were made in the 'free' zone, but lack of means hampered production and the majority of the 220 films made during the war came out of Paris, often from the German-owned firm Continentale. Despite material hardship, French cinema prospered. Films were closely monitored by German and Vichy censorship, prompting directors to avoid contemporary subjects, but few films were actual propaganda. British and American films were banned, French movies dominated screens. Cinemas were warm, attendance had never been higher.

The dominant genres of the war years were escapist: light comedies (*L'Honorable Catherine*, 1943); thrillers (*L'Assassin habite … au 21*, 1942); musicals, costume dramas (*Pontcarral, colonel d'Empire*, 1942; *Les Enfants du paradis*, 1943–45), including a rare 'fantastic' trend: *La Nuit fantastique* (1941), *L'Eternel retour* (script by Jean Cocteau*). Although the films were on the whole 'just entertainment', some have been read as critiques of the Germans and of Pétain's regime, an ambiguity which perhaps characterises most Vichy cinema: Henri-Georges Clouzot's* *Le Corbeau* (1943), found offensive by the Germans, was criticised at the Liberation as anti-French and pro-Nazi. An interesting generic development of the time was the rise of the 'woman's film', with melodramas like Gance's *Vénus aveugle* (1940), Pagnol's *La Fille du puisatier/The Well-Digger's Daughter* and Jean Stelli's *Le Voile bleu* (1942). While these films may have been vehicles for the reactionary Vichy ideology, they featured strong women characters and weak father figures who can be understood in relation to a defeated collective masculinity. However, when *Les Enfants du paradis* came out on 9 March 1945, to huge popular and critical acclaim, its two central characters, Baptiste (Jean-Louis Barrault*) and Garance (Arletty), were seen as the embodiment of the indestructible 'spirit of France'.

A Committee for the Liberation of French Cinema was set up at the Liberation, and a journal, *L'Ecran français*, founded. Jewish personnel returned, while as part of the *épuration* Guitry, Clouzot, Arletty, Chevalier and others were punished for fraternising with the Germans. French cinema briefly dealt with the war trauma. Documentaries and fiction films were made to glorify the Resistance, notably René Clément's* 1945 *La Bataille du rail/Battle of the Rails*, while others, such as Christian-Jaque's* *Boule de suif/Angel and Sinner* (1945), Claude Autant-Lara's* *Le Diable au corps/Devil in the Flesh* (1946) and Clément's *Jeux interdits/Forbidden Games* (1951) dealt with the topic more obliquely. Soon, however, the war theme receded, with exceptions such as Alain Resnais'* *Nuit et brouillard/Night and Fog* (1955) and *Hiroshima mon amour* (1959), partly as a result of censorship. Significantly, though, the war became a favourite subject of comedies for the next four decades.

The cinema of the Fourth Republic started off on a platform of change. The Centre National de la Cinématographie (CNC), founded in 1946, laid the foundations of modern French cinema, including the principle of a degree of state control, box-office levies and aid to non-commercial cinema which, in the long run, ensured its livelihood. Substantial efforts were made to rebuild and modernise French cinemas. Film culture prospered with the revival of the ciné-clubs under the aegis of André Bazin*, new analytical film journals such as *Les Cahiers du cinéma**, and popular screenings at the Cinémathèque. The French film industry, however, had to face a flood of American films. As part of the settlement of the French war debt to the US, the 'Blum–Byrnes agreements' of 1946 granted generous import quotas to American films in return for US imports of French luxury goods – anticipating the GATT negotiations of 1993.

French production returned to its 100–120 films yearly average in 1950, helped by co-productions, especially with Italy. From the late 1940s to the late 1950s, French cinema experienced its period of greatest stability and popularity. Audiences peaked between 1947 (423m) and 1957 (400m), after which permanent decline set in (television was not a significant rival until the 1960s). The industry was highly organised and well equipped, with a large reserve of experienced professionals. There were twelve sound stages in 1950; art directors such as Alexander Trauner, Jean d'Eaubonne, Léon Barsacq, Max Douy and Georges Wakhévitch created decors in every style; cinematographers like Henri Alekan*, Armand Thirard, Christian Matras and Louis Page were in great demand, their polished photography one of the hallmarks of what came to be known as the 'tradition of quality'* (the period also saw the introduction of colour and wide screen). This was also the era of scriptwriters Jean Aurenche* and Pierre Bost*, and later Michel Audiard*. Prewar directors like Clair, Duvivier, Renoir, Carné and Ophuls were back at work, joined by the 'war generation': Jacques Becker*, Yves Allégret*, Autant-Lara, Christian-Jaque, Clouzot and Clément. The French film industry was at its peak.

As in the 1930s, a 'dark' and a 'light' tradition divided popular French cinema of the 1940s and 1950s. Dark became excessively *noir*, especially in the films of Yves Allégret and Clouzot, in Carné and Prévert's epitaph to Poetic Realism, *Les Portes de la nuit* (1946), and in the 'social problem' films of André Cayatte (*Avant le déluge*, 1954). The *noir* idiom fed into the *policier**, partly inspired by the success of crime literature, as well as the popularity of Eddie Constantine* spoof thrillers (directed by Bernard Borderie). Becker's 1954 masterpiece *Touchez pas au grisbi/Honour Among Thieves* initiated a true renaissance of the genre, in which aging gangsters (typically Gabin or Lino Ventura*) and their male 'families' roamed the cobbled streets of Montmartre in black Citroëns. But if, as in the 1930s, the *noir* tradition is the best known, the 'light', in the shape of costume dramas and comedies, was the mainstay of the popular cinema. Sumptuous period reconstructions, often based on literary classics, demanded studio work and careful planning as well as big stars (Gérard Philipe*, Martine Carol*, Danielle Darrieux, Michèle Morgan, Micheline Presle*, Maria Schell). Many directors – mainstream and *auteurs* – worked in costume drama (Renoir, Clair, Ophuls, Jacqueline Audry*, Christian-Jaque). Martine Carol, then the biggest female star, smouldered in 'risqué' costume films like *Caroline chérie* (1950) and *Nana* (1955). But changes were afoot; in the mid-1950s, Carol was displaced as top French sex goddess by Brigitte Bardot* in *Et Dieu ... créa la femme/And God Created Woman* (1956). The prominence of Carol and Bardot at the box office is noteworthy, as both *policiers* and comedies were male-oriented. Comic stars included, apart from Fernandel, Noël-Noël, Darry Cowl and Francis Blanche, the two biggest new post-war comics, Bourvil* and Louis de Funès*. While these comics were strictly for home consumption, Jacques Tati* became a much loved international star with *Jour de fête*, 1949, *Les Vacances de Monsieur Hulot/Mr Hulot's Holiday*, 1951, and *Mon Oncle*, 1958.

Tati was not just a comic; his originality was that he worked on the margins of the industry. Other such independent figures began to appear in the postwar period: Agnès Varda*, Alain Resnais*, Robert Bresson*, Jean-Pierre Melville*, Roger Leenhardt, Georges Rouquier, Louis Malle*. These directors were disparate aesthetically and ideologically, but they were united in their distance from the mainstream. Their independence, their emphasis on personal 'vision' and the relative austerity of their practice marked them as *auteurs*, the precursors of (Varda, Resnais, Malle) or models for (Bresson, Melville) the forthcoming New Wave*. *Auteur* cinema was increasingly recognised by the French film industry as a vital aesthetic and marketing category, as able to compete with Hollywood as, on a different terrain, the 'tradition of quality'. A series of government measures, starting with the *loi d'aide* (1948) and culminating in the *avance sur recettes** (1960), institutionalised *auteur* cinema as a vital force in France, paving the way for the New Wave.

The New Wave, May 1968 and after

During the years 1959 to 1962, spearheaded by François Truffaut's* *Les Quatre cents coups/The 400 Blows* (1959) and Jean-Luc Godard's* *A bout de souffle/Breathless* (1960), there appeared a 'New Wave' of stylistically innovative (though on the whole 'a-political') films directed by former critics of *Cahiers du cinéma* (Truffaut, Godard, Eric Rohmer*, Jacques Rivette*, Claude Chabrol*, Pierre Kast, Jean Daniel Pollet) and classically trained independent film-makers like Varda, Resnais, Malle, Jacques Demy* and others. Several reasons explain the 'newness' of the phenomenon: the advent of de Gaulle's Fifth Republic, heralding a desire for modernity and renewal; changes in film technology (lightweight cameras, Nagra sound, location shooting); new producers (Georges de Beauregard*, Pierre Braunberger*, Anatole Dauman*, Alexandre Mnouchkine) who saw the financial possibilities in making small-budget films for small audiences. Film practice also fitted the new *politique des auteurs**. One of the New Wave's lasting achievements was to initiate new modes of spectatorship; another was to create new kinds of stars: the directors themselves, and those in front of the camera: Jean-Paul Belmondo*, Jean-Claude Brialy*, Jean-Pierre Léaud*, Jeanne Moreau*, Anna Karina*, Stéphane Audran*.

Contrary to the legend which sees the New Wave wiping the slate clean, popular genres continued successfully. However, the impact of the new *auteur* cinema was such that one history of French cinema could be written as geological layers of individual film-makers who won critical recognition and public sponsorship, if not always popular approval: those of the New Wave itself who continued to work; those in the 'spirit' of the New Wave who started later: Nelly Kaplan*, Jacques Rozier, Luc Moullet, Philippe Garrel, Jacques Doillon*, André Téchiné*; the 'classical *auteurs*': Bertrand Tavernier*, Claude Sautet*, Michel Deville*; finally, the inevitable 'unclassifiables': Maurice Pialat*, Jean Eustache*, Luis Buñuel*, Georges Franju*, Marguerite Duras*. A new generation of producers supported them (Paulo Branco, Jean-Pierre Rassam, Margaret Menegoz, Marin Karmitz*), as did film journals *Cahiers du cinéma*, *Positif** and *Cinématographe*.

Even though initially its impact appeared limited (the events have been the subject of very few films, one being Romain Goupil's *Mourir à trente ans*, 1982), the political and social upheaval of May 1968 brought changes to both French cinema and film theory. The 1970s saw a continued decline in audiences and numbers of cinemas. Mainstream genres continued to flourish, however, especially the *policier* and comedy. Belmondo and Alain Delon* were the major stars of the former, Bourvil and de Funès of the latter (especially in the films of Gérard Oury), followed by the *café-théâtre* generation [> COMEDY (FRANCE)]. At the same time, societal changes (libertarianism, feminism) found an echo in the increased naturalism of French cinema, especially after the virtual abolition of censorship from 1967. At the two extremes appeared pornographic and militant cinema. Porn films flooded cinemas for a few years (in 1975 the 'X' category was created which instituted a heavy financial penalty for porn, though there was no official censorship), and were for a time distinguished by extremely witty titles, if nothing else. The plainly titled *Emmanuelle* (1973) and its sequels represented the mainstream end of that market, the films of Walerian Borowczyk* its *auteur* manifestation. On the militant side, film cooperatives sprang up, such as Godard's Dziga Vertov group and Chris Marker's* SLON. A generation of women film-makers emerged, as did women's festivals [> CRÉTEIL], and several of these film-makers have now built important careers (Yannick Bellon, Diane Kurys*, Coline Serreau*). Militant cinema found its popular expression in the political thrillers of Costa-Gavras* and Yves Boisset*, and in many less commercial productions. There was also a renewed interest in history, especially that of the German occupation, initiated by two key films, Marcel Ophuls' *Le Chagrin et la pitié/The Sorrow and the Pity* (1971) and Malle's *Lacombe Lucien* (1974). Directors such as René Allio, Tavernier and Téchiné participated in this movement, which was connected to the popularisation of the 'new history' in social sciences and the media. As World War II began finally to be talked about openly, so (timidly) was the Algerian war, for instance in René Vautier's *Avoir vingt ans dans les Aurès* (1972).

The 1980s and 1990s are marked by schizophrenia. With television viewing at a maximum, expansion of the video market, development of multi-screens and quick rotation of films (making it increasingly difficult for small, marginal *auteur* productions to survive), and with, for the first time, an audience market share for Hollywood higher than for French films, a sense of doom set in. On the other hand, an unparalleled amount of state help under the Socialist government (1981–95), the continued strength of both popular and learned film culture, maintained production in contrast to collapsing film industries in the rest of Europe, the (perhaps temporary) success of the GATT negotiations to preserve the 'cultural exception' of the cinema, and the international success of a number of French films and stars – all this gave rise to optimism and celebration, symbolised by the Césars* awards. French reactions to the numerous Hollywood remakes of French films epitomise this split: anger at being stolen from, pride at being copied. French initiatives in television production, especially with the rise of Canal Plus, proved imaginative and fruitful. In the early 1990s, over 60 per cent of films were financed with some television input, although the vast majority were for theatrical release. Three major generic trends have emerged.

First, the continuity of *auteur* cinema. Most New Wave film-makers are still at work, as well as many from subsequent generations: Tavernier, Téchiné, Sautet, Alain Cavalier, Jean-Pierre Mocky*, Jean-Charles Tacchella, Jean-Claude Brisseau, Claude Miller, Andrzej Zulawski, Leos Carax*, Claire Denis, Catherine Breillat, Euzhan Palcy, Diane Kurys, Tonie Marshall, Eric Rochant, and more recently Cedric Kahn, Patricia Mazuy, Marion Vernoux and Olivier Assayas (many trained at FEMIS*). A notable trend in the younger generation is a return to the New Wave's detachment from social and political issues, with some exceptions provided by the second-generation immigrant directors of the *cinéma beur**. The commercial, critical and symbolic importance of *auteur* cinema in 1990s France is best illustrated by the extraordinary media attention given to young directors such as Carax and Cyril Collard, whose *Les Nuits fauves/Savage Nights* (1992), released shortly before he died of AIDS, was one of the film events of these years. Secondly, popular genres and especially comedy have proved their durability. Serreau's *Trois hommes et un couffin/Three Men and a Cradle* (1985), Jean-Marie Poiré's* *Les Visiteurs* (1993) and Josiane Balasko's* *Gazon maudit* (1995) were popular triumphs, as have been films by Francis Veber, Patrice Leconte and Claude Zidi*. Thirdly, what might be called 'new spectacular cinema' is French cinema's response to the threat of television, making use of increasingly large budgets, major stars, highly skilled technicians and technologies. The new spectacular cinema takes two major forms: the *cinéma du look** on the one hand (glossy, youth-oriented; dirs. Jean-Jacques Beineix*, Luc Besson*) and, on the other hand, costume 'super-productions' [> HERITAGE CINEMA IN EUROPE], films such as Claude Berri's* *Jean de Florette* (1986), Yves Robert's *La Gloire de mon père* (1990), Jean-Paul Rappeneau's* *Cyrano de Bergerac* (1990) and Jean-Jacques Annaud's* *L'Amant* (1991). Often critically disparaged, the 'heritage' films combine popularity at home with exportability.

A century of 'real' cinema, a century of 'French' cinema

Co-productions are a characteristic of French production in the 1990s, together with a new internationalism; Krzysztof Kieślowski*, Nikita Mikhalkov, Manoel de Oliveira, Raul Ruiz*, Pedro Almodóvar and others make films in France or with French money. Conversely, Besson and Malle have made 'French' films in English. Has Delluc's notion of a 'really French' cinema been forgone? Perhaps not entirely. French cinema, across its breadth and diversity, still occupies some spaces where its national identity may be found. One is realism, according to Jean Grémillon 'the grandeur, the meaning, the significance of French cinema', a national cinema which never really developed non-realistic genres (horror, science-fiction, the fantastic, the peplum); another is its continued foregrounding of performance (if there is no European star system, there is arguably a French one); and finally there is the lasting popularity of indigenous comedy. Though some would argue that key to the identity of French cinema – both insti-

tutionally and aesthetically – are its *auteurs*, the true exponents of the 'real cinema' advocated by Delluc, the strength of its popular traditions also underpins – though for how long? – its survival.
[> COMEDY IN FRANCE; POLICIER; FRENCH AVANT-GARDE; POPULAR FRONT CINEMA; TRADITION OF QUALITY; POLITIQUE DES AUTEURS]

FRENCH CINEMA: PERSONNEL, INSTITUTIONS, KEY CRITICAL CONCEPTS

ADJANI, Isabelle
AIMÉE, Anouk
ALEKAN, Henri
ALLÉGRET, Marc
ALLÉGRET, Yves
ALMENDROS, Nestor
ANNABELLA
ANNAUD, Jean-Jacques
ANTOINE, André
ARLETTY
AUDIARD, Michel
AUDRAN, Stéphane
AUDRY, Jacqueline
AURENCHE, Jean
AUTANT-LARA, Claude
AUTEUIL, Daniel
AVANCE SUR RECETTES
BAKER, Joséphine
BALASKO, Josiane
BARDÈCHE, Maurice
BARDOT, Brigitte
BARRAULT, Jean-Louis
BAUR, Harry
BAYE, Nathalie
BAZIN, André
BEART, Emmanuelle
BEAUREGARD, Georges de
BECKER, Jacques
BEINEIX, Jean-Jacques
BELMONDO, Jean-Paul
BENOÎT-LÉVY, Jean
BERNARD, Raymond
BERRI, Claude
BERRY, Jules
BESSON, Luc
BINOCHE, Juliette
BLANCHAR, Pierre
BLIER, Bernard
BLIER, Bertrand
BOISSET, Yves
BONNAIRE, Sandrine
BOST, Pierre
BOURVIL
BOYER, Charles
BRASILLACH, Robert
BRASSEUR, Pierre
BRAUNBERGER, Pierre
BRESSON, Robert
BRIALY, Jean-Claude
CAHIERS DU CINÉMA
CANNES
CANUDO, Ricciotto
CARAX, Leos
CARETTE, Julien
CARNÉ, Marcel
CAROL, Martine
CÉSARS
CHABROL, Claude
CHATILIEZ, Etienne
CHENAL, Pierre
CHEVALIER, Maurice
CHRISTIAN-JAQUE
CINÉMA *BEUR*
CINÉMA DU LOOK
CINÉMA VÉRITÉ
CINEMATHÈQUE FRANÇAISE
CLAIR, René
CLÉMENT, René
CLOUZOT, Henri-Georges
COCTEAU, Jean
COHL, Emile
COLETTE
COMEDY IN FRANCE
COMIQUE TROUPIER
CONSTANTINE, Eddie
CORNEAU, Alain
COSTA-GAVRAS, Constantin
COUTARD, Raoul
CRÉTEIL
DALIO, Marcel
DALLE, Béatrice
DARRIEUX, Danielle
DAUMAN, Anatole
DECOIN, Henri
DEED, André

DELANNOY, Jean
DELLUC, Louis
DELON, Alain
DEMY, Jacques
DENEUVE, Catherine
DEPARDIEU, Gérard
DEVILLE, Michel
DOILLON, Jacques
DULAC, Germaine
DURAS, Marguerite
DUVIVIER, Julien
EPSTEIN, Jean
EPSTEIN, Marie
EUSTACHE, Jean
FEMIS
FERNANDEL
FEUILLADE, Louis
FEUILLÈRE, Edwige
FEYDER, Jacques
FILM D'ART
FRANJU, Georges
FRENCH AVANT-GARDE
FRESNAY, Pierre
FUNÈS, Louis de
GABIN, Jean
GANCE, Abel
GARAT, Henri
GAUMONT, Léon
GIRARDOT, Annie
GODARD, Jean-Luc
GRÉMILLON, Jean
GRIMAULT, Paul
GUITRY, Sacha
GUY (BLACHÉ), Alice
HUPPERT, Isabelle
IDHEC
JAQUE-CATELAIN
JAUBERT, Maurice
JEANSON, Henri
JOUVET, Louis
KAPLAN, Nelly
KARINA, Anna
KARMITZ, Marin
KOSMA, Joseph
KURYS, Diane
LAFONT, Bernadette
LANGLOIS, Henri
LE VIGAN, Robert
LÉAUD, Jean-Pierre
LECLERC, Ginette
LEGRAND, Michel
LELOUCH, Claude
L'HERBIER, Marcel
LINDER, Max
LUMIÈRE, Louis and Auguste
MALLE, Louis
MARAIS, Jean
MARCEAU, Sophie
MARIANO, Luis
MARKER, Chris
MEERSON, Lazare
MELIÈS, Georges
MELVILLE, Jean-Pierre
MILTON, Georges
MIOU-MIOU
MOCKY, Jean-Pierre
MODOT, Gaston
MONTAND, Yves
MOREAU, Jeanne
MORGAN, Michèle
MORLAY, Gaby
MUSIDORA
NEW WAVE
NOIRET, Philippe
PAGNOL, Marcel
PATHÉ, Charles
PHILIPE, Gérard
PIALAT, Maurice
PICCOLI, Michel
POETIC REALISM
POIRÉ, Jean-Marie
POLICIER
POLITIQUE DES AUTEURS
POPULAR FRONT CINEMA
POSITIF
PRÉJEAN, Albert
PRESLE, Micheline
PRÉVERT, Jacques and Pierre
PRINCE-RIGADIN
RAIMU
RAPPENEAU, Jean-Paul
RENAUD, Madeleine
RENOIR, Jean
RESNAIS, Alain
RICHARD-WILLM, Pierre
RIVETTE, Jacques

ROHMER, Eric
ROMANCE, Viviane
ROSAY, Françoise
ROUCH, Jean
SADOUL, Georges
SAUTET, Claude
SCHROEDER, Barbet
SERREAU, Coline
SEYRIG, Delphine
SIGNORET, Simone
SIMENON, Georges
SIMON, Michel
SIMON, Simone
TATI, Jacques
TAVERNIER, Bertrand
TÉCHINÉ, André
TOURNEUR, Maurice
TRADITION OF QUALITY
TRAUNER, Alexander
TRINTIGNANT, Jean-Louis
TRUFFAUT, François
VADIM, Roger
VALENTIN, Albert
VANEL, Charles
VARDA, Agnès
VENTURA, Lino
VERNEUIL, Henri
VIGO, Jean
ZIDI, Claude

ADJANI, Isabelle

Paris 1955

French actress. Though Adjani has starred in relatively few major films, her talent, glamour and tumultuous personality have made her a top French star since the late 1970s. She started very young in film (1969) and on stage, joining the Comédie Française in 1973. Claude Pinoteau's comedy *La Gifle/The Slap* (1974) and François Truffaut's* drama *L'Histoire d'Adèle H/The Story of Adèle H* (1975) were her first important films. Though she continued making comedies (Jean-Paul Rappeneau's* *Tout feu tout flamme*, 1981, Philomène Esposito's *Toxic Affair*, 1993), her dominant image is one of intensity, mystery and high drama, usually in *auteur* cinema. Her arresting beauty and assertiveness predisposed her for passionate and rebellious (often self-destructive) heroines, such as the daughter figures in Jean Becker's *L'Eté meurtrier/One Deadly Summer* and Claude Miller's *Mortelle Randonnée/Deadly Circuit* (both 1983). Adjani was the target of a right-wing smear campaign in 1986, after she took up anti-National Front positions by claiming her Algerian antecedents. She nevertheless successfully produced (and starred in) Bruno Nuytten's *Camille Claudel* (1988), her powerful performance earning her her third César*. While defining glamorous French femininity, Adjani, like Catherine Deneuve*, projects a Hollywood-type aura of stardom, playfully evoked in Luc Besson's* *Subway* (1985). Despite a three-year absence from the screen in the early 1990s and the failure of *Toxic Affair*, her place in the firmament of French stars is confirmed by her highly charged performance as the heroine of Patrice Chéreau's *La Reine Margot* (1994). She has subsequently taken part in several international productions, such as Jeremiah Checkhik's *Diabolique* (1996, US/Fr.), a remake of the 1955 *Les Diaboliques* by Henri-Georges Clouzot*, and Ivan Passer's *Benia ou le cavalier rouge* (1996, Fr./Yu.).

Other Films Include: *Le Locataire/The Tenant, Barocco* (1976); *Violette et François* (1977); *The Driver* (1978, US); *Nosferatu – Phantom der Nacht/Nosferatu the Vampyre* [Ger./Fr.], *Les Soeurs Brontë/The Brontë Sisters* (1979); *Quartet* [UK/Fr.], *Possession* [Fr./Ger.] (1981); *Ishtar* (1987, US).

AIMÉE, Anouk

Françoise Dreyfus, Paris 1932

French actress known internationally as a star of 1960s European art cinema, with especially, Jacques Demy's* *Lola* (1961), Federico

Fellini's *La dolce vita* (1960) and *8½* (1963) and André Delvaux's *Un soir, un train* (1968), though she had been acting in French film since 1946. In particular, she appeared in André Cayatte's *Les Amants de Vérone* (1949), Alexandre Astruc's *Le Rideau cramoisi* (1953) and Jacques Becker's* *Montparnasse 19/Modigliani of Montparnasse* (1958), with Gérard Philipe*. These films established her as an ethereal, sensitive and fragile beauty with a tendency for tragic destinies or restrained suffering. This persona was popularised by the enormous success of Claude Lelouch's* *Un homme et une femme/A Man and a Woman* (1966), co-starring Jean-Louis Trintignant*. Lelouch tried to revive the Aimée-Trintignant couple (not so successfully this time) in *Un homme et une femme 20 ans après/A Man and a Woman: 20 Years later* (1986). With a few exceptions, Aimée has remained the star of art films rather than popular ones, her career ranging from France and Italy to the US. She appears in Robert Altman's *Prêt-à-porter* (1994, US).

AKERMAN, Chantal – see 'French Cinema in Europe', page 150

ALEKAN, Henri — Paris 1909

French cinematographer. After studying at the Paris Conservatoire des Arts et Métiers and the Institut d'Optique, and working as a puppeteer, Alekan was camera assistant on French films from 1929, including two – Marcel Carné's* *Drôle de drame* (1937) and *Quai des brumes* (1938) – with Eugen Schüfftan*, a great influence. Alekan's career took off with the resistance drama *La Bataille du rail/Battle of the Rails* (dir. René Clément*) and Jean Cocteau's* fairy tale *La Belle et la bête* (both 1946). He subsequently worked on numerous films with distinguished directors, including Yves Allégret*, Abel Gance*, Joseph Losey* and Jules Dassin*, but *La Bataille du rail* and *La Belle et la bête* epitomised his mastery of black and white photography, his preferred medium: as he declared in 1993, 'I absolutely prefer black and white. [...] I believe film should transcend the banal world.' This was literally the case in Wim Wenders' *Der Himmel über Berlin/Wings of Desire* (1987, Ger./Fr.) in which he filmed angels. In his later career, Alekan worked on other Wenders films and with Raul Ruiz*; he appears as an actor in Wenders' *In weiter Ferne, so nah!/Far Away, So Close* (1993, Ger.).

Bib: Henri Alekan, *Des lumières et des ombres* (1984).

ALLÉGRET, Marc

Basel, Switzerland 1900 – Paris 1973

French director. The older brother of Yves Allégret*, Marc Allégret was a prolific and skilled mainstream director whose disparate work included documentaries (*Voyage au Congo*, 1927, with the writer André Gide, whose nephew, contrary to legend, he was *not*), comedy – adapted operettas (*Mam'zelle Nitouche*, 1931), a Fernandel* vehicle (*Pétrus*, 1947) – and melodrama (*Orage*, 1937). He also directed Marcel Pagnol's* *Fanny* (1932). Dominant themes emerge, however: an interest in youth often combined with artistic milieux is evident from *Zouzou* (1934, with Josephine Baker*) and *Entrée des artistes/The Curtain Rises* (1938, starring Louis Jouvet*) to *Les Parisiennes* (1962, with Catherine Deneuve* and the singer Johnny Halliday). Allégret also showed an interest in women characters, giving Micheline Presle*, for instance, one of her best parts in *Félicie Nanteuil* (1942, rel. 1945). He acquired a reputation as a 'discoverer' of stars, launching Simone Simon in *Lac aux dames* (1934) and Michèle Morgan* in *Gribouille/Heart of Paris* (1937). He spotted Brigitte Bardot's* potential from a magazine cover, later casting her as the star of *En effeuillant la marguerite/Please Mr Balzac* (1956).

ALLÉGRET, Yves

Asnières 1907 – Paris 1987

French director. Brother of Marc Allégret*, on some of whose films he worked as assistant in the 1930s. Yves Allégret was part of the generation who emerged during the German occupation. His main contribution to the history of French film is as one of the exponents of postwar French *noir* cinema with a small body of films made in the late 1940s. *Dédée d'Anvers* (1948), *Une si jolie petite plage/Riptide* (1949) and *Manèges/The Cheat* (1950) fixed the Allégret universe – a dystopian vision of postwar France which evoked prewar Poetic Realism* without the 'poetry', and in which Marcel Carné's* and Jacques Prévert's* romantic belief in fate had been replaced by an emphasis on the sordid; indeed Allégret was attacked by left-wing critics for his negative and backward-looking portrayal of the period. Nevertheless, the films were seductive, wonderful lighting effects moulding the chiselled features of Gérard Philipe* in *Une si jolie petite plage* and *Les Orgueilleux/The Proud Ones* (1953, from a script by Jean-Paul Sartre) and those of Simone Signoret* (then Allégret's wife) in *Dédée d'Anvers* and *Manèges*. The performances of the superb Signoret concealed the films' deep misogyny, which can be seen as part of a backlash following the (relative) prominence of women in wartime French cinema and society. Allégret and Signoret had a daughter, Catherine Allégret, who is also an actress.

Bib: Noël Burch and Geneviève Sellier, *Le Ciné-roman familial de la société traditionnelle* (1996).

ALMENDROS, Nestor

Barcelona, Spain 1930 – New York 1992

French-based cinematographer of Spanish origin. One of the most renowned postwar cinematographers. After studying in Cuba, New York and Rome, and working on short films in Cuba (where he founded Havana's first film club), Almendros moved to Paris. He worked on a late New Wave* project, the collective *Paris vu par…* (1965), and became a regular collaborator with Eric Rohmer* and François Truffaut*. His impressive filmography includes Rohmer's *Le Genou de Claire/Claire's Knee* (1970) and *Pauline à la plage* (1982), and Truffaut's *L'Enfant sauvage/The Wild Child* (1970) and *Le Dernier métro/The Last Metro* (1980), for which Almendros received a César*. He also worked with Jean Eustache*, Marguerite Duras* and Vicente Aranda, and in the US with Terrence Malick (*Days of Heaven*, 1978, which won him an Oscar), Alan Pakula (*Sophie's Choice*, 1982) and Martin Scorsese (*New York Stories*, ep. 'Life Lessons', 1989), among others. He directed documentaries in Cuba and the US and worked for French television. An advocate of realism, he excelled in using natural light, finding inspiration in painters and taking, as he put it, 'a "window" light from Vermeer, a "candle" light from De la Tour, a chiaroscuro from Rembrandt'.

Bib: Nestor Almendros, *A Man With a Camera* (1980).

ANNABELLA

Suzanne Charpentier; Paris 1909

French actress. Annabella was the biggest female French star of the early and mid-1930s. She appeared in Abel Gance's* *Napoléon* (1927) and Jean Grémillon's* *Maldone* (1928), but her fame came from two René Clair* films, *Le Million* (1931) and *Quatorze juillet* (1932). She starred in European productions made in Britain, Germany, Hungary (Paul Féjos' *Tavaszi zapor/Marie légende hongroise*, 1932) and Austria (Féjos' *Sonnenstrahl/Gardez le sourire*, 1933). In France, she was the star of popular comedies, such as *Paris-Méditerranée* (1931, co-starring her husband Jean Murat), and melodramas like Anatole Litvak's* *L'Equipage* (1935). She was one of the few French stars invited to Hollywood who actually made films there, in particular Allan Dwan's *Suez* (1938; she subsequently married her co-star, Tyrone Power) and Henry Hathaway's *13 Rue Madeleine* (1946). She appeared as an 'Arab' woman in Julien Duvivier's* *La Bandera* (1935) and as the doomed lover in Marcel Carné's* *Hôtel du Nord* (1938). Petite and delicately pretty, Annabella embodied shy and sentimental heroines, epitomising – especially in the Clair films – a romantic type close to the operatic *midinette*. Such a screen persona did not age well, and her career quickly declined after the war.

ANNAUD, Jean-Jacques Juvisy-sur-Orge 1943

French director, one of the few truly international French film-makers. A graduate of IDHEC*, Annaud had a highly successful career in commercials before his first feature, *La Victoire en chantant/Black and White in Colour* (1976, Fr./Ger.), a sardonic view of colonialism, won an Oscar for Best Foreign Film in 1977. After *Coup de tête* (1979), he moved on to large budgets and spectacular *mise-en-scène*, with *La Guerre du feu/Quest for Fire* (1981, Fr./Canada), *Le Nom de la rose/Der Name der Rose/The Name of the Rose* (1986, based on Umberto Eco's novel) and *L'Ours/The Bear* (1988). *L'Amant/The Lover* (1991), from Marguerite Duras' novel aroused controversy for its 'betrayal' of Duras, its glossy orientalism and, not least, its use of the English language. It encapsulates the Annaud paradox: low critical esteem (Serge Daney called Annaud a 'post-film-maker'), but huge commercial success in France and abroad. He followed *L'Amant* with two US productions in 1995, *Wings of Courage*, with Val Kilmer and Charlie Sheen, and *Seven Years in Tibet*, with Brad Pitt.

ANTOINE, André Limoges 1858 – Le Pouliguen 1943

French director. A great pioneer of French theatre, founder of the Théâtre Libre in 1897, where he applied principles of literary naturalism. Signed on by SCAGL (Société cinématographique des auteurs et gens de lettres) in 1914, he directed *Les Frères corses/The Corsican Brothers* (based on Alexandre Dumas) in 1917, and directed nine films altogether, mostly adaptations of novels (Victor Hugo, Emile Zola) and plays. *L'Hirondelle et la mésange/The Swallow and the Bluetit*, from an original script, was shot in 1920–21 on a barge in Belgium and northern France. A disappointed SCAGL left it unfinished; it was rediscovered by the Cinémathèque française* in 1982 and re-released in 1983. Its use of locations, canal-side milieux and a blend of actors and non-professionals make it a key work in early realist French cinema. Between 1924 and 1940 Antoine was theatre and film critic for a number of publications, including *Le Journal* and *Comœdia*.

ARLETTY

Léonie Bathiat; Courbevoie 1898 – Paris 1992

French actress. In the pantheon of film culture, Arletty has her place as the heroine of two wartime classics by Marcel Carné* and Jacques Prévert*: *Les Visiteurs du soir* (1942) and, especially, *Les Enfants du paradis* (1943–45), in which as Garance she achieves a rare combination of romantic beauty and humour. While her wit and accent locate her as unmistakably working-class and Parisian, her performance owed much to her early career in music hall and boulevard theatre. Her 1930s film career was mainly in comedy: in the popular classic *Hôtel du Nord* (1938), she and Louis Jouvet outclassed Annabella* and Jean-Pierre Aumont, the romantic leads. Similarly, in *Le Jour se lève* (1939), a classic of Poetic Realism*, she was more of a match for Jean Gabin* than the bland Jacqueline Laurent. Despite her spirited defence that 'my heart is French but my body is international', her career suffered badly because of her wartime liaison with a German officer, though she went on to make a few films, including Jacqueline Audry's* *Huis-clos* (1954) and the underrated *L'Air de Paris* (1954, dir. Marcel Carné). She also acted on stage until blindness forced her to retire in the 1960s.

If Arletty rarely got the top billing she deserved in her films, the impact of her performances, full of heart and wisecracks, ensured her place as one of the great populist stars of French cinema.

Bib: Arletty, *La Défense* (1971).

Other Films Include: *Pension Mimosas* (1934); *La Garçonne* (1936); *Les Perles de la couronne, Désiré* (1937); *Fric-Frac, Circonstances atténuantes* (1939); *Madame Sans-Gêne* (1941); *Le Grand jeu* (1954).

AUDIARD, Michel

Paris 1920 – Dourdan 1985

French scriptwriter. A journalist, novelist and scriptwriter, Audiard's chief claim to fame derives from his work in a category peculiar to the French cinema: *dialoguiste* (dialogue writer). Like his illustrious predecessors Henri Jeanson* and Jacques Prévert*, Audiard mixed classic French and slang and delighted in derision and *bons mots*, though his dialogue was coarser (a sign of the times) and more shocking. Like theirs, his humour had an edge of bitterness ('the trouble with life is that you don't get out of it alive'). Audiard's witty, hard-hitting dialogue underpins much of the best popular French cinema from the late 1950s to the mid-1980s, notably in his collaborations with Jean Gabin*, for whom he wrote tailor-made dialogue for, among many other films, *Gas-oil* (1955), *Les Grandes familles* (1958), *Le Président* (1961), *Un singe en hiver/A Monkey in Winter* (1962) and

Mélodie en sous-sol/The Big Snatch (1963) – actor and *dialoguiste* constituting the true *auteurs* of the films. He directed nine features between 1968 and 1974. His son Jacques Audiard is also a scriptwriter and has directed two features.

AUDRAN, Stéphane

Colette Dacheville; Versailles 1932

French actress. Audran is, with Jeanne Moreau* and Anna Karina*, a key actress of the French New Wave*, especially in the films of her then husband Claude Chabrol*. A woman of elegant beauty, she projected an image of the cool yet sensual bourgeoise; her talent was to inject emotion and humour into such characters. She is integral to the appeal of Chabrol's bourgeois dramas of the 1960s and 1970s, especially *Les Biches* (1968), *La Femme infidèle* (1969) and *Le Boucher* (1970), and of Luis Buñuel's* *Le Charme discret de la bourgeoisie/The Discreet Charm of the Bourgeoisie* (1972). After smaller roles, for instance in *Violette Nozière* (1978) and Bertrand Tavernier's* *Coup de torchon/Clean Slate* (1981), she revived her international fame in Gabriel Axel's *Babettes Gæstebud/Babette's Feast* (1987, Den.). She has meanwhile continued to appear in numerous French films.

AUDRY, Jacqueline

Orange 1908 – Poissy 1977

French director. Audry followed the classic route of continuity and assistantship to (among others) Jean Delannoy* and Max Ophuls* before directing her first short, *Les Chevaux du Vercors*, in 1943. Her well-made literary adaptations belong to the 1950s 'tradition of quality'*; not so her choice of subject matter, however. Adaptations from Colette* (*Gigi*, 1949, *Minne, l'ingénue libertine/Minne*, 1950, *Mitsou*, 1956) and Victor Marguerite (*La Garçonne*, 1957), and her portrayal of lesbian relationships in *Olivia/Pit of Loneliness* (1951), show her consistent interest in transgressive women. Even though their subversiveness is constrained by conventional narratives and the titillating potential of the subjects, Audry's women are never treated as perverse curiosities. Though several of her films were box-office successes, she suffered setbacks in her career; that she managed to make as many as eighteen features is remarkable. Apart from the celebrated *Olivia*, which has aroused feminist interest, her work is still in need of critical reappraisal.

Other Films: *Les Malheurs de Sophie* (1946); *Sombre dimanche* (1948); *La Caraque blonde, Huis-clos* (1954); *L'Ecole des cocottes, C'est la faute d'Adam* (1958); *Le Secret du chevalier d'Eon* (1960); *Les Petits Matins* (1962); *Cadavres en vacances* (1963); *Cours de bonheur conju-*

gal (1964, TV); *Fruits amers (*also *Soledad,* 1967); *Le Lys de mer* (1969); *Un Grand Amour de Balzac* (1972, TV).

AURENCHE, Jean — Pierrelatte 1904 – Bandol 1992
and
BOST, Pierre — Lasalle 1901 – Paris 1975

French scriptwriters. Aurenche worked in advertising in the early 1930s. He co-scripted films with Jean Anouilh, Marcel Achard and Henri Jeanson* as well as writing his own screenplays. Bost wrote plays and novels from the 1920s, adding film dialogues in the late 1930s. Aurenche and Bost met in 1943; their partnership as script/dialogue writers, starting with Claude Autant-Lara's* *Douce* (1943), lasted thirty years. 'Aurenche-et-Bost' films, typically directed by Autant-Lara, were the epitome of 'tradition of quality'* French cinema: carefully structured, studio-shot literary adaptations performed by bankable French stars. Notable examples among many are *Le Diable au corps/Devil in the Flesh* (1947), *L'Auberge rouge/The Red Inn* (1951), *Gervaise* (1956) and *La Traversée de Paris/A Pig Across Paris* (1956). François Truffaut* singled out Aurenche and Bost for special attention in his famous 1954 assault on the quality tradition, denouncing them as 'nothing but the Viollet-Leduc of adaptation' after the painstaking nineteenth-century restorer of gothic architecture. Aurenche and Bost's work is nonetheless testimony to the importance of the word in classic French cinema. Bertrand Tavernier* later reclaimed this heritage, inviting them to script *L'Horloger de Saint-Paul/The Watchmaker of Saint-Paul* (1973). Aurenche scripted other films by Tavernier, who also adapted a novella by Bost for *Un dimanche à la campagne/Sunday in the Country* (1983).

AUTANT-LARA, Claude — Claude Autant; Luzarches 1901

French director. Autant-Lara came from an artistic milieu and made his debut in the avant-garde of the 1920s, working in set and costume design, and as assistant to Marcel L'Herbier* and René Clair*. His early short, *Construire un feu* (1928, rel. 1930), was notable for its use of the Hypergonar, an early version of CinemaScope. From 1930 to 1932 Autant-Lara was in Hollywood, making French versions of American films. He directed his first feature, *Ciboulette* (scripted by Jacques Prévert*), in 1933 and worked on some films uncredited. His wartime costume dramas established him as a leading exponent of the 'tradition of quality'*. They were distinguished by a bleak vision of the French bourgeoisie, but also by complex and strong women characters (especially in *Douce*, 1943). The controversial *Le Diable au corps/*

Devil in the Flesh (1947), seen as anti-clerical and anti-war, confirmed Autant-Lara's status and won many prizes. He continued alternating costume films with comedies such as *L'Auberge rouge/The Red Inn* (1951) and *La Jument verte/The Green Mare's Nest* (1959), earning much hostility from New Wave* critics. François Truffaut*, however, applauded *La Traversée de Paris/A Pig Across Paris* (1956), a war comedy starring Jean Gabin* and Bourvil*, admiring both its ferocity and the precision of its *mise-en-scène*. Autant-Lara worked less successfully in the mainstream French cinema of the 1960s. In 1984 he published the first volume of his memoirs, remarkable for its vituperation, bitterness and extreme right-wing views. He remains, however, one of the most gifted and provocative film-makers of classical French cinema.

Other Films Include: *Le Mariage de Chiffon, Lettres d'amour* (1942); *Sylvie et le Fantôme* (1946); *Occupe-toi d'Amélie* (1949); *Le Blé en herbe/The Game of Love, Le Rouge et le noir/Scarlet and Black* (1954); *Marguerite de la nuit* (1956); *En cas de malheur/Love is My Profession* (1958); *Le Comte de Monte-Cristo* (1961); *Tu ne tueras point/Non uccidere/Thou Shalt Not Kill* (1963); *Le Journal d'une femme en blanc* (1965); *Le Franciscain de Bourges* (1968).

AUTEUIL, Daniel — Algiers, Algeria, 1950

French actor. Originally a singer and stage actor, Auteuil started his film career in the mid-1970s. It was not until 1986, however, that he made his mark, with his part as the cunning, yet tragic, farm simpleton Ugolin in Claude Berri's* *Jean de Florette* and *Manon des sources* (both 1986), in which he co-starred with Gérard Depardieu*, Yves Montand* and Emmanuelle Béart*. Though a-typical of his range, his strong character performance as Ugolin established him as one of the most popular French actors. In a line of French stars such as Jean-Louis Trintignant*, he plays the not conventionally handsome, yet seductive, male lead. He has appeared in comic roles, such as the harrassed executive of Coline Serreau's* *Romuald et Juliette* (1989), but his dominant persona emerged as one of quiet charm and interiority, displayed in Patrice Chéreau's *La Reine Margot* (1994, as Henri de Navarre) but especially in Claude Sautet's* *Un coeur un hiver/A Heart in Winter* (1993, also with Béart) and Christian Vincent's *La Séparation*, co-starring Isabelle Huppert*, which both display his sensitive, minimalist style of performance. He created and runs his own production company (D.A. Films).

AVANCE SUR RECETTES (Advance on box-office receipts)

French funding system designed to promote *auteur* films and usually thought of (not entirely correctly) as a key element in the New Wave*. The *avance*, set up in 1960, complemented existing state support measures funded from box-office levies by putting in place more selective financing for the promotion of 'original', especially first, films. It was granted by a commission, nominated by the Minister of Culture, which made decisions predominantly on script submission. Its other novelty was that it did not entail repayment unless the film made money. The system has been criticised for its occasional support of 'commercial' film-makers (Yves Robert, Claude Lelouch*), while the likes of Eric Rohmer* often failed to qualify. The *avance* budget (over FF100m [c. £12m] in the early 1990s) is modest by French production standards, yet enviable relative to other European countries; it is only part of the substantial aid package available to film production every year. Altogether, over 1,000 films, often low-budget or 'difficult', have benefited from the *avance*, which as part of the increasingly complex financing system of the 1980s and 1990s remains a force in the promotion and survival of *auteur* cinema.

Bib: René Prédal, *Le Cinéma français depuis 1945* (1991).

BAKER, Josephine

St Louis, Missouri 1906 – Paris 1975

American-born performer who moved to France in 1925. Baker's beauty, allied to her astonishing 'dislocated' dancing in the *Revue nègre*, clad only in a string of bananas, made her the toast of European capitals. Although her 'exoticism' was fetishised, she found in France a relatively racist-free environment. She starred in music hall, had her own cabaret in Paris and launched a successful recording career with Vincent Scotto's song *J'ai deux amours* ('My country and Paris'). Her brief filmography is notable for *Zouzou* (Marc Allégret*, 1934, co-starring Jean Gabin*) and *Princesse Tam-Tam* (Edmond T. Gréville, 1935), musicals showcasing her performance and bearing ample witness to her impact on French culture. Her support for the Resistance and founding of a children's home (a financial catastrophe) turned her into a French folk heroine. She performed on stage to the very end of her life.

BALASKO, Josiane

Paris 1951

French actress, director and scriptwriter. Known outside France for her part as the ostentatiously plain secretary in Bertrand Blier's* *Trop belle pour toi!* (1989), Balasko has been an important force in French comedy since her training in *café-théâtre* in the early 1970s [> COMEDY (FRANCE)]. Within this irreverent tradition, she has turned her plump physique and considerable wit to a type of comedy which, while not strictly feminist, consistently deflates the excesses of French machismo – sometimes as actress (Patrice Leconte's *Les Bronzés*, 1978), sometimes as scriptwriter (the successful *Les Hommes préfèrent les grosses/ Men Prefer Fat Girls*, dir. Jean-Marie Poiré*, 1981). Balasko has written, starred in and directed several plays and films, such as *Les Keufs/Flatfoots* (1987). In *Gazon maudit* (1995; the title – literally 'cursed lawn' – is a sexual joke), she turned a lesbian comedy into a family film and box-office hit. Together with Coline Serreau*, Balasko is one of the significant women film-makers in popular French cinema, and as such deserves more attention than she has had so far.

BARDÈCHE, Maurice and BRASILLACH, Robert

Dun-sur-Auron 1909

Perpignan 1909 – Fresnes 1945

French film historians. With their *Histoire du cinéma* (translated as *The History of Motion Pictures*), first published in 1935, revised in 1943 and reprinted many times since, Bardèche and Brasillach inaugurated the pioneering wave of French film historiography which also included Jean Mitry and Georges Sadoul*. Ideologically opposed to the communist Sadoul, Bardèche and Brasillach were overtly fascistic and anti-semitic, not least in their opinions on film. They shared with Sadoul, however, an enthusiasm for silent cinema and *auteur* films and a distrust of popular entertainment. They were particularly hostile to the coming of sound, seeing it – like many then – as 'the agony of an art'. But they could rise above their political bias to recognise artistic value, for instance in Jean Renoir*. Brasillach was an intellectual and novelist (Bardèche, an academic, was his brother-in-law), and a literary and film critic for the royalist *L'Action française* and the fascist *Je suis partout*. He was executed for collaboration and 'intellectual crime'. Bardèche was imprisoned and deprived of his university chair but continued to write, notably on fascism.

BARDOT, Brigitte

Paris 1934

French actress. One of the very few French stars to achieve equivalent world fame, Bardot was propelled to stardom by *Et Dieu … créa la femme/And God Created Woman* (1956), directed by her then husband Roger Vadim*. While the film has been hailed – somewhat exaggeratedly – as a precursor of the New Wave*, it launched 'BB', a former model, as the most potent female sexual myth in 1950s France and a valuable export commodity. Bardot's screen persona defined the sex-kitten, wedding 'natural' and unruly sexuality with childish attributes – slim but full-breasted, blonde with a girlish fringe, the pout and the giggle. After her spectacular breakthrough, she went on to star in many unremarkable vehicles, with a few intelligent exceptions: Henri-Georges Clouzot's* *La Vérité* (1960), a courtroom drama in which her sexuality itself is on trial, Louis Malle's* semi-biographical *Vie privée* (1962), and Jean-Luc Godard's* *Le Mépris/Contempt* (1963). She was idolised – her gingham dresses, hairstyle and pout were copied by millions of women, and she modelled for the effigy of the French Republic – but also viciously attacked and abused. The archetypal object of male fantasies, Bardot was also a rebel (on and off screen), delighting in her own body and sexuality: 'as much a hunter as she is a prey,' as Simone de Beauvoir put it. As a result she was box-office although she wasn't always popular. Unlike her contemporaries Marilyn Monroe and Diana Dors, Bardot showed stamina and a shrewd business sense. She retired from acting in 1973 and is now a devoted campaigner for animal rights.

Bib: Simone de Beauvoir, *Brigitte Bardot and the Lolita Syndrome* (1960).

Other Films Include: *Le Trou normand/Crazy for Love* (1952); *Doctor at Sea* [UK], *Les Grandes manoeuvres, Helen of Troy* [US] (1955); *La Lumière d'en face/The Light Across the Street, Cette sacrée gamine/Mam'zelle Pigalle, La Mariée est trop belle/The Bride is Too Beautiful* (1956); *Une Parisienne* (1957); *Les Bijoutiers du clair de lune/The Night Heaven Fell, En cas de malheur/Love is My Profession* (1958); *La Femme et le pantin/A Woman Like Satan, Babette s'en va-t-en guerre/Babette Goes to War* (1959); *Les Amours célèbres* (1961); *Le Repos du guerrier/Warrior's Rest* (1962); *Une ravissante idiote/A Ravishing Idiot* (1964); *Viva Maria!* (1965); *Histoires extraordinaires/Spirits of the Dead, Shalako* [UK] (1968); *L'Ours et la poupée/The Bear and the Doll* (1970); *Boulevard du rhum/Rum Runner, Les Pétroleuses/The Legend of Frenchie King* (1971); *Don Juan 1973 ou si Don Juan était une femme/Don Juan or if Don Juan were a woman…* (1973).

BARRAULT, Jean-Louis

Le Vésinet 1910 – Paris 1994

French actor, who made his mark primarily in the theatre. His performance in Marcel Carné's* *Les Enfants du paradis* (1943–45) alone ensured his place in film history. Barrault studied acting and mime. He met Madeleine Renaud* in 1936 and married her in 1940; they founded a long-lived stage company. Barrault's thin physique, feverish look and theatrical performance style destined him for romantic parts such as Berlioz in *La Symphonie fantastique* (1942) and the poet in Max Ophuls'* *La Ronde* (1950). He also played mannered cynics – the killers of *Drôle de drame* and *Le Puritain* (both 1937) – and the dual hero of Jean Renoir's* *Le Testament du Dr Cordelier* (1961). His triumph was Baptiste in *Les Enfants du paradis*, based on the mime Debureau, a character he suggested to Carné and Jacques Prévert*, thus also reviving popular interest in pantomime. His last important part was in Ettore Scola's *La Nuit de Varennes* (1982).

BAUR, Harry

Henri Baur; Montrouge 1880 – Paris 1943

French actor. A prominent stage actor who became one of the most popular stars of the 1930s. After a few silent parts, Baur's film career proper started with the coming of sound, in Julien Duvivier's* *David Golder* (1930). He then embarked on a prolific screen career, including many films with Duvivier. A corpulent man with a resonant voice, his stagey performance style ranged from the hammy (as in Granowsky's *Tarass Boulba*, 1936, or Duvivier's *Un carnet de bal*, 1937) to the soberly moving, especially as Jean Valjean in Raymond Bernard's* *Les Misérables* (1933), as the judge in Pierre Chenal's* *Crime et châtiment/Crime and Punishment* (1935), and in Robert Siodmak's* *Mollenard* (1937).

Baur died horrifyingly after torture by the Gestapo (though, ironically, he had worked for the German firm Continental).

BAYE, Nathalie

[Judith Mesnil?] Mainneville 1948

French actress, trained in theatre and dance and launched in film by François Truffaut's* *La Nuit américaine/Day for Night* (1973), in which she plays the continuity person. With Miou-Miou*, Isabelle Huppert* and Isabelle Adjani*, Baye became one of the quartet of strong French actresses of the 1970s and 1980s. Truffaut's *La Chambre verte/The Green Room* (1978), Bertrand Tavernier's* *Une semaine de vacances* and Jean-Luc Godard's* *Sauve qui peut (la vie)/Slow Motion* (1980, Best Actress César*) established her screen persona.

Capitalising on her discreet good looks, they revealed a vulnerable yet determined personality whose naturalistic performances are characterised by graceful gestures, a shy smile and occasional tearfulness. This image endures even in against-the-grain roles like the prostitute in Bob Swaim's *La Balance* (1982, Best Actress César) or the sensual heroine of *Le Retour de Martin Guerre/The Return of Martin Guerre* (1982).

Baye's brief marriage to pop star Johnny Halliday in the early 1980s was newsworthy, but her career declined somewhat in the latter part of the decade. She has, however, successfully reappeared in 'independent yet vulnerable' roles in Diane Kurys'* *La Baule-les-Pins/C'est la vie* (1989) and Nicole Garcia's *Un Week-end sur deux* (1990). She starred in *Mensonge/The Lie* (1993), one of the first French AIDS movies.

BAZIN, André — Angers 1918 – Bry-sur-Marne 1958

French film critic and theoretician. An eminent film critic and educator in France in the 1940s and 1950s (he taught at IDHEC* among other institutions), Bazin is the single most influential writer in film studies, 'as central a figure in film aesthetics as Freud is in psychology' (Andrew Sarris). Although he had predecessors – Louis Delluc*, Rudolf Arnheim, Béla Balázs, Paul Rotha – Bazin's uniqueness was to combine rigorous film analysis, militant pedagogic vocation and popularising journalism (as film critic for *Le Parisien libéré*). His intellectual training was a blend of Catholicism, Catholic-inspired philosophy and socialist commitment. Working for *Travail et Culture*, he took the cinema to factories, trade union halls and the *ciné-clubs* which he did much to develop, tirelessly commenting and stimulating discussion; some of his best essays are the result of these activities, such as his celebrated analysis of *Le Jour se lève* (1939), published in 1947. Working during the war and the period of liberation, a time of unparalleled enthusiasm for the cinema, Bazin charted the main areas of film studies as we know them, effectively creating the discipline: authorship (a pioneering study of Orson Welles, a defence of Chaplin, writings on Jean Renoir* and new independent film-makers such as Jean-Pierre Melville* and Jacques Tati*, which led Bazin's disciples to develop the *politique des auteurs**), realism (sparked by his interest in documentary and neo-realism*), stars (Humphrey Bogart, Jean Gabin*), the notion of a 'classical' Hollywood cinema. His idea of cinema as a 'window on the world' and his defence of long takes and deep-focus cinematography against Soviet montage are his best known (sometimes reductively) and most controversial views – even at the time, when Bazin was accused of 'formalism' by critics such as Georges Sadoul*. It is also the case that for all his openness to the social and historical world Bazin was oblivious of the male bias of his milieu and filmic interests. Bazin's theoretical work came under renewed attack in the

1970s, when his 'bourgeois' emphasis on *auteurs* and his belief in the integrity of visual space were out of step with new thinking inspired by psychoanalysis, semiology and Marxism. However, these critiques, initiated at *Cahiers du cinéma**, contained more than a hint of Oedipal rebellion; they could not have existed without the solid foundations that Bazin had laid down. Furthermore, as Dudley Andrew points out, some of the concerns of 1980s and 1990s film studies, such as the status of images, are indebted to his work on the 'ontology' of the image. By all accounts a captivating, generous personality, Bazin acted as mentor to the New Wave* and was an adoptive father to François Truffaut*, who characterised him as 'intelligence itself'. He died prematurely just before the release of Truffaut's first feature, *Les Quatre cents coups/The 400 Blows* (1959), which was dedicated to him.

Bib: Dudley Andrew, *André Bazin* (1978, reprinted 1990).

BÉART, Emmanuelle — Saint-Tropez 1964

French actress (daughter of singer Guy Béart) who rose to prominence as the young heroine of Claude Berri's* *Manon des sources* (1986), for which she was awarded a César* in 1987. At that point, her fame rested mainly on her exquisite beauty, later prominently displayed in Jacques Rivette's* *La Belle Noiseuse* (1991), where she plays a nude model to Michel Piccoli's* obsessive painter. She subsequently matured into the archetypal sensitive young woman of art cinema, especially with her role in the internationally successful *Un coeur en hiver/A Heart in Winter* (1993, directed by Claude Sautet*, co-starring, as in *Manon des sources*, Daniel Auteuil*) and in Sautet's *Nelly et M. Arnaud* (1995). She also starred in Claude Chabrol's* *L'Enfer* (1994). Her part in the US production *Mission Impossible* (1995) alongside Tom Cruise may signal a new departure.

BEAUREGARD, Georges de — Edgar de Beauregard; Marseilles 1920 – Paris 1984

French producer, who became a key player in the development of *auteur* cinema in France. Beauregard earned the sobriquet 'father of the New Wave*' for his work with Jean-Luc Godard*, especially their legendary collaboration on *A bout de souffle/Breathless* (1960). A former journalist, Beauregard had worked in French film export, especially to Spain, which had led him to produce two of Juan Antonio Bardem's films. He introduced Godard to Raoul Coutard* and saw them through the difficult shoot of *A bout de souffle.* He produced many of Godard's subsequent films, as well as films by Jacques Demy*, Agnès Varda*, Jean-Pierre Melville*, Jacques Rivette* and Eric Rohmer*, among others. A cinema in Paris bears his name.

BECKER, Jacques

Paris 1906–60

French director. The son of an Anglo-French upper middle-class family, Becker acted as assistant to Jean Renoir* in the 1930s. This was a key influence on his work and critical reputation, locating him within the realist-humanist tradition of French cinema.

A co-director of the communist propaganda film *La Vie est à nous* (1936) and a number of short films, Becker started making features in 1942 with the thriller *Dernier atout,* and *Goupi Mains-rouges/It Happened at the Inn* (1943), a sombre peasant saga. *Falbalas*, an elegant yet acid-tinged portrait of a fashion house, followed in 1945. Although lacking a clear social agenda, Becker's work can be seen, like Renoir's, as an ethnocentric panorama of his time: *Rendez-vous de juillet* (1949) is a study of the postwar generation; *Antoine et Antoinette* (1947), *Édouard et Caroline* (1951) and *Rue de l'Estrapade* (1953) are light comedies which gently interrogate their popular and bourgeois settings; as Becker put it, 'I am French, I work on Frenchmen, I look at Frenchmen, I am interested in Frenchmen.' At the same time, Becker's two greatest films were genre works. *Casque d'or/Golden Marie* (1952, with Simone Signoret*) is a romantic costume drama set in turn-of-the-century Paris; undercutting the ostentation of the genre with the sobriety of its performances, it provides a rare sympathetic portrait of female desire. *Touchez pas au grisbi/ Honour Among Thieves* (1954), starring Jean Gabin*, defined the postwar *policier**, with its families of Parisian gangsters for whom loyalty and conviviality were as important as the heists. In the 1950s, Becker also made star vehicles such as *Montparnasse 19/Modigliani of Montparnasse* (1958, with Gérard Philipe*) and comedies, before the tense prison drama *Le Trou/The Night Watch* (1960), finished by his son Jean Becker (who as a director in his own right made *L'Été meurtrier/One Deadly Summer* with Isabelle Adjani* in 1982).

Underlying Becker's diversity were a vision of 'French-ness' in its quotidian dimension and the qualities of classical French cinema: 'professionalism, forthrightness, authenticity' (Dudley Andrew).

Other Films Include: *Ali Baba et les 40 voleurs/Ali Baba* (1954); *Les Aventures d'Arsène Lupin/The Adventures of Arsène Lupin* (1956).

BEINEIX, Jean-Jacques

Paris 1946

French director. Beineix's career is marked by spectacular successes – *Diva* (1981), *37°2 le matin/Betty Blue* (1986) – and equally spectacular commercial failures: *La Lune dans le caniveau/The Moon in the Gutter* (1983, Fr./It.), *Roselyne et les lions/Roselyne and the Lions* (1989), *IP5* (1992). An eclectic transatlantic training with directors ranging from Jerry Lewis to Claude Berri*, and extensive work in advertising (post-

Diva), are regularly cited by critics to account for Beineix's penchant for non-naturalistic colours, object fetishism and startling framings, and have led to accusations of 'style over substance', connecting him to the *cinéma du look** and film-makers such as Luc Besson* and Leos Carax*.

Beineix has convincingly argued that advertising is *the* idiom of youth culture, but has rarely successfully 'spoken' to that youth culture, except in *Diva*, a cult film of the 1980s, and *37°2 le matin* (thanks largely to the exuberant performance of Béatrice Dalle*). Despite a coherent aesthetic programme, Beineix has failed to win over critics in France, where he is rarely considered an *auteur*. Yet his work combines the baroque *mise-en-scène* and romantic streak characteristic of many European film-makers whose work he vigorously defended during the 1993 GATT negotiations. In 1994 he made *Otaku*, a video documentary on obsessive Japanese male hobbyists.

BELMONDO, Jean-Paul — Neuilly-sur-Seine 1933

French actor and producer. Jean-Paul Belmondo will always be remembered for his embodiment of the emblematic anti-heroes of the New Wave* in Jean-Luc Godard's* *A bout de souffle/Breathless* (1960) and *Pierrot le fou* (1965), but he has also been a pillar of the French mainstream cinema for over two decades.

Belmondo's early success stemmed from stage-bred acting skills and unconventional looks: his engagingly lived-in face, dangling *gauloise* and casually insolent delivery memorably defined the persona of his early films, from Claude Sautet's* *Classe tous risques/The Big Risk* (1960) and the Godard films to Peter Brook and Marguerite Duras'* *Moderato Cantabile* (1960) and Jean-Pierre Melville's* *Léon Morin, prêtre* (1961). Like his rival Alain Delon*, Belmondo turned away from *auteur* cinema towards popular genres after the success of the swashbuckler *Cartouche* (1961) and especially *L'Homme de Rio/That Man from Rio* (1964). Also like Delon, Belmondo favoured stories of virile adventure and friendship, but laced with humour and famously undoubled stunts (if Delon emulated Clint Eastwood, Belmondo was in the James Bond mode). 'Bébel' became one of the populist heroes of French cinema in a series of vehicles such as *Borsalino* (1970, with Delon), *Le Casse* (1971, Fr./It.), *Le Magnifique* (1973) and *L'As des as* (1982). But again like Delon, his popularity declined in the late 1980s and his output slowed. Apart from producing his own as well as some *auteur* films (Alain Resnais'* *Stavisky...*, 1974, Claire Denis' *Chocolat*, 1988), he has triumphantly returned to the Parisian stage. He starred in a multi-layered role (as Jean Valjean, but also as a wrongly accused convict and a boxer/removal man who becomes a resistance hero) in Claude Lelouch's* version of Victor Hugo's novel, *Les Misérables du XXe siècle.*

Other Films Include: *Les Tricheurs, Charlotte et son Jules* [short] (1958); *A double tour/Web of Passion* (1959); *Une femme est une femme* (1961); *Un singe en hiver* (1962); *Le Doulos, L'Aîné des Ferchaux* (1963); *Cent mille dollars au soleil, Week-end à Zuydcoote/Weekend at Dunkirk* (1964); *Les Tribulations d'un Chinois en Chine/Up to His Ears* (1965); *Tendre voyou* (1966); *Le Voleur/The Thief of Paris* (1967); *Le Cerveau, La Sirène du Mississipi/Mississippi Mermaid* (1969); *Docteur Popaul* (1972); *Peur sur la ville/The Night Caller* (1975); *L'Alpagueur* (1976); *L'Animal* (1977); *Flic ou voyou* (1979); *Le Guignolo* (1980); *Le Professionnel* (1981); *Le Marginal* (1983); *Les Morfalous, Joyeuses Pâques* (1984); *Hold-up* (1985); *Le Solitaire* (1987); *L'Itinéraire d'un enfant gâté* (1988).

BENOÎT-LÉVY, Jean – see EPSTEIN, Marie

BERNARD, Raymond

Paris 1891–1977

French director, son of playwright Tristan Bernard. Bernard's acting debut was in *Jeanne Doré* with Sarah Bernhardt (play 1913, film 1915). He joined his father at Gaumont*, where both worked with Jacques Feyder*, and started directing in 1917. After *Le Petit café* (1919) with Max Linder*, and other mainstream films, Bernard achieved prominence in historical dramas, starting with *Le Miracle des loups/The Miracle of the Wolves* (1924), a spectacular medieval epic with battle scenes shot in Carcassonne, more impressive, according to Kevin Brownlow, than its model, D. W. Griffith's *Intolerance* (1916). *Le Joueur d'échec/The Chess Player* (1927), set in Poland, was equally successful. Bernard skilfully made the transition to sound, joining Pathé*-Natan. *Les Croix de bois/The Wooden Crosses* (1931, based on Roland Dorgelès' best-selling novel), a haunting World War I story starring Pierre Blanchar*, was lent authenticity by the fact that Bernard, Blanchar and other members of the cast were themselves war veterans. Bernard directed probably the best version of *Les Misérables* (1933, in three parts), starring Harry Baur* and Charles Vanel*. His 1930s films also include the excellent populist melodrama *Faubourg-Montmartre* (1931) and the spy story *Marthe Richard au service de la France/Marthe Richard* (1937), with Edwige Feuillère* and Erich von Stroheim. With the exception of the war years, Bernard worked until the late 1950s.

Other Films Include: *Tarakanova* (1930); *Tartarin de Tarascon* (1934); *J'étais une aventurière* (1938); *Adieu chérie* (1946); *La Dame aux camélias* (1953); *La Belle de Cadix* (1953).

BERRI, Claude

Claude Langman; Paris 1934

French director, producer and actor, internationally famous as the director of *Jean de Florette* and *Manon des sources* (1986), the lyrical and nostalgic recreations of Marcel Pagnol's* Provençal universe [> HERITAGE CINEMA IN EUROPE]. Berri started with an Oscar-winning short, *Le Poulet/The Chicken* (1963), and semi-autobiographical films such as *Le Vieil homme et l'enfant/The Two of Us* (1967), *Mazel Tov ou le mariage/Marry Me! Marry Me!* (1968) and *Sex-shop* (1972). There followed 'socio-comic' films, notably *Le Maître d'école/The Schoolmaster* (1981) and *Tchao Pantin* (1983), both starring Coluche, and the Catherine Deneuve* vehicle *Je vous aime* (1980). Since the triumph of *Jean de Florette* and *Manon des sources*, Berri has continued to make high-budget literary adaptations with *Uranus* (1990) and a lavish version of *Germinal* (1993), the latter released in France at the same time as Steven Spielberg's *Jurassic Park* and a totem in the battle to defend European audio-visual culture against American 'cultural imperialism' during the GATT negotiations. Across the different genres he has worked in, Berri's cinema is populist and popular, recalling, as in the title of his 1971 film *Le Cinéma de papa/Daddy's Cinema*, a classic heritage of realism, high production values, solid plots and popular stars.

Berri is also an important producer. He has worked with film-makers like André Téchiné*, Jacques Rivette* and Roman Polanski* (*Tess*, 1979), and produced two French 'super-productions' of the 1990s: *L'Amant/The Lover* (1991) and *La Reine Margot* (1994) as well as a number of other successful French films, such as Christian Vincent's *La Séparation* (1994) and Josiane Balasko's* *Gazon maudit/French Twist* (1995). His sister, Arlette Langman, is a scriptwriter and editor.

BERRY, Jules

Jules Paufichet; Poitiers 1883 – Paris 1951

French actor. Berry's flourishing career in Parisian *boulevard* theatre was paralleled by appearances in almost a hundred films, mostly in the 1930s. He transposed to the screen his elegant cad in countless examples of *théâtre filmé* (filmed theatre), such as *Arlette et ses papas* (1934) or *L'Habit vert* (1937), brilliantly reciting – and sometimes improvising – sparkling dialogue in a blur of frenetic gestures. But Berry's comic persona could also take on sinister tones, as in his most celebrated dramatic films, Jean Renoir's* *Le Crime de Monsieur Lange* (1935), Marcel Carné's* *Le Jour se lève* (1939) and *Les Visiteurs du soir* (1942, as the devil), and Albert Valentin's* *Marie-Martine* (1943). Whatever the genre or quality of the film, Berry's performances were always a delight, making him one of the most popular and instantly recognisable French film actors.

BESSON, Luc

Paris 1959

French director. Besson served his assistantship in film, advertising and music videos, shooting the critically successful *Le Dernier combat/The Last Battle* (1982) at the age of twenty-three. Gaumont* then lined up stars Isabelle Adjani* and Christophe Lambert and gave him a huge budget for his first major feature, *Subway* (1985). This modish mix of thriller and post-modern *cinéma du look**, set in a Paris métro recreated by Alexandre Trauner*, was disliked by critics but won huge popular acclaim, particularly among the young. This was echoed by Besson's next feature, *Le Grand bleu/The Big Blue* (1988), one of the French film events of the 1980s. If *Le Grand bleu* was almost pure image and no plot in its celebration of the ecstasy of deep-sea diving, *Nikita* (1990) heralded a return to narrative, in science-fiction thriller mode. The tensions in Besson's work are emblematic of a strand in late 1980s/early 1990s French cinema: the youth appeal of US genres (rock music, thriller) is balanced by the iconography of Frenchness (restaurants, fashion, Paris métro), while the much-feared contamination of cinema by 'impure' forms (video, advertisements) is offset by an insistence on spectacular techniques which demand – so far successfully – that audiences actually sit in a cinema to appreciate them. Besson's latest film, *Leon* (1994), shot in English in New York, was a major international success.

BINOCHE, Juliette

Paris 1964

French actress. After a spell in theatre and television, Binoche emerged around 1985 with small parts in Jean-Luc Godard's* *Je vous salue, Marie/Hail Mary!* (1984) and Jacques Doillon's* *La Vie de famille* (1985), and the lead in André Téchiné's* *Rendez-vous* (1985). Her gamine looks and seductive combination of spontaneity and sensuality recalled New Wave* actresses, especially in Leos Carax's* *Mauvais sang/The Night is Young* (1986) and *Les Amants du Pont-Neuf* (1991). Lately, she has moved towards more 'mature' parts and an international career, with Philip Kaufman's *The Unbearable Lightness of Being* (1987, US), Louis Malle's* *Damage/Fatale* (1992, UK/Fr.), Krzysztof Kieślowski's* *Trois couleurs bleu/Three Colours: Blue* (1993), Anthony Minghella's *The English Patient* (1995, US) and Chantal Akerman's* *Un divan à New York* (1996, Fr./Bel.). Jean-Paul Rappeneau's* *Le Hussard sur le toit/The Horseman on the Roof* (1995) extended her range further into French popular cinema.

BLANCHAR, Pierre

Pierre Blanchard; Philippeville [Skikda], Algeria 1892 – Paris 1963

French actor. Like many French actors of the classical period, Blanchar pursued a dual career on stage and screen. He shared with Jean-Louis Barrault* piercing eyes and a feverish, mannered acting style, well suited to tormented heroes such as Raskolnikov in Pierre Chenal's* *Crime et châtiment/Crime and Punishment* (1935, for which he was awarded a prize at Venice). His good looks won him romantic leads, often in costume, as in *L'Affaire du courrier de Lyon/The Courier of Lyons* (1937). His powerful incarnation of the tragic World War I hero of Raymond Bernard's* *Les Croix de bois/The Wooden Crosses* (1931) gave him a powerful aura of authenticity (he had himself been wounded in the trenches). During World War II, Blanchar played the emblematic Pontcarral in Jean Delannoy's* *Pontcarral, colonel d'Empire* (1942), a film widely considered as obliquely 'resistant'. At the liberation he headed the film industry's Liberation Committee and read the voice-over commentary for the collective *Libération de Paris* (1944–45). With a few exceptions, such as Delannoy's *La Symphonie pastorale* (1946), he then mostly devoted himself to the theatre.

BLIER, Bernard

Buenos Aires, Argentina 1916 – Paris 1989

French actor. Blier was the archetype of the character actor who, despite few leading roles, ranked high in the French star firmament (he was tenth in the overall postwar French box-office popularity rankings). Blier trained in the theatre with Louis Jouvet*, a relationship portrayed in Marc Allégret's* *Entrée des artistes/The Curtain Rises* (1938), though his first important part was in *Gribouille* (1937). With his unglamorous physique, he cornered the market in sympathetic humiliated husbands, as in *Hôtel du Nord* (1938) and *Quai des Orfèvres* (1947). He ventured into dramatic parts as well as sinister ones, epitomised by his excellent Inspector Javert of *Les Misérables* (1958). Generally, though, he played comic roles and became a pillar of French postwar comedies, such as those of Georges Lautner and Jean Yanne, appearing in over 200 films [> COMEDY IN FRANCE].

Blier also appeared in films directed by his son Bertrand Blier*, in particular *Buffet froid* (1979). He received a César* for life achievement in 1988.

BLIER, Bertrand

Boulogne-Billancourt 1939

French director, son of actor Bernard Blier*. Blier made his first feature, *Hitler, connais pas!*, in 1963, but his career took off with the spectacularly successful *Les Valseuses/Going Places* (1973). Inspired by the libertarian *café-théâtre*, *Les Valseuses* also launched Gérard Depardieu*, Miou-Miou* and Patrick Dewaere. This picaresque saga of two hoodlums on the run encapsulates the features of Blier's subsequent (and self-referential) work: an ability to capture *'l'air du temps'* – here post-1968 societal changes – a desire to shock, and a misogyny 'justified' by women's extravagant sexual demands and men's fear of inadequacy (as in *Calmos/Femmes Fatales*, 1975, and *Préparez vos mouchoirs/Get Out Your Handkerchiefs*, 1977, which won an Oscar for best foreign film). Technically accomplished and by turns brilliantly funny and gruesome, Blier's cynical, absurdist and comic cinema is often popular at the French box office, in particular *Tenue de soirée/ Ménage* (1986, special jury prize at Cannes and Best film César*). The more arty *Trop belle pour toi* (1989) was an international hit.

Bib: Jill Forbes, *The Cinema in France After the New Wave* (1992).

Other Films: *Si j'étais un espion/If I Was a Spy* (1967); *Buffet froid* (1979); *Beau-père* (1981); *La Femme de mon pote/My Best Friend's Girl* (1983); *Notre histoire/Our Story* (1984); *Merci la vie* (1991); *Un, deux, trois soleil (*1993); *Mon homme* (1995).

BOISSET, Yves

Paris 1939

French director, a graduate of IDHEC*, former film critic and admirer of American cinema, who started making films in the late 1960s. Boisset worked in the *policier** genre from the start, but in his most interesting work of the 1970s he used it to raise topical social issues in the manner of André Cayatte, but also of the politicised cinema of the period in France and especially Italy. He dealt, for instance, with corruption in the police (*Un Condé/The Cop*, 1970) and in government (*L'Attentat/The French Conspiracy*, 1972), with racism in *Dupont Lajoie* (1975), with the Algerian war in *R.A.S.* (1973), and with fascist secret police groups in *Le Juge Fayard dit 'Le Shérif'* (1976) – films that presented their argument in a direct, clear-cut (some say overly black-and-white) and entertaining way. They were often subject to political censorship, Boisset acquiring a solidly left-wing reputation. *La Femme flic/Female Cop* (1980), about a policewoman (played by Miou-Miou*), added the impact of feminism and signalled a move to more psychological subject matter. Boisset is a prolific director, making films at the rate of almost one a year, though except for *Allons z'enfants* (1980) and *Bleu comme l'enfer* (1986) none has lately achieved the success of his earlier work. In 1994 he replaced Costa-Gavras* as director of *L'Affaire Dreyfus*.

BONNAIRE, Sandrine Clermont-Ferrand 1967

French actress. Picked out of hundreds of adolescent hopefuls, Bonnaire was an overnight sensation in Maurice Pialat's* *A nos amours/To Our Loves* (1983). Her lack of training and working-class origins added authenticity to her talented performance as the unruly heroine, and to her portrayal of a tragic drop-out in Agnès Varda's* *Sans toit ni loi/Vagabonde* (1985). Bonnaire (who received a César for both films) has become a major figure among young French actors, injecting into her heroines a toughness recalling the young Jeanne Moreau*. Her career has gone from strength to strength, and she received an international accolade with an award at the 1995 Venice film festival for her performance in Claude Chabrol's* *La Cérémonie/Judgement in Stone* (1995), co-starring Isabelle Huppert*.

Other Films Include: *Blanche et Marie* (1984); *Police* (1985); *Sous le soleil de Satan/Under Satan's Sun* (1987); *Monsieur Hire, Peaux de vaches* (1989); *Jeanne la pucelle* (1994).

BOROWCZYK, Walerian – see 'French Cinema in Europe', page 151

BOST, Pierre – see AURENCHE, Jean

BOURVIL André Raimbourg; Petrot-Vicquemare 1917 – Paris 1970

French actor. One of the best-loved popular French film comedians, Bourvil started as an accordionist in Normandy dance halls and later sang in Parisian cabarets and on the radio, where he was discovered. From his first lead in *La Ferme du pendu* (1945), a peasant melodrama, he drew on his origins as a farmer's son to develop his early persona of the 'village idiot'. He emerged as a star in Claude Autant-Lara's* *La Traversée de Paris/A Pig Across Paris* (1956), for which he won a prize at Venice. From then on he broadened his comic peasant to embody the 'average Frenchman' duped by more aggressive middle-class partners (Jean Gabin* in *La Traversée*, Louis de Funès* in the hits *Le Corniaud/The Sucker*, 1965, and *La Grande vadrouille/Don't Look Now, We're Being Shot At*, 1966).

Like many comics, Bourvil had ambitions to play serious roles, which he did as the brilliantly sinister Thénardier of *Les Misérables*

(1958) and in Jean-Pierre Melville's* thriller *Le Cercle rouge/The Red Circle* (1970), made shortly before his death. But for French audiences his enduring appeal was comic, the not-so-simple peasant and epitome of the man in the street, vindicated through stardom.

Other Films Include: *Miquette et sa mère* (1950); *Le Passe-muraille* (1950); *Le Trou normand* (1952); *Si Versailles m'était conté* (1954); *Le Miroir à deux faces* (1958); *Le Chemin des écoliers* (1959); *Tout l'or du monde* (1961); *La Cuisine au beurre* (1963); *Les Grandes gueules* (1965); *Le Cerveau* (1969).

BOYER, Charles

Figeac 1897 – Phoenix, Arizona 1978

French actor. Boyer, along with Maurice Chevalier*, was one of the only French stars to make a really successful career in Hollywood. A cultured and classically trained actor, Boyer possessed distinguished looks, dark eyes and a famous velvety voice. He emerged in the 1920s, but fame came with sound. He appeared in proletarian roles in Franco-German productions such as *Tumultes* (1931) and Fritz Lang's* French film *Liliom* (1934). However, his real register was that of the lover in romantic (often costume) melodrama; notably with Danielle Darrieux* in *Mayerling* (1936) and Michèle Morgan* in *Orage* (1937), embodying a man consumed by love, the object of desire of the heroine and of the camera. This is also his Hollywood image, in melodramas such as *All This and Heaven Too* (1940) with Bette Davis and *Back Street* (1941) with Margaret Sullavan. He also conveyed the sinister aspect of male seduction, especially in *Gaslight* (1944, with Ingrid Bergman). Boyer took American citizenship in 1942 and was active in promoting Franco-American relations. The antithesis of Chevalier's caricatural Frenchman, Boyer nevertheless owed much of his success in Hollywood to a romantic notion of 'Frenchness'. He kept up French connections, acting in films directed by exiles such as Julien Duvivier* (*Tales of Manhattan*, 1942) and remakes of French films (*Algiers*, 1938, after *Pépé le Moko*; *The Thirteenth Letter*, 1951, after *Le Corbeau*). He continued his international career after the war, with notable parts in Max Ophuls'* *Madame de...* (1953), Christian-Jaque's* *Nana* (1954) and Alain Resnais'* *Stavisky...* (1974). He killed himself two days after the death of his wife of forty-four years, the British actress Pat Paterson, perhaps his most romantic gesture.

BRASILLACH, Robert – see BARDÈCHE, Maurice

BRASSEUR, Pierre

Pierre-Albert Espinasse; Paris 1905 – Brunico, Italy 1972

French actor. A 'sacred monster' of stage and screen, whose immense filmography (over 130 titles) includes few leading parts, yet who left his mark on French cinema, especially in *Les Enfants du paradis* (1943–45). Brasseur trained at the Paris Conservatoire; he acted in, and wrote plays for, *boulevard* theatre. From the late 1920s he appeared indiscriminately in minor roles in popular movies, gradually specialising in depraved rogues (Marcel Carné's* *Quai des brumes*, 1938) and demented bohemians (Jean Grémillon's* *Lumière d'été*, 1943). Close to the Surrealists, he appeared in Pierre Prévert's* fantasy *Adieu Léonard* (1943, written 1932). He developed a baroque, rather menacing persona of seducer and/or *bon viveur* (as in Denys de la Patellière's *Les Grandes familles*, 1958). He appeared in René Clair's* *Porte des Lilas* (1957), Georges Franju's* *Les Yeux sans visage/Eyes With-out a Face* (1960) and Walerian Borowczyk's* *Goto l'île d'amour/Goto, Isle of Love* (1969). But the glory of his career remains his flamboyant incarnation of the actor Frédérick Lemaître in *Les Enfants du paradis*. His subversion of an over-the-top melodrama rehearsal is one of the great moments of French cinema.

Brasseur was once married to the actress and novelist Odette Joyeux (born Paris, 1917), who played intense young women, notably in Marc Allégret's* *Entrée des artistes/The Curtain Rises* (1938) and Claude Autant-Lara's* *Douce* (1943). Their son Claude Brasseur (Claude Espinasse, born Paris 1936) has pursued a successful career on stage and in the cinema since the late 1950s.

BRAUNBERGER, Pierre

Paris 1905–90

French producer, associated with the new breed of independent producers who supported the New Wave* (see also Georges de Beauregard* and Anatole Dauman*). Braunberger, however, was by then already a veteran, with experience of the 'first wave' of *auteur* cinema in France [> FRENCH AVANT-GARDE] during which he produced such films as René Clair's *Entr'acte* (1924), Luis Buñuel's *L'Age d'or* (1930) and Jean Renoir's* *La Chienne* (1931), as well as more mainstream films, through his company Etablissements Braunberger-Richebé. His New Wave involvements include François Truffaut's* *Tirez sur le pianiste/Shoot the Pianist* (1960) and Jean Rouch's* *Moi, un noir* (1959). He went on to produce films by Maurice Pialat* and Claude Lelouch*, among others. In 1969 he co-founded the GREC (Groupe de recherches et d'essais cinématographiques), an organisation devoted to financing short, 'uncommercial' projects. Braunberger recounted his eventful life and work in an entertaining and informative autobiography, *Cinémamémoire* (1987).

BREL, Jacques – see 'French Cinema in Europe', page 152

BRESSON, Robert
Bromont-Lamothe 1907

French director. One of the most respected *auteurs* of world cinema, described by admirer Paul Schrader as 'the most important spiritual artist' and as a 'Jansenist' by his detractors. Bresson's originality within French cinema is twofold. First, he is almost unique in pursuing a religious discourse; second, his dislike of actors and use of unknown amateurs runs counter to the great French tradition of performance- and dialogue-based cinema.

Bresson studied philosophy and was a photographer and painter before working in film. Startlingly, he began as a scriptwriter on mainstream comedies in the 1930s. His first feature, *Les Anges du péché* (1943), was a naturalistic convent drama with established actors, qualified by Bresson as 'a bit naive, too simple'. He emerged as a force in independent cinema with *Les Dames du Bois de Boulogne* (1945) and *Le Journal d'un curé de campagne/The Diary of a Country Priest* (1951), adapted from a novel by the Catholic writer Georges Bernanos. Apart from the themes of redemption and divine grace which inform all his work, *Le Journal* exemplified the power of Bresson's austere black-and-white *mise-en-scène,* in which extreme sparseness combines with an almost hyper-realist use of locations and soundtrack. Bresson's next two films, *Un condamné à mort s'est échappé/A Man Escaped* (1956) and *Pickpocket* (1959), are understated yet lyrical, offering minute observation of the gestures and sounds of a prison escape in the former, and of the techniques of picking pockets in the latter (Schrader reprised the ending of *Pickpocket* in his *American Gigolo*, 1979). Bresson went on to produce one of the most consistent bodies of films in French cinema, introducing colour in *Une femme douce/A Gentle Creature* (1969), also noteworthy for the fact that its principal 'model', Dominique Sanda, became a star in her own right (as did Anne Wiazemsky, the protagonist of *Au hasard, Balthazar*, 1966) – a phenomenon said to irritate Bresson.

Bresson's cinema, while critically acclaimed, does not attract large audiences and he has made relatively few films, putting his difficulties, not unreasonably, down to his refusal of 'performance'. His opposition to mainstream cinema, the coherence of his themes and *mise-en-scène* and his self-scripted films made him one of the models for the future New Wave* in the early 1950s. Bresson's quest for a 'pure' cinema – 'I want to be as far from literature as possible, as far from every existing art' – actually relates him to an even earlier tradition, that of the French avant-garde* of the 1920s.

Bib: Paul Schrader, *Transcendental Style in Film: Ozu, Bresson, Dreyer* (1988).

Other Films: *Le Procès de Jeanne d'Arc/The Trial of Joan of Arc* (1962); *Mouchette* (1967); *Les Quatre nuits d'un rêveur/Four Nights of a Dreamer* (1971); *Lancelot du lac* (1974); *Le Diable probablement/The Devil Probably* (1977); *L'Argent* (1983).

BRIALY, Jean-Claude

Aumale [Sour El-Ghozlan], Algeria 1933

French actor and director. Brialy was one of the totem actors of the New Wave*. Claude Chabrol's* *Le Beau Serge* (1957) and *Les Cousins* (1958) and Jean-Luc Godard's* *Une femme est une femme/A Woman is a Woman* (1961) fixed his persona as the spoilt young man roaming the streets of Paris in his sports car in search of women and fun. Though he acted in many other films – including Eric Rohmer's* *Le Genou de Claire/Claire's Knee* (1970) and Claude Miller's *L'Effrontée/An Impudent Girl* (1985) – he never regained such prominence. He is, however, a well-known stage actor, theatre owner and media personality and he has continued to feature on the cast of numerous French films, including Patrice Chéreau's *La Reine Margot* (1994) and Régis Warnier's *Une femme française* (1995). He has directed a number of films, including adaptations of classic French children's fables such as *Les Malheurs de Sophie* (1980) and *Un bon petit diable* (1983).

BUÑUEL, Luis – see 'French Cinema in Europe', page 152

C

CAHIERS DU CINÉMA

French film journal, the best-known and probably the most influential in the world, founded in April 1951 by Lo Duca and Jacques Doniol-Valcroze, and joined by André Bazin* for the second issue. *Cahiers'* fame comes from its glorious cinephile 'first period' when the *politique des auteurs** was developed, and when many of its star critics – François Truffaut*, Eric Rohmer* and Jean-Luc Godard* among them – became the film-makers of the New Wave*. *Cahiers* has known many tribulations since, which can be divided into its second and third phases. In the second period, the '*pures et dures*' post-1968 years, theories were developed under the triple aegis of Althusser, Lacan and Foucault and photographs were banned from the cover; this phase also influenced Anglo-American theory via *Screen*. The third and last period, from the late 1970s, has seen a return to cinephilia, precisely at a time when cinema was coming under threat. The critical theories debated in *Cahiers* over these years have been concerned with the status of the cinematic image in relation to television, to 'new images' and to painting, as well as, in a neat return to origins, with the place of the *auteur* in contemporary (especially French) cinema. These debates have not so far had the resonance of the earlier ones, though forthcoming translations of works by one-time editor Serge Daney, the most important film critic of the 1980s, as well as by Pascal Bonitzer and Jacques Aumont, should remedy this.

Cahiers never existed in a vacuum. Bazin wrote for the earlier *L'Ecran français*, and in the postwar years new journals appeared, some still in existence. But while its greatest critical rival remains *Positif**, competition has also emerged from glossy magazines such as *Première* (since 1976), prompting the creation of a news section (1980), with more topical items. In 1984, *Cahiers* diversified into book publishing with Editions de l'Etoile. However much these changes may owe to economic necessity, the continued existence of *Cahiers* (and *Positif*) is testimony to the relative health of French film culture.

CANNES

French film festival, founded in 1938, originally to counter fascist influences thought to contaminate Venice. The planned opening on 1 September 1939 was cancelled because of the war, and the first Cannes festival actually took place six years later. Cannes soon became one of the top world festivals: the cinema was popular, the Côte d'Azur glamorous, and the beach provided endless photo opportunities for starlets. The showbiz factor has always been high at Cannes, whether it was Sophia Loren causing a near-riot in 1958 or Quentin Tarantino's appearance in 1994. As in all such events, the list of prizes over the years reveals both masterpieces and duds. More serious arguments have agitated Cannes periodically, such as German protests over the screening of Alain Resnais'* *Nuit et brouillard/Night and Fog* in 1955 and the closure of the festival by the 'events' of May 1968. François Truffaut* called Cannes 'a failure dominated by rackets, compromises and blunders' in 1957, but two years later he was awarded the *mise-en-scène* prize for *Les Quatre cents coups/The 400 Blows*. Increasing officialdom and suspected 'corruption' has led to the creation of several parallel sections over the years – the 'Semaine internationale de la critique' in 1962 and the 'Quinzaine des réalisateurs' in 1969, generally devoted to independent and *auteur* cinema. Despite the controversies Cannes still fulfils two major functions. It is an important film market, and its awards guarantee distribution rather than oblivion for some non-mainstream, non-Hollywood films.

CANUDO, Ricciotto

Gioia del Colle, Italy 1879 – Paris 1923

Italian-born French film writer. Canudo moved to Paris in 1902 and joined the avant-garde of the 1910s and 1920s [> FRENCH AVANT-GARDE] in which intellectuals, artists and film-makers attempted to define the specificity of the moving image and struggled to assert the legitimacy of the medium. Canudo's main claim to fame is to have coined the phrase 'the seventh art', but he also edited and wrote for a number of early film publications, such as *La Gazette des sept arts,* and headed the group responsible for the first actual cine-club in 1920. In Richard Abel's words, he was 'the most flamboyant prophet of the new art'.

Bib: Richard Abel, *French Cinema, The First Wave, 1915–1929* (1984).

CARAX, Leos

Alex Dupont; Paris 1960

French director, hailed as a prodigy in the 1980s. With his tortured personality, instant success through his first feature, *Boy Meets Girl* (1984), and regular use of alter ego actor Denis Lavant, Carax has been seen as the carrier of the New Wave* inheritance. *Boy Meets Girl*, shot in black and white on location in Paris, combined New Wave romanticism with post-modernism (especially in the use of music). *Mauvais Sang/The Night is Young* (1986) added overt references to Jean-Luc Godard* with the use of primary colours and a Juliette Binoche* made to look like Anna Karina*. The extravagant (in all senses) *Les Amants du Pont-Neuf* (1991), starring Lavant and Binoche, is a sumptuous and romantic tribute to Paris, *amour fou* and Binoche. Carax figures controversially in debates over the *cinéma du look**, his cine-literacy and 'neo-baroque' *mise-en-scène* earning criticism for a beautiful but supposedly 'empty' cinema, but also passionate admiration.

CARETTE, Julien

Paris 1897 – Le Vésinet 1966

French actor, usually known simply as 'Carette'. One of the archetypal character actors or, as Raymond Chirat put it, 'eccentrics' of French cinema: never a star, yet instantly recognised and appreciated by a devoted audience. Carette, who had a long career in theatre and music hall and acted in dozens of comic films, would be just one of these talented bit-players, along with Pauline Carton, Saturnin Fabre, Marguerite Pierry, Sylvie and many others, were it not for his parts in four Jean Renoir* films – *La Grande Illusion, La Marseillaise* (both 1937), *La Bête humaine* (1938) and *La Règle du jeu/Rules of the Game* (1939) – to which he brought his inimitable working-class Parisian accent and a capacity to move and amuse at the same time. The Prévert* brothers and Claude Autant-Lara* also employed him frequently. Carette's death, set alight by his cigarette in a wheelchair, was a sad final scene for such a likeable actor.

Bib: Raymond Chirat and Olivier Barrot, *Les Excentriques du cinéma français (1928–1958)* (1983).

CARNÉ, Marcel

Paris 1909

French director. Carné's place in film history is assured as the foremost exponent of Poetic Realism*, especially in his collaborations with the poet/scriptwriter Jacques Prévert*.

Carné trained as a photographer and started in film as a journalist (for *Cinémagazine*) and assistant director to René Clair* and especially Jacques Feyder*. His first film, *Nogent, Eldorado du dimanche* (1930), was a documentary on working-class leisure, heralding his interest in 'ordinary people'; during the Popular Front* period he worked briefly with the left cooperative Ciné-Liberté. With *Jenny* (1936, starring Françoise Rosay*), Carné established his poetic-realist universe: stylised urban decors, a cast of workers and marginals, a dark and pervasive atmosphere of doom shot through with the genuine poetry of the everyday. It was followed by *Hôtel du Nord*, *Quai des brumes* (both 1938) and *Le Jour se lève* (1939). These films showcased the work of Carné's brilliant team: set designer Alexandre Trauner*, composers Maurice Jaubert* and Joseph Kosma*, émigré cameramen Eugen Schüfftan and Curt Courant, actors like Jean Gabin*, Louis Jouvet*, Michel Simon* and Michèle Morgan*. Last but not least was Prévert, who contributed sardonic humour (as in the surreal-burlesque *Drôle de drame*, 1937) and romantic fatalism, especially in *Quai des brumes* and *Le Jour se lève*, for which he wrote the dialogue.

In the constrained context of the German occupation, Carné, with Prévert, switched to costume dramas. *Les Visiteurs du soir* (1942) was a medieval fable, and *Les Enfants du paradis* (1943–45) an exuberant reconstruction of the Parisian theatre of the 1830s, with a remarkable performance by Arletty*. While these two films drew on the 'poetic' side of poetic realism, *Les Portes de la nuit* (1946) seemed the swansong of its dark populism. Carné, without Prévert, switched to natural decors (*La Marie du port*, 1950) and contemporary subjects, such as the much criticised but highly popular *Les Tricheurs* (1958), a portrait of the young generation, but he never regained his prewar status. However, *Thérèse Raquin* (1953, starring Simone Signoret*) and *L'Air* *de Paris* (1954, with Arletty and Gabin) show that Carné still excelled at evoking, respectively, doomed passion and a nostalgic popular Paris.

Bib: Edward Baron Turk, *Child of Paradise* (1989).

Other Films: *La Fleur de l'âge* (1947, unfinished); *Juliette ou la Clé des songes* (1951); *Le Pays d'où je viens* (1956); *Terrain vague* (1960); *Du mouron pour les petits oiseaux* (1963); *Trois chambres à Manhattan* (1965); *Les Jeunes loups* (1967); *Les Assassins de l'ordre* (1971); *La Merveilleuse visite* (1974); *La Bible* (TV, 1976).

CAROL, Martine

Marie-Louise Mourer; Biarritz 1920 – Monaco 1967

French actress. The most popular French female star before Brigitte Bardot*, Carol has been unjustly disparaged for her acting and for the unfashionable genres she worked in, especially the costume film. Carol began in true starlet mode, bleaching her hair and doing publicity stunts, including throwing herself into the Seine. After small parts on stage (as Maryse Arley) and in film, her career took off with *Caroline Chérie* (1950), directed by Richard Pottier from Cécil Saint-Laurent's 'scandalous' novel. This set Carol on her path as the 'ooh-la-la' star of a series of comic-erotic adventures (actually aimed at a family audience), in which period costumes showed off her ample curves – *Nana* (1955), directed by her then husband Christian-Jaque* from Zola's novel, is a good example. Criticised as 'pandering to the fantasies of Fourth Republic men', she was very popular with women, who appreciated her light touch in contemporary romantic comedies such as Christian-Jaque's *Adorables créatures/Adorable Creatures* (1952). Her sex-goddess image was to be her downfall. In the new era ushered in by Bardot she seemed old-fashioned; the disastrous reception of Max Ophuls'* *Lola Montès* (1955), in which she is presented as a fairground attraction, also affected her badly. Her last years were a sad tale of failed marriages, drink and drugs, leading to suicide. Carol was a vibrant popular performer, the first to challenge the male hegemony at the French box office.

Other Films Include: *Les Belles de nuit, Un caprice de Caroline Chérie* (1952); *Lucrèce Borgia/Sins of the Borgias* (1953); *Madame du Barry* (1954); *Nathalie, agent secret/The Foxiest Girl in Paris* (1957); *Austerlitz* (1960); *Vanina Vanini* (1961, It./Fr.).

CÉSARS

French institution. Césars, the French Oscars, were created in 1975 by advertising executive Georges Cravenne. Awards in twenty categories are determined by nomination and secret voting by members of the Académie du Cinéma (created at the same time), composed of some 2,400 French film professionals. Initially greeted with derision, and not just in the US, the Césars have proved extremely successful and are much sought after by the profession; half the French population watches the 'Nuit des Césars' on television.

CHABROL, Claude

Paris 1930

French director. One of the stable of *Cahiers du cinéma** critics, Chabrol inaugurated the New Wave* with *Le Beau Serge* (1957), *Les Cousins* (1958) and *Les Bonnes femmes* (1960). Like other early New Wave films, these were characterised by independent production, location shooting, new stars (Jean-Claude Brialy*, Stéphane Audran*) and a focus on a young, disaffected generation. Chabrol soon departed from this idiom to enter on a prolific and varied career embracing comedies (*Marie-Chantal contre le docteur Khâ*, 1965), thrillers (*A double tour/Web of Passion*, 1959), war films (*La Ligne de démarcation*, 1966), political thrillers (*Les Noces rouges/Blood Wedding*, 1973, *Nada*, 1974), a 'lesbian' drama (*Les Biches/The Does*, 1968), and more; his filmography runs to over forty features. If there is unity in Chabrol's work, it can be found along two axes. The first is his work with his main star (and for a long time, wife) Stéphane Audran, especially *Le Boucher* (1970) and their superb 'dramas of adultery': *La Femme infidèle/The Unfaithful Wife* (1969), *La Rupture/The Breakup* (1970) and *Juste avant la nuit/Just Before Nightfall* (1971). The second is Chabrol's dissection of the French bourgeoisie, which ranges from the incisive to the affectionate, usually in the thriller format. At the incisive end are *Que la bête meure/Killer!* (1969) and *Violette Nozière* (1978); more affectionate are *Poulet au vinaigre/Cop au vin* (1984), *Masques* (1987) and *Le Cri du hibou/The Cry of the Owl* (1987). With his lush adaptation of *Madame Bovary* (1991, with Isabelle Huppert*), Chabrol made an excursion into the Heritage cinema genre [> HERITAGE CINEMA IN EUROPE], though *Betty* (1992) and *L'Enfer* (1994) signal a return to the bourgeois thrillers, as does *La Cérémonie/ Judgement in Stone* (1995, based on a novel by British crime writer Ruth Rendell), starring Sandrine Bonnaire* and Isabelle Huppert, who were jointly awarded the acting prize at the 1995 Venice film festival. Ironically, given Chabrol's critical beginnings, there is a comfortable 'quality' to his films, which is, however, far from unpleasurable.

Other Films Include: *Les Godelureaux* (1961); *Landru* (1963); *Paris vu par . . .* (1965, ep. 'La Muette'); *Le Scandale/The Champagne Murders*, *La Route de Corinthe* (1967); *La Décade prodigieuse/Ten Days Wonder* (1971); *Docteur Popaul* (1972); *Une partie de plaisir* (1974); *Le Cheval d'orgueil* (1980); *Les Fantômes du chapelier/The Hatter's Ghosts* (1982); *Le Sang des autres/The Blood of Others* (1984); *Inspecteur Lavardin* (1986); *Une affaire de femmes* (1988); *Jours tranquilles à Clichy/Quiet Days in Clichy, Docteur M* (1990).

CHATILIEZ, Etienne — Roubaix 1952

French director who started his career in commercials. With only three feature films (all co-scripted by Florence Quentin), Chatiliez imposed a new type of French comedy, where social derision rests on a particularly good use of wickedly acute, though affectionate, stereotypes. *La Vie est un long fleuve tranquille/Life is a Long Quiet River* (1988) swapped the children of two families on the opposite ends of the social scale (the catholic upper-bourgeoisie and the underclass); *Tatie Danielle* (1990) subverted the stereotype of the benevolent grandmother figure, with the depiction of an old woman who is anything but nice; *Le Bonheur est dans le pré* (1995), less overtly satirical, still targets the provincial bourgeoisie of the previous two films; it features a particularly colourful cast, with Carmen Maura and footballer Eric Cantona, together with classic French actors such as Michel Serrault, Eddie Mitchell and Sabine Azéma.

CHENAL, Pierre — Philippe Cohen; Brussels 1904 – La Garenne-Colombes 1991

French director, one of the most interesting yet least known of the classical French film-makers. A talented draughtsman and poster designer, close to the Surrealists, and a communist sympathiser, Chenal started with documentaries, including on the cinema. His first feature was the extraordinary *Le Martyre de l'obèse* (1932), on the amorous tribulations of an extremely fat man. His second, *La Rue sans nom* (1933), based on Marcel Aymé's novel about a derelict Parisian street, was the first to attract the label of Poetic Realism*. Chenal's subsequent work included prestigious literary adaptations (*Crime et châtiment/Crime and Punishment*, 1935, *L'Homme de nulle part/The Late Mathias Pascal*, 1936, *L'Affaire Lafarge*, 1937) and populist films like *La Maison du Maltais/Sirocco* (1938). *L'Alibi* (1937) – starring a great Louis Jouvet*/Erich von Stroheim duo – and the (first) adaptation of James Cain's *The Postman Always Rings Twice* as *Le Dernier tournant* (1939) mark Chenal as a pioneer of French *film noir*. Chenal spent the war years in Argentina, where he made several films, returning to

France to direct the classic comedy of French provincialism, *Clochemerle* (1948), and several excellent *policiers*, in particular *Section des disparus* (1956) based on David Goodis and *Rafles sur la ville/Sinners of Paris* (1958), which were praised by Jean-Luc Godard*. He also made the anti-racist *Sangre Negra/Native Son* (1949–51, Argentina/US), based on, and starring, the novelist Richard Wright.

Bib: Pierrette Matalon, Claude Guiguet, Jacques Pinturault, *Pierre Chenal* (1987).

CHEVALIER, Maurice Paris 1888–1972

French singer and actor. The leading French male music-hall star of the twentieth century, Chevalier long embodied the international stereotype of the Frenchman. After an impoverished Parisian childhood, 'Momo' quickly graduated from local *cafés-concerts* to stardom in the great Parisian music halls. A superstar in 1920s Paris, he led stage revues with hit songs like '*Valentine*', his stage persona a winsome mixture of cocky *gavroche* and dandy. He was soon signed by Paramount. Chevalier, who had already appeared in many French shorts, made sixteen US movies between 1928 and 1935. *Innocents of Paris* and *The Love Parade* (both 1929) were his first hits, followed by many others; the best – *The Smiling Lieutenant* (1931), *One Hour With You* (1932) and *The Merry Widow* (1934) – were directed by Ernst Lubitsch. In the make-believe universe of these musicals, Chevalier epitomised the frivolously sexy Parisian, with emphatic gestures and heavy French accent. Returning to Europe in 1935, he made a few films which were (surprisingly) only moderately successful, his Hollywood glamour clashing with French populism in the underrated *L'Homme du jour* (1936, dir. Julien Duvivier*), *Avec le sourire/With a Smile* (1936, dir. Maurice Tourneur*) and *Pièges/Personal Column* (1939), Robert Siodmak's* last French film. He also starred in René Clair's* *Break the News* (1938, UK) and Curtis (Kurt) Bernhardt's *The Beloved Vagabond*, made in London in 1936. A performing tour for French prisoners of war in Germany caused Chevalier problems at the Liberation. However, he went on singing and acting, notably in René Clair's* *Le Silence est d'or/Man About Town* (1947) and Vincente Minnelli's *Gigi* (1958). Both are nostalgic pieces in which Chevalier incarnates an aging beau, symbolising a vanishing era of popular entertainment.

Bib: Gene Ringgold and DeWitt Bodeen, *Chevalier, The Films and Career of Maurice Chevalier* (1973).

CHRISTIAN-JAQUE Christian Maudet; Paris 1904–94

French director, one of the most versatile and successful French film-makers. After poster design and art direction he worked for Paramount in Joinville in 1931. A French-style Michael Curtiz, Christian-Jaque succeeded in virtually all genres. After *Les Disparus de Saint-Agil/Boys School* (1938), a boarding-school story starring Erich von Stroheim, his 1940s films are considered his best: costume dramas (*La Symphonie fantastique*, 1942, *La Chartreuse de Parme/La certosa di Parma*, 1948), literary adaptations (*Boule de suif/Angel and Sinner*, 1945), bourgeois dramas (*Un revenant/A Lover's Return*, 1946). However, his Fernandel* vehicles of the 1930s – especially *Un de la Légion* (1936) – deserve re-evaluation, as do the swashbuckler *Fanfan la Tulipe* (1952, best director at Cannes 1952) and some of his films with his then wife Martine Carol*: *Adorable créatures/Adorable Creatures* (1952), *Nana* (1955), *Nathalie/The Foxiest Girl in Paris* (1957). From the 1960s he continued in genre films with some success – for instance, *La Tulipe noire/The Black Tulip* (1964) with Alain Delon*, and the spoof Western *Les Pétroleuses/The Ballad of Frenchie King* (1971), with Brigitte Bardot* and Claudia Cardinale. He also worked in television.

CINÉMA *BEUR*

French film genre of the 1980s. '*Beur*' is French slang – a play on *arabe* – for second-generation North Africans in France, children of the 1950s and 1960s immigrants. As this generation came of age and immigration made its way up the political agenda in the mid-1980s, a number of them made films featuring *beur* characters as part of post-colonial, multi-ethnic urban France. Unlike the authors of experimental British black cinema such as Isaac Julien, *beur* film-makers chose mainstream narratives and realism to dramatise the lives of their heroes.

Though minimising racism (in contrast to the militant cinema of the earlier generation), the world of *beur* films is embedded in poverty and unemployment (Abdelkrim Bahloul's *Le Thé à la menthe/Mint Tea*, 1984; Mehdi Charef's *Le Thé au harem d'Archimède/Tea in the Harem*, 1985, and *Miss Mona*, 1987; Rachid Bouchareb's *Bâton Rouge*, 1985, and *Cheb*, 1991). Dominant themes are a desire for integration and the difficulty of belonging to either French or Arabic culture. *Beur* cinema's focus on young men is not devoid of misogyny and homophobia, and its lack of militancy arguably dilutes its impact. It nevertheless shows, in accessible form, a complex and sympathetic representation of ethnic identity in modern France, challenging traditional negative stereotypes. It looked, in the early 1990s, as if *beur* cinema might be fading away; few *beur* films came out, or when they did, like Mehdi Charef's *Camomille* (1988) and *Au pays des Juliets* (1992), they were not about specific *beur* issues. However, a number of films made by *beur* directors (or other directors of North African descent) began to appear again in the mid-1990s: Malik Chibane's *Hexagone* in 1994, in 1995, Chibane's *Douce France*, Thomas Gilou's *Raï*, Karim Dridi's *Pigalle* and *Bye-Bye*, Ahmed Bouchaala's *Krim* and in 1996 Zaïda Ghorab-Volta's *Souviens-toi de moi*. Many of these revisited the familiar territory of earlier *beur* cinema, the working-class Parisian suburbs, or *banlieues*, with various perspectives on their social and cultural deprivation as well as their racial tensions. Other films by other (non-*beur*) young directors have taken up this particular topography, in particular Mathieu Kassovitz's highly successful *La Haine/Hate* and Jean-François Richet's *Etats des lieux* (both 1995), so much so that the term '*film de banlieue*' (suburbs film), has come to characterise them, pointing to an evident social malaise as well as to the uncertain critical status of the term '*beur* cinema'.

CINÉMA DU LOOK

French film genre, which arose with Jean-Jacques Beineix's* *Diva* in 1981, designating youth-oriented films with high production values. Subsequent titles include Beineix's *37°2 le matin/Betty Blue* (1986), Luc Besson's* *Subway* (1985) and *Nikita* (1990), and Leos Carax's* *Mauvais Sang/The Night is Young* (1986). Another possible candidate is Jean-Pierre Jennet and Marc Caro's *Delicatessen* (1991). The 'look' of the *cinéma du look* refers to the films' high investment in non-naturalistic, self-conscious aesthetics, notably intense colours and lighting effects. Their spectacular (studio-based) and technically brilliant *mise-en-scène* is usually put to the service of romantic plots. The *cinéma du look* is popular at the box office but hated by critics who dislike its calculated borrowings from advertising, music videos and cartoons, summarised by *Cahiers du cinéma** as 'postcard aesthetics'. *Cahiers,* and in its wake many Anglo-American critics, see the films as typical of a post-modern, 'image for image's sake' style in their lack of social or ideological substance; other French critics more positively label them 'neo-baroque'. These debates reveal both an uneasiness about the status of cinema in the age of other media and a deep reluctance to accept forms of French cinema which do not follow the norms of *auteur* cinema. After *Nikita*, and with the failure of Beineix's *IP5* (1992), it looked like the moment had passed, but the international success of Besson's *Leon* (1994), shot in English, may yet give the *cinéma du look* a second life.

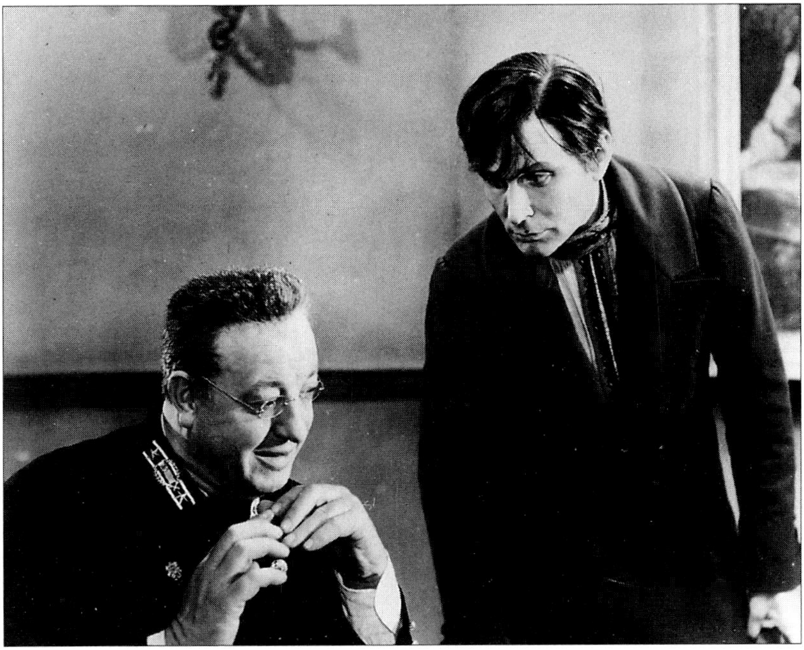

Harry Baur (left) and Pierre Blanchar in *Crime et châtiment/Crime and Punishment* (Pierre Chenal, 1935).

Pierre Brasseur (left) and Jean-Louis Barrault in *Les Enfants du paradis* (Marcel Carné, 1943–45).

Madeleine Sologne and Jean Marais in *L'Eternel retour* (Jean Delannoy, 1943).

Louis de Funès (left) and Bourvil in *La Grande vadrouille/Don't Look Now, We're Being Shot At* (Gérard Oury, 1966).

Hubert Kounde (right), Saïd Taghmaoui (centre) and Vincent Cassel (left) in *La Haine* (Mathieu Kassovitz, 1995).

Delphine Seyrig (centre) in *India Song* (Marguerite Duras, 1975).

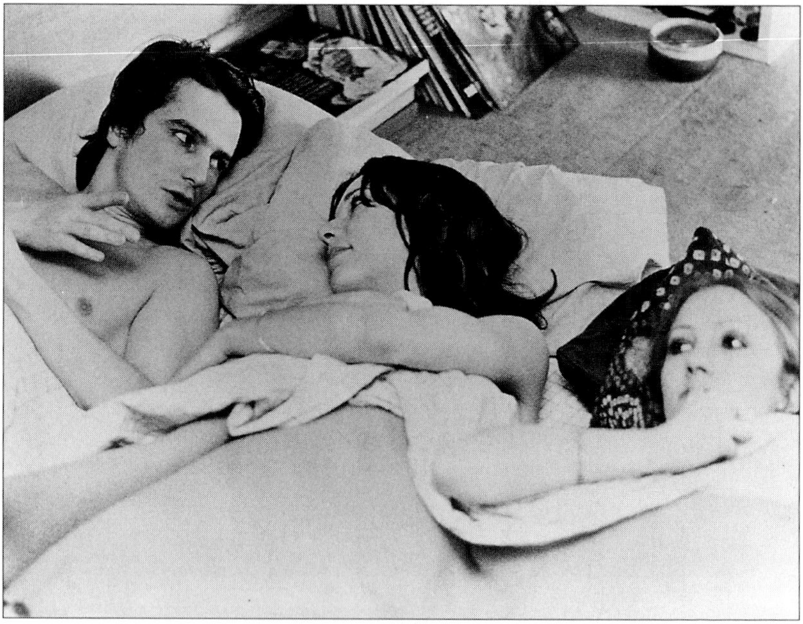

Jean-Pierre Léaud (left), Bernadette Lafont (centre) and Françoise Lebrun in *La Maman et la putain/The Mother and the Whore* (Jean Eustache, 1973).

Juliette Binoche and Michel Piccoli in *Mauvais sang/The Night is Young* (Leos Carax, 1986).

Albert Dieudonné as the eponymous hero of *Napoléon vu par Abel Gance/ Napoléon* (Abel Gance, 1972).

Julien Carette (left) and Marcel Dalio in *La Règle du jeu/ Rules of the Game* (Jean Renoir, 1939).

Béatrice Dalle in *37°2 le matin/Betty Blue* (Jean-Jacques Beineix, 1985).

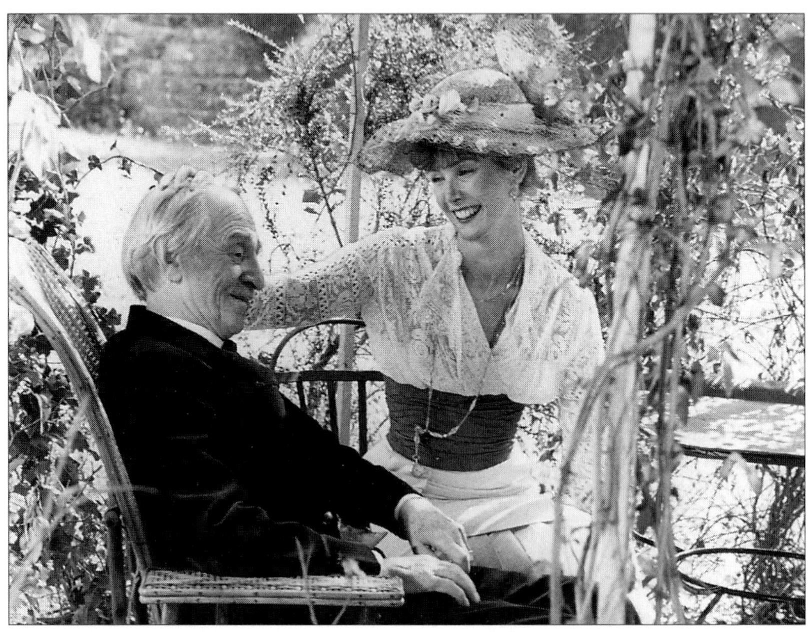

Henri Crémieux and Sabine Azéma in *Un dimanche à la campagne/ Sunday in the Country* (Bertrand Tavernier, 1984).

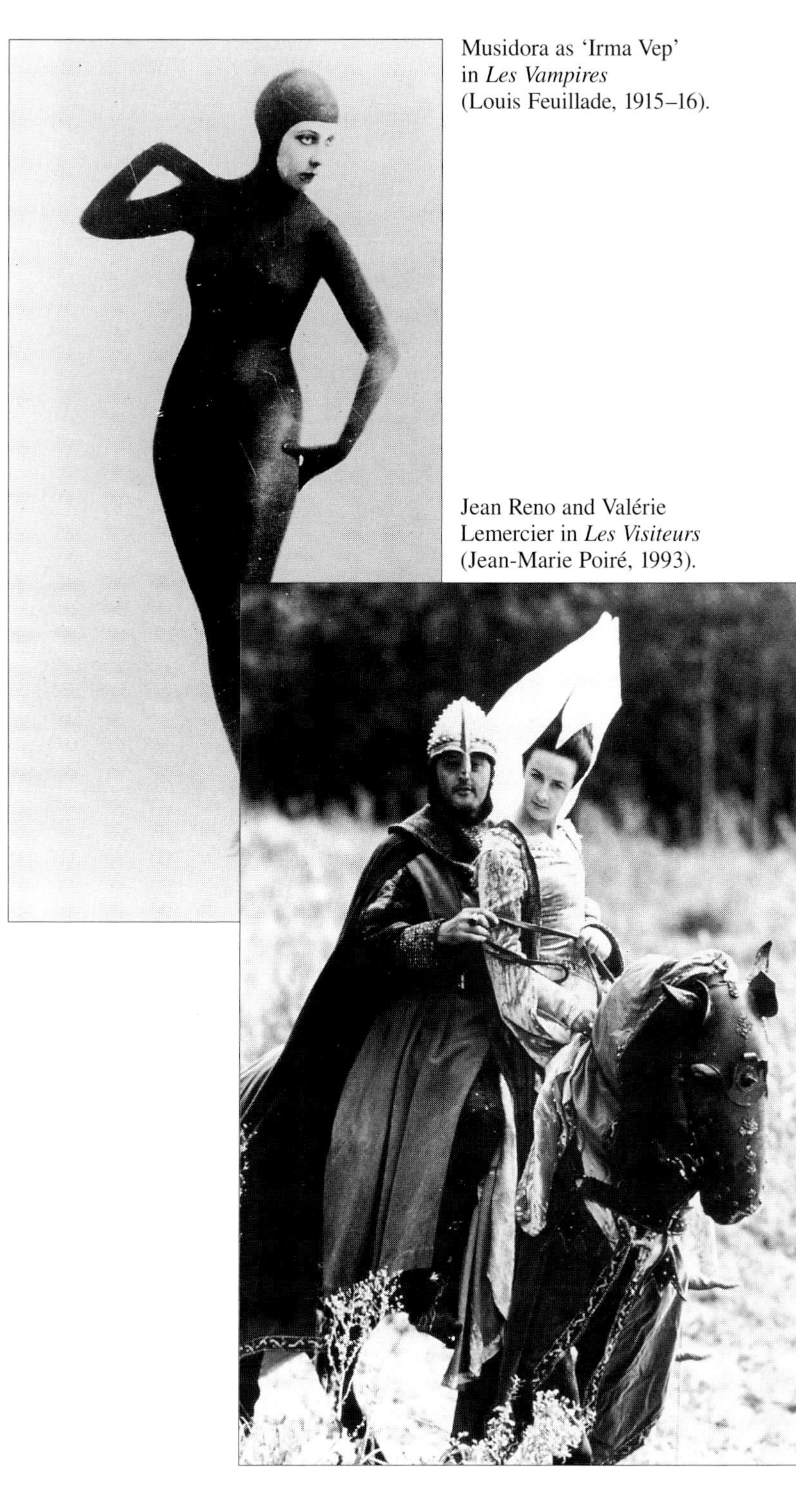

Musidora as 'Irma Vep' in *Les Vampires* (Louis Feuillade, 1915–16).

Jean Reno and Valérie Lemercier in *Les Visiteurs* (Jean-Marie Poiré, 1993).

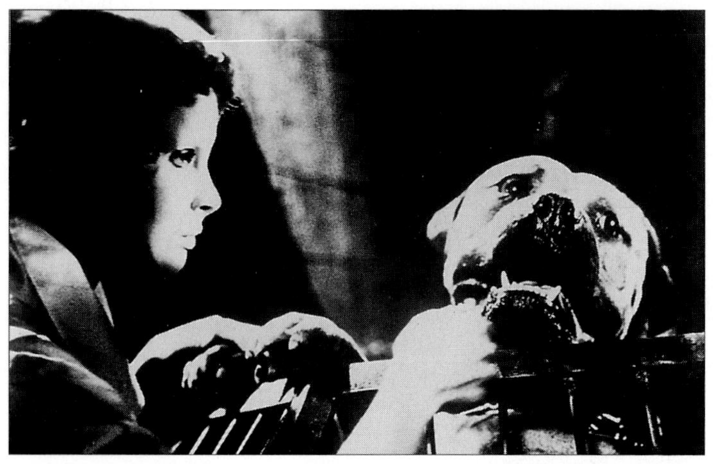

Edith Scob in *Les Yeux sans visage/Eyes Without a Face* (Georges Franju, 1960).

Martine Carol, the star of erotic costume dramas in the 1950s.

Alice Guy-Blaché, pioneer of the silent cinema.

CINÉMA-VÉRITÉ

French film term, designating an international trend in postwar documentary film-making; in Europe, a type of film making extensive use of interviews. A literal translation of Dziga Vertov's *Kino-Pravda*, the expression originated with the sociologist Edgar Morin, who, with Jean Rouch*, directed the key *cinéma-vérité* work: *Chronique d'un été/Chronicle of a Summer* (1961), in which Parisians respond to personal questions and the film-makers appear in the film, reflecting on their own practice. Other important films are Rouch's *Moi, un noir* (1959) and Chris Marker's* *Le Joli mai* (1963). *Cinéma-vérité* is indebted both to Vertov and to Robert Flaherty, a dual heritage indicative of the splits at the centre of the concept: on the Soviet side spontaneity but montage, on the American side a non-interventionist observation of the subjects' lifestyles shot in long takes. *Cinéma-vérité* raises wider issues about objectivity and 'manipulation', touching on a question central to all documentary, that of authenticity, although on the whole it aimed to reveal rather than capture 'truth'. *Cinéma-vérité* was made possible by new technologies – sensitive film stock, portable cameras and sound equipment – and coincided with the advent of television and a growing interest in sociology. Perhaps more than in the films themselves, its importance resides in its hybrid use in fiction films such as those of the New Wave*.

CINÉMATHÈQUE FRANÇAISE

French film archive. Founded in September 1936, the Cinémathèque was not the first film archive in the world, nor even the largest; but it is probably the most famous, its place in history secured by its educational function as a 'school' for generations of *cinéphiles*, including the New Wave*. For a long time, its history overlapped with that of director and co-founder Henri Langlois*, whose idiosyncratic methods and lack of administrative skills were legendary. Langlois preferred accumulation of prints and screenings to cataloguing, restoring and housekeeping; two fires destroyed important collections. The attempt by André Malraux, Minister for Culture, to impose an administrator in 1968 caused a celebrated furore in which international film personalities flocked to Langlois' defence. Partly in response, the Service des Archives du Film was created in 1969 at Bois d'Arcy for the deposit (a legal obligation since 1977), storage and restoration of film prints. Since 1981 the Socialist Ministry for Culture has funded a thorough programme of cataloguing and restoration. It has also planned a massive 'image palace' in the Palais de Tokyo, next to the Palais de Chaillot where the Cinémathèque moved in 1962, to include the Cinémathèque, the FEMIS* film school and the BIFI library (Nouvelle Bibliothèque de l'Image-Filmothèque) as well as a new museum. Since Langlois' death, presidents of the Cinémathèque have included Costa-Gavras*, Jean Rouch* and Dominique Païni.

Other major French cinémathèques are the Cinémathèque de Toulouse, headed by founder Raymond Borde, the Cinémathèque Universitaire at Paris III University, and the Musée du cinéma de Lyon [> LUMIÈRE].

CLAIR, René — René Chomette; Paris 1898–1981

French director, writer and actor. One of the first *auteurs* of world cinema, Clair epitomised a certain idea of 'Frenchess', with his light, witty and elegant films which ranged from farce to sentimental comedy. Although Jean Renoir* now stands as the greatest French director of the classical era, at the time Clair had a higher standing: André Bazin* could write in 1957, 'René Clair is probably, after Chaplin, the most esteemed director in the world' (an opinion not shared by other writers at *Cahiers du cinéma**). Clair was an actor and film critic before becoming assistant to Jacques de Baroncelli and joining the French avant-garde*. *Entr'acte* (1924) and *Paris qui dort/The Crazy Ray* (1924–25) wedded formal experimentation with Surrealist fantasy and a touch of the populism which characterised his later work. He injected movement into two Labiche farces, *Un chapeau de paille d'Italie/The Italian Straw Hat* (1928) and *Les Deux timides* (1929), especially with the comic chases inherited from early cinema which became his trademark. *Sous les toits de Paris* (1930), *Le Million* (1931) and *Quatorze juillet* (1932), all brilliantly designed by Lazare Meerson*, fixed an iconography of popular Paris – a 'sweet' version of the darker Poetic Realism*, full of street singers, irate concierges and neighbours, and pretty *midinettes* (like Annabella* in the latter two films). At the same time, *Sous les toits de Paris*, one of the first French talking pictures, was a remarkable experiment in sound, both technically and in its discourse on the *possibilities* of the new dimension. As a social satire on modernisation, *A nous la liberté* (1931) foreshadowed Chaplin's *Modern Times* (1936). By 1934, the failure of *Le Dernier milliardaire* (another social satire, about an imaginary dictatorship) hinted that Clair's style was going out of fashion. He left for Britain, where he made *The Ghost Goes West* in 1936 (lots of chases in a Scottish castle), and *Break the News* (1938) with Maurice Chevalier* and Jack Buchanan, before going on to Hollywood for another successful career (including *The Flame of New Orleans*, 1940, and *It Happened Tomorrow*, 1943). He returned to France in the 1950s, when he made elegant (and popular) costume films such as *Le Silence est d'or/Man About Town* (1947), *Les Belles de nuit* (1952) and *Les Grandes manoeuvres* (1955) [> TRADITION OF QUALITY]. Clair wrote many plays and novels and his film essays have been collected. He also wrote one of the classic texts on the coming of sound, *Cinema*

Yesterday and Today (1972). As Bazin put it, Clair's work manifested a rare 'meeting of intelligence and popularity'.

Bib: R. C. Dale, *The Films of René Clair, I: Exposition and Analysis; II: Documentation* (1986).

Other French Films: *Le Fantôme du Moulin Rouge* (1925); *Le Voyage imaginaire* (1926); *La Proie du vent* (1927); *La Tour* (1928, short); *Air Pur* (1939, unfinished); *La Beauté du diable/Beauty and the Devil* (1950); *Porte des Lilas* (1957); *La Française et l'amour* (1960, ep. 'Le mariage'); *Tout l'or du monde* (1961); *Les Quatre Vérités* (1962, ep. 'Les Deux Pigeons'); *Les Fêtes galantes* (1965).

CLÉMENT, René   Bordeaux 1913 – Monte Carlo 1996

French director, one of the most successful yet least celebrated postwar French film-makers. Clément studied architecture, made an animation film, directed several shorts – including *Soigne ton gauche* (1936) with Jacques Tati* – and documentaries before making his first feature, the remarkable Resistance film *La Bataille du rail/Battle of the Rails* (1946), with non-professional actors and photography by Henri Alekan*. He also acted as 'technical consultant' on Jean Cocteau's* *La Belle et la bête* (1946). Although *Le Père tranquille/Mr Orchid* (1946) and *Jeux interdits/Forbidden Games* (1952) return to the war, there is little common thread through Clément's films: 'I want to explore all genres and in each of my films I look for a new tone, a different style.' But if there is no thematic link between *Au-delà des grilles/Le mura di Malapaga/The Walls of Malapaga* (1949, a populist drama which attempts to rewrite the prewar Jean Gabin* myth in a postwar environment), *Jeux interdits* (the war through children's eyes), *Gervaise* (1956, a costume Zola adaptation) and *Plein Soleil/Purple Noon/Lust for Evil* (1960, a Patricia Highsmith adaptation with Alain Delon*), there is the impeccable *mise-en-scène*, care for detail and solid scripts of the Tradition of Quality*, which ensured Clément a large audience and numerous prizes (including Oscars for *Au-delà des grilles* and *Jeux interdits*). Towards the end of his career he turned to large-scale productions with international stars, such as *Paris brûle-t-il?/Is Paris Burning?* (1966).

Other Films Include: *Les Maudits/The Damned* (1947); *Le Château de verre/The Glass Castle* (1950); *Knave of Hearts/Monsieur Ripois* (1954, UK/Fr.); *Les Félins/The Love Cage* (1964); *Le Passager de la pluie/ Rider on the Rain* (1970).

CLOUZOT, Henri-Georges

Niort 1907 – Paris 1977

French director and scriptwriter, one of the most controversial film-makers of the postwar period. Clouzot's early activities were devoted to writing. After an early short (*La Terreur des Batignolles*, 1931), he began adapting thrillers in the 1940s, a genre he pursued throughout his career. The first was his debut feature *L'Assassin habite ... au 21* (1942). *Le Corbeau* (1943, produced by the German-owned Continentale) turned him into both a celebrity and an object of scandal. Its vicious portrait of a strife-ridden small town was deemed 'anti-French' and Clouzot was suspended from the film industry in 1944. Ironically, historians now read the film as anti-German. Clouzot resumed film-making in 1947, shooting a small but significant and highly successful body of films epitomising (with such directors as Yves Allégret*) the French *noir* tradition. Most, like *Quai des Orfèvres* (1947) and *Les Diaboliques* (1955), combine tight, suspenseful crime narratives with critical depictions of bourgeois milieux. *Le Salaire de la peur/The Wages of Fear* (1953), the ultra-tense story of two men delivering a lorry-load of nitro-glycerine, was a triumph at home and abroad. Clouzot directed one of Brigitte Bardot's* best films, *La Vérité* (1960). His films also include *Manon* (1949) and *Les Espions* (1957), and a documentary on Picasso, *Le Mystère Picasso* (1955). Ironically for a film-maker who wrote all his scripts and insisted that a director 'be his own *auteur*', Clouzot suffered at the hands of New Wave* critics, who saw him as a mere '*metteur-en-scène*' [> POLITIQUE DES AUTEURS] and disliked the black misanthropy of his vision. A reassessment of his work is long overdue.

COCTEAU, Jean

Maisons-Lafitte 1889 – Milly-la-Forêt 1963

French artist, writer and director. Cocteau's artistic output was prodigious – poems, plays, opera libretti, essays, drawings, church murals – and the cinema was only one aspect of it. Yet on account of their beauty and singularity his relatively few films have had a disproportionate impact. Cocteau introduced a rare element of the fantastic in French cinema, reworking myths and fairy tales which he rendered with a 'magic' imagery of mirrors, baroque objects and architecture and fabulous creatures. Apart from his avant-garde short feature *Le Sang d'un poète/The Blood of a Poet* (1930), Cocteau's cinematic activity was confined to the 1940s and 1950s. *La Belle et la bête*, starring Jean Marais* (1946, 'technical consultant' René Clément*, cinematographer Henri Alekan*), is one of the most beautiful French films ever made, a cult movie for *cinéphiles* and children alike. Cocteau pursued two main avenues in his films: myth, with *L'Eternel Retour* (1943, dir. Jean Delannoy*), *Orphée* (1950) and *Le Testament d'Orphée*

(1960); and Oedipal drama, with *Les Parents terribles/The Storm Within* (1948, described by André Bazin* as Cocteau's most theatrical *and* most cinematic work) and *Les Enfants terribles/The Strange Ones* (directed by Jean-Pierre Melville*, 1950).

Other Films as Director: *L'Aigle à deux têtes* (1948); *La Villa Santo-Sospir* (1952, short). **As scriptwriter**: *La Comédie du bonheur* (1942; dir. Marcel L'Herbier*); *Le Baron fantôme* (1943; dir. Serge de Poligny); *Les Dames du Bois de Boulogne* (1945; dir. Robert Bresson*); *Ruy Blas* (1948; dir. Pierre Billon).

COHL, Emile

Emile Courtet; Paris 1857–1938

French animation pioneer. After studying drawing, Cohl did political cartoons. He belonged to 'The Incoherents', an iconoclastic avant-garde artists' group, and was also variously a stage costume designer, vaudeville author, photographer and inventor of games. Noticing that a Gaumont* film had 'stolen' one of his ideas, he secured a contract in 1905 and began a fruitful new career in 'animated cartoons'. Although the American James Stuart Blackton had made an animated film, *The Haunted Hotel*, in 1906, historians agree that Cohl, starting with *Fantasmagorie* (1908), was the real father of animation, developing it both technically and aesthetically. He created characters such as the 'fantoche' (puppet) and built comically anarchic series round them, experimenting with techniques: movable cut-outs, three-dimensional animation, single-frame exposure. While at Gaumont he also wrote scripts and directed live-action films and animated scenes for other films. He moved to Pathé* in 1910 and Eclair in 1912, and in September 1912 to Eclair's New York premises. There he made more series (including the 'Newlyweds') and, it appears, had his equipment and methods widely copied. Back in Paris in 1914, he experienced difficulties in the face of increased competition; as he said, 'Father of animated cartoons, today I see my offspring returning from America resurfaced, gilded, thanks to the fabulous dollar.' Increasingly marginalised, he died destitute. Though Walt Disney always acknowledged his debt to Cohl, it is only recently that scholars have recognised his importance as a pioneer and his influence on all subsequent animation.

Bib: Donald Crafton, *Emile Cohl, Caricature, and Film* (1990).

COLETTE

Sidonie-Gabrielle Colette;
Saint-Sauveur en Puisaye 1873 – Paris 1954

French novelist and film critic, one of the most popular writers of the twentieth century. Many of her works focusing on women – *La*

Vagabonde, *Chéri* – have been adapted for the cinema: by Musidora* in the 1910s, Simone Bussi in the 1930s and Jacqueline Audry* in the 1940s and 1950s; *Gigi* (her portrait of the archetypal gamine) was filmed by Audry (1949) and Vincente Minnelli (1958). Colette wrote film criticism from 1914 to 1939, and contributed scripts and dialogues, notably for Marc Allégret's* *Lac aux dames* (1934) and Max Ophuls'* *Divine* (1935), the latter based on her own experience of the music-hall stage. She was the subject of Yannick Bellon's documentary *Colette* (1950).

COMEDY IN FRANCE

Alice Guy's* *La Fée aux choux/The Cabbage Fairy* (1896) was a farce about babies popping out of cabbages. Almost a century later, *Les Visiteurs* (1993, dir. Jean-Marie Poiré*) demolished all previous box-office records. Between these two titles, comedy has consistently been the most popular genre in France. Yet despite its high cultural status in literature (Rabelais, Molière), comedy has also been the most despised and ignored French film genre, with the exception of a few star-*auteurs*: Max Linder*, René Clair*, Sacha Guitry*, Jacques Tati*, Pierre Etaix. *Auteur*-oriented critics mistrust a genre based on performers, who moreover often come from other media (theatre, music hall, radio, song), and consider French comedy to be socially irrelevant, undemanding and lacking in subversiveness.

Comics sustained a large amount of silent French cinema, especially during the 'golden age' of 1907–15 when numerous series were produced, dominated by André Deed* and Max Linder*. If the 1920s saw the rise of the avant-garde and of bourgeois melodrama, sound firmly re-established comic genres, deriving either from the theatre (directors Clair, Guitry, Marcel Pagnol*; actors Raimu*, Michel Simon*, Jules Berry*) or the music hall (actors/singers Fernandel*, Bach and Georges Milton*, Arletty*), and included sub-genres such as the *comique troupier**. French directors also emulated American-style light comedy (directors Marc Allégret*, Christian-Jaque*, Henri Decoin*; actors André Luguet, Fernand Gravey, Danielle Darrieux*, Micheline Presle*, Edwige Feuillère*). The postwar period saw the even greater popularity of Fernandel, while dramatic actors like Jean Gabin* joined the ranks of comedy alongside new ones such as Noël-Noël, Darry Cowl, Robert Lamoureux, Bernard Blier*, Francis Blanche, Jean Poiret, Michel Serrault, and especially Bourvil* and Louis de Funès*, the latter surpassing all others at the box office and causing most critical consternation. Directors such as Yves Robert (especially with *La Guerre des boutons/War of the Buttons*, 1962), Georges Lautner, Gilles Grangier and Gérard Oury achieved huge success. While these comics and their films were for domestic consumption only, Jacques Tati's success was international, his humour built on universal sight gags. Later Pierre Etaix took up the

Linder–Tati tradition in such films as *Le Soupirant/The Suitor* (1963), although his fame was mainly national. The 1960s and 1970s saw the rise of a fresh generation of comic stars such as Jean Yanne, Michel Galabru, Annie Girardot* and Jean-Paul Belmondo* (*L'Homme de Rio/That Man from Rio*, 1964), the worldwide success of Edouard Molinaro's *La Cage aux folles/Birds of a Feather* (1978), and the appearance of the 'flaky' Pierre Richard, often in a duo with Gérard Depardieu* (in films directed by Francis Veber). A new generation of stars, scriptwriters and directors from the libertarian *café-théâtre* also appeared, bringing a sexually more explicit and stylistically more naturalistic humour, and a sharper social mockery (though the films toned down the politics of the original plays): directors such as Coline Serreau* (whose *Trois hommes et un couffin/Three Men and a Cradle*, 1985, was a huge hit), stars such as Coluche, Michel Blanc, Thierry Lhermitte, Christian Clavier, Miou-Miou* and Josiane Balasko*. Directors Patrice Leconte and Jean-Marie Poiré* popularised this tradition, while Bertrand Blier's* early work represented its *auteur* manifestation. From the 1980s, other influences shaped French comedy, notably television, with comics such as 'Les Nuls', and advertising (for instance Etienne Chatiliez's *La Vie est un long fleuve tranquille/Life is a Long Quiet River*, 1988, and *Tatie Danielle*, 1990).

Three aspects of French film comedy may explain its lasting popularity: its overwhelming maleness, which has gone hand in hand with the hegemony of male stars at the box office (with a few exceptions: Annie Girardot, Josiane Balasko, Anémone, Valérie Lemercier); the importance of language and word-play in French culture [> JACQUES PRÉVERT, HENRI JEANSON, MICHEL AUDIARD]; and the taste for deriding social and regional types. Although the conventional image of French cinema is centred on dramatic trends such as Poetic Realism* and *auteur* cinema, the importance of comedy shows that the construction of national identity by French cinema should rather be sought in comedy – the only domestic genre to resist Hollywood, as confirmed by the 1995 French box office, when Poiré's *Les Anges gardiens* (with Depardieu and Christian Clavier) and Balasko's *Gazon maudit* (starring herself and Victoria Abril) beat Hollywood blockbusters such as *Die Hard III.*

COMIQUE TROUPIER

French genre. The *comique troupier*, or military comedy, once one of the most popular French genres, reached its peak in the 1930s. It remained strictly for national consumption, addressing barrackfuls of conscripts and family audiences. With roots in the music hall and the theatre (in particular the plays of Georges Courteline, whose *Les Gaietés de l'escadron/The Joys of the Squadron* was filmed twice, in 1912 and 1932), the genre depended on songs and comic routines by the likes of Bach, Carette*, Roland Toutain and Raimu*. Its undis-

puted star, however, was Fernandel*, whose prototypical *Ignace* was the most popular French film of 1937 (alongside, ironically, the war drama *La Grande illusion*). *Comique troupier* humour is regressive, chaotic and bawdy; it relies on male ineptitude and ritual humiliation, transvestism and petty rule-breaking. Though order eventually prevails, the attraction of the *comique troupier* is to offer ordinary soldiers the brief chance to outwit or annoy their superiors. It was also the only genre which could mock the French army, 'serious' war films being subjected to the close scrutiny of the censors. Though it waned with World War II, the *comique troupier* had a revival in the 1970s, thanks to singers Les Charlots (especially in Claude Zidi's* *Les Bidasses en folie/Soldiers Freaking Out*, 1971), to Robert Lamoureux's *Mais où est donc passée la 7e compagnie?/Whatever Happened to the 7th Company?* (1973) and its sequels, and to the soft porn boom. Such films as *Les Filles du régiment/The Girls of the Regiment* (1979) can occasionally be seen on European cable channels.
[> COMEDY IN FRANCE, FINNISH MILITARY FARCE]

CONSTANTINE, Eddie

Edward Constantine; Los Angeles, California 1917 – Wiesbaden, Germany 1993

French actor and singer, American by birth. Like Yves Montand*, Constantine launched a singing career through a meeting with the singer Edith Piaf. He became a French film star in a series of parodic thrillers based on Peter Cheyney, initiated by Bernard Borderie's *La Môme vert-de-gris/Poison Ivy* (1953). As Lemmy Caution, Constantine embodied the French idea of a hard-boiled American hero: tall, handsome, cynical, hard-drinking and irresistible to women. He appeared in many films subsequently, as Caution or Caution-clones, as in émigré John Berry's skilful *noir* thriller *Je suis un sentimental* (1955). Michel Deville's* *Lucky Jo* (1964) was a departure, as was Jean-Luc Godard's* *Alphaville* (1965), a typical Godardian commentary on the star's image, which actually marked the end of his popular career. He tried unsuccessfully to work in the US, finishing his career as a nostalgic icon for European art film directors such as Rainer Werner Fassbinder, Ulrike Ottinger and Chris Petit.

CORNEAU, Alain

Orléans 1943

French director. An IDHEC* graduate, Corneau was always interested in music, the subject of his international hit *Tous les matins du monde* (1992, winner of seven Césars*). Previously, however, Corneau was one of the main exponents of the French thriller of the 1970s and 1980s, which he employed in the style of the period to diagnose the ills of French society [> POLICIER]. *France, société anonyme* (1974), *Série noire* (1979), *Le Môme* (1986), *Police Python 357* (1975) and *Le Choix des armes* (1981) continued this trend, although moving towards the mainstream, with more schematic narratives, larger budgets and major stars. Apart from the more personal *Nocturne indien* (1989), which combines a thriller format with an unusual Indian setting, Corneau seems to have opted for Heritage cinema*, with *Fort Saganne* (1984), a colonial saga starring Depardieu, *Tous les matins du monde*, the story of baroque composer Marin Marais, and arguably *Le Nouveau Monde* (1995), which recreates French relationships with American culture of the 1950s.

COSTA-GAVRAS, Constantin

Konstantinos Gavras; Athens 1933

French director of Greek origin. A graduate of IDHEC*, Costa-Gavras' first feature *Compartiment tueurs/The Sleeping Car Murders* (1965), based on Sébastien Japrisot's popular thriller, is usually considered routine. However, it already heralds two characteristics of his later work: gripping narrative and major stars (here Yves Montand* and Simone Signoret*). His greatest critical and popular success came with three of his next films, *Z* (1969), *L'Aveu/The Confession* (1970) and *Etat de siège/State of Siege* (1973). All three star Montand; all three combine the clarity, pace and drama of popular cinema with political issues (respectively Greek dictatorship, Communist totalitarianism and American imperialism) in the manner of the French *film à thèse* and the Italian 'political cinema' of the time. As is often the case with 'liberal' films, the ideological positions are clear-cut and unobjectionable. Nevertheless, the films exposed huge audiences to important topical issues. Costa-Gavras' subsequent career in France has been uneven, but in the 1980s he made successful Hollywood films, in particular *Missing* (1982), *Betrayed* (1988) and *Music Box* (1989). In contrast to the male world of his French films, these are movies distinguished by an emphasis on women. Costa-Gavras and his wife Michèle Ray are producers. Between 1982 and 1987 he was director of the Cinémathèque française*.

Other Films: *Un homme de trop/Shock Troops* (1967); *Section spéciale* (1975); *Clair de femme* (1979); *Hanna K* (1983); *Conseil de famille/Family Business* (1986); *Petite apocalypse* (1993); *A propos de Nice* (1994, one ep.); *L'Affaire Dreyfus* (1994, taken over by Yves Boisset); *Raspoutine* (1995).

COUTARD, Raoul

Paris 1924

French cinematographer, celebrated for his New Wave* work, especially with Jean-Luc Godard*. Coutard started as a photographer-reporter, then became a cinematographer with Pierre Schoendorffer, whose producer Georges de Beauregard* introduced him to Godard. Coutard was a key element in Godard's first feature *A bout de souffle/ Breathless* (1960), using a hand-held camera to achieve the improvised look of the film, pushing the unorthodox black-and-white Ilford stock to its limits and making imaginative use of natural and ceiling light. Coutard lit most Godard films until the late 1960s, and again worked with him on *Passion* (1982) and *Prénom Carmen* (1983), as well as with other New Wave directors such as François Truffaut*. Though Coutard is associated with the black-and-white luminosity of *A bout de souffle*, *Jules et Jim* (1962) and *Alphaville* (1965), he also worked in colour, for instance on *Le Mépris* (1963), in which he appears in the credit sequence. He has directed a few features, including *Hoa-Binh* (1970) and *SAS à San Salvador* (1982).

CRETEIL (Festival International de Films de Femmes)

French film festival. Originally held in Sceaux from 1979, the French International Women's Film Festival moved to Créteil (another suburb of Paris) in 1985, where it is now housed in the Maison des Arts, part-financed by local funds. This annual ten-day event takes place in late March/early April and has become the world's largest women's film festival; in 1994 it drew a mixed audience of over 50,000 spectators and showed over a hundred films whose common denominator was a woman director. Créteil's trajectory reflects that of women's cinema in Europe since the 1970s: from an explicitly feminist ethos, the event has moved towards more mainstream film, privileging art-house, *auteur*-oriented cinema over experimental and video work. Despite the toning down of its feminism, the festival has met with limited success in its aim of improving women's standing in the film industry. Professional and media resistance to feminism, strong in France, makes the continued existence and scope of the festival all the more impressive.

DALIO, Marcel

Israel Moshe Blauschild; Paris 1899–1983

French actor. Dalio came from the music hall and theatre and was typecast in most of his huge 1930s filmography (thirty films in 1936–38 alone) in minor roles which exploited his Semitic features – a casting which was both racist and a source of employment. The cowardly L'Arbi in Julien Duvivier's* *Pépé le Moko* (1936) and Mattéo in Pierre Chenal's* *La Maison du Maltais* (1938, a rare leading part) are the epitome of this stereotyping. His role as the rich and generous Jewish prisoner in Jean Renoir's* *La Grande illusion* (1937), clearly meant as positive, still appeared as racist to some. As the cultured Marquis de la Chesnaye in Renoir's *La Règle du jeu/Rules of the Game* (1939), Dalio at last escaped the stereotype. But when the war forced him to emigrate to Hollywood, he found himself playing another: the 'Frenchie' in US films which, however, included distinguished titles such as *Casablanca* (1942) and *To Have and Have Not* (1944). Dalio acted in small parts in many popular French and US movies until 1980.

DALLE, Béatrice

Brest 1964

French actress. Dalle was 'discovered' on the streets of Paris and cast by Jean-Jacques Beineix* as Betty in *37°2 le matin/Betty Blue* (1985). The film was a massive success, and Dalle the most explosive revelation of a new generation of actresses. With her blatant sensuality and popular wit (on and off the screen), Dalle projects provocative sexuality, insolence and spontaneity in the Brigitte Bardot* mould. Like BB, she has found it hard to escape typecasting. Her subsequent films, including Claire Devers' intelligent *Chimères* (1989), which works against her *Betty Blue* image, and Diane Kurys'* *A la folie* (1994), have failed at the box office. So far she remains, unfortunately, a one-film star despite intellligent performances in small parts in a variety of films, including Jim Jarmusch's *Night on Earth* (1992, US) and Claire Denis' *J'ai pas sommeil* (1993).

DARRIEUX, Danielle

Bordeaux 1917

French actress. The embodiment of the 'sophisticated Frenchwoman', Darrieux has had one of the longest and most distinguished film careers of all French actresses. While studying music and singing, she was cast from a newspaper advertisement in Wilhelm Thiele's *Le Bal*

(1931, the French version of his *Der Ball*) at the age of fourteen. Her part as the unruly daughter who throws her parents' invitations in the Seine rather than post them set the foundations of her early persona: the pretty, bubbly and impertinent young woman, her heart-shaped mouth in a permanent pout. A successful career followed in comedies and musicals, such as Robert Siodmak's* *La Crise est finie* (1934), Billy Wilder's *Mauvaise graine* (1934), and in *Battement de coeur* (1939, directed by Henri Decoin*, her first husband). Unusually, she alternated between this light tradition and melodrama – *Mayerling* (1936), co-starring Boyer*, *Katia* (1938). Darrieux's dominant 1930s image, however, was that of the modern young woman: a lawyer in *Un mauvais garçon* (1936), wearing up-to-date swimsuits in the extraordinary *Club de femmes* (1936, in which no man appears except her transvestite boyfriend) or fashionable berets and shiny raincoats in the melodramatic *Abus de confiance* (1937). Her success attracted the attention of Hollywood, but her American career was lacklustre. Her postwar films capitalised on her melodramatic, sophisticated image. In Max Ophuls'* *La Ronde* (1950) and *Madame de.../The Earrings of Madame de...* (1953), she epitomised another stereotype of French femininity: the elegant and knowing adulteress. She starred in other popular costume films like *Le Rouge et le noir* (1954) and *Pot-Bouille/The House of Lovers* (1957), both with Gérard Philipe*. Her post-1950s film career was less successful, with exceptions such as Jacques Demy's* *Les Demoiselles de Rochefort* (1967) and *Une chambre en ville* (1982), and André Téchiné's* *Le Lieu du crime/The Scene of the Crime* (1986). Meanwhile she has pursued a very successful career on television and on stage.

DAUMAN, Anatole — Warsaw, Poland 1925

French producer. With Georges de Beauregard* and Pierre Braunberger*, Dauman is a key figure in French *auteur* cinema. His company, Argos Film (founded 1951 with Philippe Lifchitz), was notable for taking on 'risky' and 'difficult' films, including Alain Resnais'* *Nuit et brouillard/Night and Fog* (1955) and *Hiroshima, mon amour* (1959), Robert Bresson's* *Mouchette* (1967), and Chris Marker's* *La Jetée* (1962). Since the 1970s Argos has taken on an international dimension, producing Nagisa Oshima's *Ai no corrida/In the Realm of the Senses* (1976, Jap./Fr.), Andrey Tarkovsky's *Offret/The Sacrifice* (1986) and several films by Wim Wenders among many others.

DECOIN, Henri — Paris 1896–1969

French director. Prolific director of the classical period, known especially for a series of films starring Danielle Darrieux*. Decoin was also a sports journalist and scriptwriter and worked on French versions of multi-language films. His long and varied filmography – forty-nine titles as director – makes it difficult to categorise his work generically. The 1930s, however, are dominated by bitter-sweet comedies and melodramas with Darrieux, then his wife. The former are epitomised by *Mademoiselle ma mère* (1937) and *Battement de coeur* (1939), in which Decoin successfully blended the American-style light comedy at which Darrieux excelled (and on the strength of which she was invited to Hollywood) with classic performances from French character actors such as Saturnin Fabre and Carette*. *Abus de confiance* (1937), on the other hand, belonged to the tradition of the French populist drama, a trend Decoin pursued during the war, notably with a first-class adaptation of Georges Simenon's* *Les Inconnus dans la maison/Strangers in the House* (1942), starring Raimu* and scripted by Henri-Georges Clouzot*. Decoin's two notable postwar films are another Simenon adaptation, *La Vérité sur Bébé Donge* (1952), with Darrieux and Jean Gabin*, a sombre psychological drama, and *Razzia sur la chnouf* (1955), an excellent *policier**, in which Gabin and Lino Ventura* haunt Parisian cabarets and the drugs underworld. Decoin's last film, *Nick Carter va tout casser*, starring Eddie Constantine*, was made in 1964.

DEED, André

André [de?] Chapuis, Le Havre 1884 – Paris 1938 [some sources: 1879–1931]

French actor, one of the major comic stars of early world cinema. Like many comics, Deed came from the music hall, where he had been a singer and an acrobat. At Pathé*, he starred in a popular comic series as the character Boireau (1906–09). His fame greatly increased when he was lured to Giovanni Pastrone's Itala studios in Turin in 1909, where under the pseudonym of Cretinetti he starred in more than a hundred films, some directed by himself (in Spain he was Torribo or Sanchez, in English-speaking countries Foolshead or Jim). Typical of early farce and chase films, his humour was physical and violent, based on a character who gets into trouble and makes things worse in his struggle to escape the consequences. He is described by Richard Abel as 'a grotesquely bewildered clown and a skilful practitioner of physical gags'. As the popularity of the early comic genres waned, so did Deed's and he died in neglect and poverty.

Bib: Richard Abel, *The Ciné Goes to Town: French Cinema 1896–1914* (1994).

DELANNOY, Jean

Noisy-le-Sec 1908

French director, who began as an actor and editor in the late 1920s and worked as an assistant director before making his directing debut in 1935. His real prominence came during the war with *L'Eternel Retour* (1943), from a script by Jean Cocteau, and the costume drama *Pontcarral, colonel d'Empire* (1942); both were extemely successful, as was the prize-laden *La Symphonie pastorale* (1946), from the novel by André Gide and starring Michèle Morgan*. Delannoy continued working successfully in mainstream genres through the 1940s and 1950s (in fact until the early 1990s, though never regaining the status of the earlier decades). His reliance on literary texts (and often dialogues by Jean Aurenche* and Pierre Bost*) and major stars, and his elegant though impersonal *mise-en-scène*, situated him within the tradition of quality*, earning him the contempt of the New Wave* critics. Among his most interesting films, *Les Jeux sont faits/The Chips Are Down* (1947), *La Minute de vérité/The Moment of Truth* (1952), *Chiens perdus sans collier* (1955), *Notre-Dame de Paris/The Hunchback of Notre Dame* (1956) and *Maigret tend un piège/Inspector Maigret* (1958) are testimony to a high degree of professionalism and understanding of popular tastes.

DELLUC, Louis

Cadouin 1890 – Paris 1924

French theoretician and director. Inspired by Cecil B. DeMille's *The Cheat* (1915), Delluc (originally a literary critic) became a key figure in the French avant-garde*, especially for his writing. He edited a number of film journals, including the ambitious *Cinéa*, and pioneered film criticism in his regular column for *Paris-Midi*; his essays were the first to be collected in France, in *Cinéma et cie* (1919), *Photogénie* (1920), and other volumes. A great admirer of Hollywood, Delluc also advocated a specifically French cinema: 'Let French cinema be real cinema, let French cinema be really French.' Like the future practitioners of the New Wave*, he moved on to film-making, writing scripts for Jean Epstein* and Germaine Dulac*, and directing seven films between 1920 and 1923. Of these the best are *Fièvre* (1921), an atmospheric drama set in a studio-reconstructed Marseilles bar, and *La Femme de nulle part* (1922), an exploration of subjectivity past and present; both star his wife Ève Francis. Contemporary critic Léon Moussinac's description of *Fièvre* encapsulates Delluc's 'impressionist' cinema: 'From faces and gestures, from expressive movements in a completely integrated decor, [Delluc] can produce emotional effects of real power ... even poetry.'

The Louis Delluc Prize was created in 1937, awarded annually to a French film considered an artistic achievement (that year it went to Jean Renoir's* *Les Bas-fonds/The Lower Depths*).

DELON, Alain

Sceaux 1935

French actor, director and producer. When the exceptionally handsome young Alain Delon started acting in the 1950s, he bypassed the New Wave*, unlike his contemporary Jean-Paul Belmondo*. Instead, he came to prominence in René Clément's* *Plein Soleil/Purple Noon/Lust for Evil* (1960), based on a Patricia Highsmith novel, and his career took off in prestigious Italian *auteur* films (*Rocco e i suoi fratelli/Rocco and His Brothers*, 1960, *L'eclisse/The Eclipse*, 1962, *Il gattopardo/The Leopard*, 1963), in which he combined charismatic but ambiguous sex appeal with a hint of corruption. His success in the thriller *Mélodie en sous-sol/The Big Snatch* (1963, with Jean Gabin*) steered him away from playboys towards increasingly tough and monosyllabic gangsters or *flics* in films directed by Jean-Pierre Melville* (*Le Samouraï*, 1967, *Le Cercle rouge/The Red Circle*, 1970), Henri Verneuil* (*Le Clan des Siciliens/The Sicilian Clan*, 1969), Jacques Deray (*Borsalino*, 1970), or himself (*Pour la peau d'un flic/For a Cop's Hide*, 1981, *Le Battant/The Cache*, 1983). Delon failed in Hollywood but reigned over French cinema in the 1960s and 1970s, sharing top box-office ranking with Belmondo and Louis de Funès*, his image apparently unaffected by off-screen liaisons, scandals and right-wing politics. He also founded his own production company. Delon's popularity then declined with that of the traditional *policier**, prompting, perhaps, his return to art cinema: *Un Amour de Swann/Swann in Love* (1984), *Notre histoire/Our Story* (also 1984, for which he won a César*), and, ironically, Jean-Luc Godard's *Nouvelle Vague* (1990). He received a special tribute at the 1995 Berlin film festival.

Other Films Include: *Sois belle et tais-toi, Christine* (1958); *Faibles femmes, Le Chemin des écoliers* (1959); *Che gioia vivere* (1961, It./Fr.); *La Tulipe noire/The Black Tulip, L'Insoumis, Les Félins/The Love Cage* (1964); *Les Aventuriers* (1966); *Adieu l'ami, La Piscine/The Swimming Pool* (1968); *La Veuve Couderc (*1971); *L'Assassinio di Trotsky/The Assassination of Trotsky* [It./Fr.], *Un flic/Dirty Money* (1972); *Traitement de choc, Les Granges brûlées, Deux hommes dans la ville* (1973); *La Race des 'seigneurs', Les Seins de glace, Borsalino & Co* (1974); *Flic story* (1975); *Mr Klein* (1976); *Armaguedon, L'Homme pressé* (1977); *Le Toubib* (1979); *Trois hommes à abattre* (1980); *Le Choc* (1982); *Parole de flic* (1985); *Le Passage* (1986); *Dancing Machine* (1990); *Le Retour de Casanova* (1992); *Un crime, L'Ours en peluche* (1993).

DEMY, Jacques

Pontchâteau 1931 – Paris 1990

French director. One of the outstanding film-makers of postwar France, Demy is best known for his first feature *Lola* (1961) and for

Les Parapluies de Cherbourg/The Umbrellas of Cherbourg (1964), his first musical proper.

Demy was brought up in Nantes, a city he loved (the affection is well captured in Agnès Varda's* moving film portrait *Jacquot de Nantes,* 1991), and where he made his earliest amateur movie. He studied cinema in Paris, training in short films with Georges Rouquier and later in animation with Paul Grimault*. *Lola*, a lyrical poem to Nantes and the cabaret artiste played by Anouk Aimée*, shared some of the aesthetic concerns of the New Wave* (although Demy was not strictly part of it): location shooting, exuberant *mise-en-scène* – especially stunning camerawork by Raoul Coutard* – and love for the American cinema. *Les Parapluies de Cherbourg* inaugurated the 'bitter-sweet' Demy universe, with sentimental music by Michel Legrand*, pastel colour-scheme, and the innovation of all-sung dialogue. The film turned Catherine Deneuve* into a star and was awarded a prize at Cannes, but Demy never matched its popular success in his subsequent chequered career, although *Peau-d'Ane/Donkey Skin* (1970), a sumptuous adaptation of the Perrault fairy tale, came near. Nevertheless, *Les Demoiselles de Rochefort* (1967) and *Une chambre en ville* (1982), like *Les Parapluies*, beautifully illustrate Demy's original, if not totally satisfactory, pursuit of a specifically French musical genre.

Other (Feature) Films: *Les Sept péchés capitaux/The Seven Deadly Sins* (1962, ep.); *La Baie des Anges* (1963); *Model Shop* (1969, US); *The Pied Piper* (1972, UK); *L'Événement le plus important depuis que l'homme a marché sur la lune/A Slightly Pregnant Man* (1973); *Lady Oscar* (1978); *Trois places pour le 26* (1988).

DENEUVE, Catherine — Catherine Dorléac; Paris 1943

French actress. Declared by *Newsweek* 'the most beautiful woman in the world', and like Bardot* a model for Marianne, the effigy of the Republic, Catherine Deneuve has embodied, on and off screen, an ideal of elegant French womanhood since the early 1960s. With Isabelle Adjani*, she is France's top female star of the 1980s and early 1990s.

After small parts in comedies with her sister Françoise Dorléac and a short spell with Roger Vadim*, Deneuve triumphed in Jacques Demy's* *Les Parapluies de Cherbourg/The Umbrellas of Cherbourg* (1964). This entirely sung melodrama popularised her image of the demure middle-class *jeune fille*, solidified in Demy's *Les Demoiselles de Rochefort* (1967) and other light comedies such as *La Vie de château* (1965). Roman Polanski's* *Repulsion* (1965, UK) and Luis Buñuel's* *Belle de jour* (1967) added a layer of 'perverse' sexuality, producing the figure of the ice maiden, a bait for sadistic male fantasies. This was further exploited in the 1970s in Buñuel's *Tristana* (1970, Sp.) and

Marco Ferreri's* *Liza/La cagna* (1971, It.). Deneuve's Italian and Hollywood films (*Hustle*, 1975, *The Hunger*, 1984), and her role as ambassador of French chic (Saint-Laurent clothes, Chanel perfume) internationalised her. In France in the 1980s she continued an active career in mainstream (*Je vous aime*, 1980, *Fort Saganne*, 1984) and *auteur* cinema (with François Truffaut*, André Téchiné*, Jean-Pierre Mocky*, François Dupeyron and Nicole Garcia), evolving towards figures of independence and stoic suffering, of greater appeal to women and more in tune with her off-screen feminism. But although her status remained intact in the 1980s, her parts tended to become symbolic rather than actual leads. Her success in *Indochine* (1992), a popular colonial melodrama [> HERITAGE CINEMA IN EUROPE], may herald more substantial mature roles, as does Manoel de Oliveira's *O Convento/Le Couvent* (1995, Port.).

Other Films Include: *Les Portes claquent* (1960); *Les Parisiennes* [ep.] (1962); *Le Vice et la vertu* (1963); *Les Créatures* (1966); *Benjamin ou les mémoires d'un puceau, La Chamade* (1968); *La Sirène du Mississipi/The Mississippi Mermaid* (1969); *Peau-d'Ane* (1970); *Ça n'arrive qu'aux autres* (1971); *Un flic/Dirty Money* (1972); *L'Événement le plus important depuis que l'homme a marché sur la lune/A Slightly Pregnant Man* (1973); *Touche pas la femme blanche* (1973); *Le Sauvage* (1975); *L'Argent des autres* (1978); *Le Dernier métro/The Last Metro* (1980); *Hôtel des Amériques, Le Choix des armes* (1981); *Le Bon Plaisir, Paroles et musique* (1984); *Le Lieu du crime/The Scene of the Crime, Speriamo che sia femmina/Let's Hope It's a Girl* (1985, It.); *Drôle d'endroit pour une rencontre/A Strange Place to Meet* (1988); *La Reine blanche* (1991); *Ma saison préférée* (1993); *La Partie d'échecs, Petites heures du matin* (1994); *L'Enfant de la nuit, Place Vendôme* (1995).

DEPARDIEU, Gérard — Châteauroux 1948

French actor, the biggest star in France since the mid-1970s. With more than fifty leading roles under his belt at the age of 47, Gérard Depardieu has also achieved worldwide stardom.

Depardieu's adolescence in working-class Châteauroux was marked by delinquency, which later haunted him when (unresolved) allegations of rape ruined his chances of an Oscar for *Green Card* (Aust./Fr.) in 1990. The theatre (a continuing passion) led him to the straight and narrow and to Paris, where he briefly joined the libertarian *café-théâtre*, meeting fellow actors Coluche, Patrick Dewaere and Miou-Miou*. After a dozen minor film parts, his co-starring role in Bertrand Blier's* *Les Valseuses/Going Places* (1973) turned him into France's young male sensation. Since then, his star has hardly stopped rising. Apart from exceptional talent and energy, a key to Depardieu's success is his versatility. Equally at ease in broad farce and romantic leads (despite unconventional features), he has been a mainstay of popular cinema (*Préparez vos mouchoirs/Get Out Your Handkerchiefs*, 1977, *Inspecteur La Bavure/Inspector Blunder*, 1980, *Les Fugitifs*, 1986, etc.), a supporter of *auteur* films by Marguerite Duras*, Marco Ferreri* and Maurice Pialat*, and of major art films like *1900* (1976), *Le Dernier métro/The Last Metro* (1980) and *Cyrano de Bergerac* (1990). Out of this diversity a strong star persona has emerged, made up of an intensely male physical presence, combined with surprising and, according to him, 'feminine' gentleness. Depardieu's bulky physique and earthy off-screen activities (tending a vineyard) evoke a popular longing for ancestral roots (crystallised in *Jean de Florette*, 1986), while his cultural aura projects a modernist personality. Like Jean Gabin* before him, Depardieu sums up an idealised French masculinity, merging working-class virility with romanticism. Exporting himself has meant losing some of these complexities, since Depardieu's global stardom is, so far, dependent (as was Maurice Chevalier's*) on playing a rather clichéd Frenchness, as in *Green Card*, or even Europeanness, as in Ridley Scott's *1492 Conquest of Paradise* (1992, UK/Fr./Sp.). Already a star of 'heritage' cinema* with *Jean de Florette* and *Cyrano*, Depardieu has moved increasingly to this type of film in the 1990s, notably with *Germinal* (1993) and *Le Colonel Chabert* (1994), while retaining an interest in *auteur* cinema, as shown by his starring role in Jean-Luc Godard's *Hélas pour moi* (1993) and Pialat's *Le Garçu* (1995). A remarkably eclectic star, Depardieu at the same time confirmed his popularity in comedy, with Jean-Marie Poiré's* *Les Anges gardiens*, which topped the 1995 French box-office.

Bib: Paul Chutkow, *Gérard Depardieu* (1994).

Other Films Include: *L'ultima donna/The Last Woman, Barocco* (1976); *Le Camion* (1977); *Mon oncle d'Amérique/My American Uncle* (1980); *La Femme d'à côté/The Woman Next Door, Le Retour de Martin Guerre/The Return of Martin Guerre* (1981); *Danton* (1982); *Fort Saganne, Le Tartuffe* (1984); *Police* (1985); *Tenue de soirée* (1986); *Sous le soleil de Satan/Under Satan's Sun* (1987); *Camille Claudel* (1988); *I Want to Go Home, Trop belle pour toi* (1989); *Tous les matins du monde* (1992); *Mon père, ce héros* (1993); *My Father, The Hero*, *La Machine* (1994); *Elisa*, *Bogus* [US] (1995).

DEVILLE, Michel — Boulogne-sur-Seine 1931

French director. Although contemporary with the New Wave*, Deville (trained as an assistant) worked parallel to it. He made light comedies, including, with Anna Karina*, *Ce soir ou jamais* (1961) and with Brigitte Bardot*, *L'Ours et la poupée* (1970); thrillers, either 'classic', such as *Lucky Jo* (1964, with Eddie Constantine*), or 'political', such as *Le Dossier 51* (1978); and erotic costume films, like

Benjamin ou les mémoires d'un puceau (1968) and *Raphaël ou le débauché* (1970), many co-written by Nina Companeez. His career took a different course in the 1980s and 1990s with a series of glossy art-house hits: *Péril en la demeure* (1985, awarded a César*), *Le Paltoquet* (1986), and *La Lectrice* (1988), in which he developed a cool, mannered style and a distanced eroticism.

DOILLON, Jacques

Paris 1944

French director. Since the early 1970s, Jacques Doillon has occupied a marginal yet not negligible place in French *auteur* cinema. He co-directed *L'An 01* (1973) with Jean Rouch* and Alain Resnais*, and came to prominence with his first feature, *Les Doigts dans la tête* (1974). His intimate, small-scale films are marked by recurrent themes of oedipal and gender conflicts – especially between fathers and daughters – which, although not strictly autobiographical, often re-work events from his life. Doillon tends to concentrate on female characters and prefers working with actresses; he is also a gifted director of young actors, as in the excellent *Le Jeune Werther* (1993). Doillon's *mise-en-scène* favours pared-down, claustrophobic settings and situations, contrasting with the violent emotions depicted. His films have a steady, if restricted, appeal; as he aptly said, 'I'm afraid I will remain an unsettling film-maker interested in complexity.'

Other Films: *Un sac de billes* (1975); *La Femme qui pleure* (1978); *La Drôlesse* (1979); *La Fille prodigue* (1981); *La Pirate, La Vie de famille, La Tentation d'Isabelle* (1985); *La Puritaine* (1986); *Comédie!* (1987); *L'Amoureuse* [TV] (1987, rel. 1993); *La Fille de quinze ans, La Vengeance d'une femme, Le Petit criminel* (1990); *Amoureuse* (1992); *Un homme à la mer, Du fond du cœur* (1994).

DULAC, Germaine

Germaine Saisset-Schneider; Amiens 1882 – Paris 1942

French director, and key figure in the 'first' avant-garde [> FRENCH AVANT-GARDE] of the 1920s. Dulac started as a photographer and wrote for two feminist journals, *La Fronde* and *La Française*. In her thirties she began her own production company, Delia Film. Her first films were conventional melodramas, but a chance meeting with theoretician Louis Delluc* led to them formulating the tenets of the avant-garde. Dulac was at the heart of this group of intellectuals devoted to the promotion of art film-making, film education and film criticism.

From *Ames de fous* (1917), Dulac increasingly privileged the representation of impressions and inner feelings over narrative. Her first critical success was *La Fête espagnole* (1920), but her major work is *La*

Souriante Mme Beudet/The Smiling Mrs Beudet (1923), a sympathetic portrayal of the frustrations, desires and revolt of a bourgeois housewife, which uses superimpositions, dissolves and slow motion. Dulac alternated avant-garde productions with mainstream films like *Gossette* (1923), but aspired to a more abstract style, 'the integral film ... a visual symphony made of rhythmic images'. A supreme expression of this is the controversial *La Coquille et le clergyman/The Seashell and the Clergyman* (1928), a rare attempt at rendering the unconscious on screen. She went on to make abstract and documentary films, including *Germination d'un haricot* (1928), the stop-motion record of the germination of a seed, and she also lectured on film. She was head of Gaumont* newsreels until her death. Dulac was deeply committed to both feminist issues and the search for a new cinematic language.

Bib: Sandy Flitterman-Lewis, *To Desire Differently: Feminism and the French Cinema* (1990).

Other Films Include: *Les Soeurs ennemies, Vénus victrix* (1917); *La Cigarette* (1919); *La Belle dame sans merci* (1920); *La Mort du soleil* (1922); *Ame d'artiste* (1925); *La Princesse Mandane, Thèmes et variations* (1928).

DURAS, Marguerite

Marguerite Donnadieu; Gia-dinh, Indo-China [now Vietnam] 1914 – Paris 1996

French novelist, playwright and director, a major figure in French and feminist culture. Duras wrote screenplays, notably for Alain Resnais* (*Hiroshima mon amour*, 1959), and co-directed an adaptation of her play *La Musica* (1967, with Paul Seban), before directing *Détruire, dit-elle/Destroy She Said* in 1969. She has since engaged in writing and film-making as parallel and cross-referencing activities: *La Femme du Gange/Woman of the Ganges* (1974) and *India Song* (1975) rework the same events and characters as her novels *The Vice-Consul*, *The Ravishing of Lol V. Stein* and *L'Amour*.

Duras is a modernist who works on sound and image with equal intensity; her lyrical soundtracks – sometimes featuring her own mesmerising voice, as in *Le Camion* (1977) – may even assume a separate identity: *Son nom de Venise dans Calcutta désert* (1976) matches a new set of images to the soundtrack of *India Song*. Duras' approach is minimalist and allusive, and she has been criticised for her a-historical characters. While her vision of women's 'suicidal' condition is bleak, her films nevertheless concentrate on female desire and women's experience. She strongly disapproved of Jean-Jacques Annaud's* lavish adaptation of her Goncourt prize-winning autobiographical novel *L'Amant/The Lover* (1991).

Bib: Lesley Hill, *Duras* (1993).

Other Films (as Director) Include: *Jaune le soleil* (1971); *Nathalie Granger* (1972); *Des journées entières dans les arbres/Whole Days in the Trees* (1976); *Baxter, Vera Baxter* (1977); *Le Navire night, Aurélia Steiner – Vancouver* (1979); *Les Enfants* (1984).

DUVIVIER, Julien

Lille 1896 – Paris 1967

French director. One of the great French directors of the classical era, Duvivier was revered in the 1930s but later unfavourably compared with Jean Renoir*. Assistant to André Antoine*, he started making silent films in 1919, mostly melodramatic literary adaptations such as *Poil de carotte* (1926, which he remade with sound in 1932). From his prolific 1930s output, four films stand out: an excellent early Simenon adaptation, *La Tête d'un homme* (1932), in which Harry Baur* stalks shady bars in Montparnasse as Inspector Maigret; and (especially) three films which created and fixed the Jean Gabin* 'myth', *La Bandera* (1935), *La Belle équipe* (1936) and *Pépé le Moko* (1936). Beyond their different genres (respectively a foreign legion drama, a tale of male solidarity at the time of the Popular Front*, and a thriller set in Algiers), these films illustrate the dominant Duvivier universe of that period: pessimistic proletarian tales of loyalty and betrayal, 'men's stories', as he put it. Also characteristic was his extraordinary technique, especially his signature virtuoso camera movements combined with extremely long takes. Duvivier's two other notable 1930s films are *Un carnet de Bal* (1937), a series of episodes around an actress (Marie Bell) and a galaxy of male stars (including Raimu* and Pierre Blanchar*), and *La Fin du jour* (1938), about an actors' retirement home (with, among others, Michel Simon*), both displaying his skilled use of stars. Duvivier also worked in Hollywood, making (among other films) *The Great Waltz* (1938), *Tales of Manhattan* (1942) and *The Imposter* (1944, with Gabin). *Panique* (1947) continued his 1930s pessimistic vein, as did the virulently misogynist *Voici le temps des assassins* (1956), which is partly redeemed by the presence of Jean Gabin. Duvivier's postwar career was distinguished by the immense success of the Franco-Italian *Don Camillo* series starring Fernandel* and Gino Cervi* (five films from 1952 to 1965, of which Duvivier directed the first two, with a sixth in 1972 with Cervi alone), and by the Zola adaptation *Pot-bouille/The House of Lovers* (1957, with Gérard Philipe*).

EPSTEIN, Jean

Warsaw, Poland 1897 – Paris 1953

French director and theoretician. Epstein moved to Paris in 1921, after studies in Switzerland and Lyons. Like his contemporary Louis Delluc* he was first a film theoretician, publishing several books (including *Bonjour cinéma*, 1921); he became a prominent director of the French avant-garde*. Although best known for his experimental films, such as *La Chute de la maison Usher/The Fall of the House of Usher* (1928), Epstein was also interested in realism – his first film was a documentary on *Pasteur* (1922). For Pathé*, he made three fiction films which combine melodramatic narratives with formal concerns: *L'Auberge rouge*, *Cœur fidèle* (both 1923) and *La Belle Nivernaise* (1924). *Cœur fidèle*, described as a 'symbolic melodrama', is the most original, with fast editing and unusual use of close-ups. After a spell at the Russian émigré studio Albatros, where he made popular films, Epstein ran his own production company (1926–30), giving free rein to his formal preoccupations. In its complex narrative structure *La Glace à trois faces* (1927) anticipates Alain Resnais*. It was one of the earliest films made for the new 'art' cinema circuit, and is considered the culmination of the French narrative avant-garde. *La Chute de la Maison Usher*, which employs slow motion, illustrated Epstein's theories of time in the cinema. On the other hand *Finis terrae* (1929), filmed on a remote Brittany island, anticipated neo-realism* and inaugurated Epstein's 'Breton cycle'. His career in the 1930s and 1940s was difficult, alternating commercial features and documentaries.

His sister, the film-maker Marie Epstein*, wrote scripts for him, co-directed and acted in some of his early films.

EPSTEIN, Marie

Marie-Antonine Epstein; Warsaw, Poland 1899 – Paris 1995

and

BENOÎT-LÉVY, Jean

Paris 1888–1959

French directors and scriptwriters. When not ignored by film history, the Polish-born Epstein is overshadowed by her collaborators, her brother Jean Epstein*, and Jean Benoît-Lévy. Marie and her brother were part of the French avant-garde* of the 1920s. She was assistant director and acted in Jean's *Cœur fidèle* (1923) and wrote scripts for some of his best films. Her major work, however, was as scriptwriter and co-director with Benoît-Lévy in sound films, starting with *Le Coeur de Paris* (1931). Their second film, *La Maternelle* (1933), adapted from Léon Frapié's populist novel, is one of the best early

French sound films, an extraordinary combination of social propaganda (for state nursery education), naturalism and lyricism, with a luminous performance by Madeleine Renaud*. Epstein worked with Benoît-Lévy throughout the 1930s. Their work shows concern for popular milieux and for the young – as in *Peau de pêche* (1929), *La Maternelle*, and *Altitude 3200* (1938) – as well as, unusually for the period, women (*Hélène*, 1936, *Le Feu de paille*, 1939). Epstein made a documentary on atomic energy in 1953 and worked at the Cinémathèque Française* restoring silent films, including some of her brother's and Abel Gance's* *Napoléon*.

Bib: Sandy Flitterman-Lewis, *To Desire Differently: Feminism and the French Cinema* (1990).

EUSTACHE, Jean Pessac 1938 – Paris 1981

French director. A peripheral yet important figure in *auteur* cinema, Eustache was an editor and worked for television; he made several films, including *Les Mauvaises fréquentations/Bad Company* (1967, made up of two episodes, one being *Le Père Noël a les yeux bleus/Father Christmas Has Blue Eyes*, 1965), *La Rosière de Pessac* (1969, a documentary), *Mes Petites amoureuses* (1975) and *Une sale histoire/A Dirty Story* (1977). His outstanding film, however, was the extraordinary *La Maman et la putain/The Mother and the Whore* (1973), the intense, epic yet intimate story of one man (Jean-Pierre Léaud*) and two women (Bernadette Lafont* and Françoise Lebrun). Characteristic of the sexual utopias and dystopias of the 1970s, it remains one of the best cinematic documents of that decade, not least in its awareness of, and complicity with, male self-centredness. A film 'as autobiographical as fiction can be', in Eustache's words, it had serious repercussions for at least two people: the woman on whom the 'whore' was based committed suicide the day after the premiere, and Eustache himself took his own life in 1981.

F

FEMIS (formerly IDHEC)

French film school (Institut de Formation et d'Enseignement pour les Métiers de l'Image et du Son/Institute for the training and teaching of audio-visual professions), which incorporated and replaced IDHEC

(Institut des Hautes Etudes Cinématographiques) in 1986. Situated in the Palais de Tokyo in Paris, near the Cinémathèque Française*, and endowed with enviable resources, FEMIS takes on fifty to sixty students a year to study theoretical film analysis alongside practical work. The present (1994–95) President is the scriptwriter Jean-Claude Carrière. The so-called Vaugirard school, officially the Lycée Louis Lumière, provides more technically oriented training. IDHEC/FEMIS and Vaugirard have produced many noted French and European film-makers and technicians (Alain Resnais*, Louis Malle*, Jacques Demy*, Anja Breien, Henri Decae, Claude Zidi*), although plenty of great film-makers did not attend such schools, and the practice of assistantship has remained the accepted way for people (whether school-trained or not) to gain entry to film-making.

FERNANDEL

Fernand Contandin; Marseilles 1903 – Paris 1971

French actor. One of the great French comic stars, with over 150 films from 1930, Fernandel started in the Marseilles music hall, singing and clowning in soldier disguise, and exploiting his two greatest assets: his horse-like features, especially his huge teeth, and a strong southern accent.

In over forty movies in the 1930s alone, Fernandel evolved two types familiar from Provençal folklore. On the one hand he was the poignant simpleton of Marcel Pagnol's* *Angèle* (1934), *Regain/Harvest* (1937) and *Le Schpountz* (1937). On the other, he played (and sang) the idiotic proletarian of countless farces, especially the military vaudevilles of the *comique troupier**, of which the epitome was *Ignace* (1937). His humour was a mixture of physicality and innuendo, well illustrated by *Le Rosier de Madame Husson/The Virtuous Isidore* (1931), in which, lauded as the virgin of the village, he celebrates by (accidentally) visiting the brothel. The public adored him while officials were appalled by the success of his 'despicable vulgar comedies which are the shame of our production'. He continued working with Pagnol in *La Fille du puisatier/The Well-Digger's Daughter* (1940) and *Topaze* (1951) and made countless other successful comedies, including *L'Auberge rouge/The Red Inn* (1951), *Le Mouton à cinq pattes/The Sheep Has Five Legs* (1954) and *La Vache et le prisonnier/The Cow and I* (1959). His popularity reached new heights with *Le Petit monde de Don Camillo/The Little World of Don Camillo* (1952), directed by Julien Duvivier* in Italy and followed by four sequels up to 1965 (a last film in 1972 starred Gino Cervi* alone). As Don Camillo, the priest who 'talked to God' and fought with Cervi's Communist mayor, Fernandel capitalised on his irrepressible grin and his accent. He directed three films, and in the 1960s co-founded a production company, Gafer, with Jean Gabin*. One of his sons, Franck Fernandel, was a moderately successful pop star in the 1960s.

FERRERI, Marco – see 'French Cinema in Europe', page 155

FEUILLADE, Louis

Lunel 1873 – Nice 1925

French director. One of the great pioneers of French cinema, Feuillade started out as a wine merchant, wrote poetry and journalism on topics ranging from a defence of Catholicism to bull-fights and created a short-lived satirical magazine, *La Tomate*. He was hired by Alice Guy* at Gaumont* in 1905 and became artistic director in 1907 when Guy left France. He wrote and directed hundreds of comic films, melodramas, biblical scenes, trick films, etc. His stupendous activity encompassed the long-running children's series *Bébé* and *Bout-de-Zan*; the ambitious art series 'Le Film esthétique', based on original subjects and with sophisticated decors; and the realist series 'La Vie telle qu'elle est' ('Life as it is'), meant to give 'an impression of truth never seen before'. This 'impression of truth', based on location shooting, informs Feuillade's most famous films, the extraordinary *Fantômas* (five feature-length films, 1913–14), a baroque crime series set in Paris which mixes the everyday with the delirious, based on phenomenally successful novels by Marcel Allain and Pierre Souvestre. *Fantômas* combines anarchist and bourgeois sensibilities, a duality which also informs *Les Vampires* (1915–16), starring Musidora*. Both series were immensely popular, an object of fascination for artists, and the target of Establishment disapproval. Feuillade responded with *Judex* (1917), another series in which the hero was, nominally, on the side of the law. He also made *Vendémiaire* (1919), *Tih-Minh* (1919) and *Barrabas* (1920). His filmography includes almost 400 titles.

FEUILLÈRE, Edwige

Caroline Cunati; Vesoul 1907

French actress. Trained in classical theatre and a member of the Comédie Française, Feuillère, as Cora Lynn, appeared initially in films chiefly interested in her statuesque body. She made some American-style sophisticated comedies, such as *Mister Flow* (1936) and *L'Honorable Catherine* (1943), but specialised in costume dramas like *Lucrèce Borgia* (1935), *De Mayerling à Sarajévo* (1940), *L'Idiot* (1946) and *L'Aigle à deux têtes* (1948), in which she excelled with her majestic beauty and deep, melodious voice. By the early 1950s she was a *grande dame* of French cinema, epitomising for François Truffaut* the staginess of the tradition of quality*, but appealing to a popular audience, especially women, with her erotically charged portrayals of mature women, as in *Olivia/The Pit of Loneliness* (1951) and *Le Blé en herbe/The Game of Love* (1954). She still pursues a successful stage career. She received an honorary César* in 1984.

FEYDER, Jacques

Jacques Frédérix; Ixelles, Belgium 1885 – Prangius, Switzerland 1948

French director of Belgian origin. Feyder worked as an actor in and director of mainstream French silent films. Three of them raised him to the status of a major director. *L'Atlantide* (1921), based on Pierre Benoît's melodramatic novel, was an unusually long film for the time, shot on location in North Africa; *Crainquebille* (1923), a dramatic tale set in popular Paris, prefigured Poetic Realism*; and *Visages d'enfants* (1923–25, shot in Switzerland) was praised for its realism, especially in its use of children and the Swiss countryside. Feyder was hired by MGM and went to Hollywood, directing *The Kiss* (1929) with Greta Garbo and foreign versions of American films, including *Anna Christie* (1930), also with Garbo. His reputation, back in France, traditionally rests on *La Kermesse héroïque/Carnival in Flanders* (1935), a humorous though formal costume drama starring Françoise Rosay* and Louis Jouvet*; nowadays *Le Grand jeu* (1933) and *Pension Mimosas* (1934) seem more interesting with their 'poetic realist' sensibility – their seedy decors and world-weary characters, greatly enhanced by wonderful performances, especially by Rosay.

FILM D'ART

French movement and production company. 'Le Film d'Art' designates: (1) a company founded in February 1908, partly with funds from Pathé*. The company acquired a studio in Neuilly and hired playwright Henri Lavedan and Comédie Française actor Charles Le Bargy to produce quality filmed drama. *L'Assassinat du Duc de Guise* (1908) remains the classic Film d'Art product, and the symbol of the strategy to move the cinema firmly into the realm of 'bourgeois' narrative. High production costs pushed the company into debt, however, and it closed in 1911. Meanwhile Pathé created a similar company, SCAGL (Société cinématographique des auteurs et gens de lettres), which produced such films as *L'Arlésienne* (1908). Other companies or departments within companies (such as Gaumont*) were created with similar aims. (2) The Film d'Art as a genre, and more specifically the historical film, set in place new trends for French cinema: bringing in and promoting well-known stage actors, introducing more sober performance styles, and developing more sophisticated narratives and film language.

Bib: Richard Abel, *The Ciné Goes to Town: French Cinema 1896–1914* (1994).

FRANJU, Georges

Fougères 1912 – Paris 1987

French director. An original figure in French cinema, Franju worked in set design and scientific film and was one of the co-founders of the Cinémathèque Française*. His first documentary short, *Le Sang des bêtes* (1949), shot in a Parisian slaughterhouse, had an enormous impact, revealing Franju's acute perception of the cruel and the uncanny within a realistic setting, as did *Hôtel des Invalides* (1952). This prepared the terrain for his best-known features which, rarely for French cinema, worked within the genre of the 'fantastic', especially *Les Yeux sans visage/Eyes Without a Face* (1960) and *Judex* (1963), a tribute to Louis Feuillade's* 1917 series (Franju also directed a film on Georges Méliès* in 1952). Among his other features are some distinguished literary adaptations, notably *Thérèse Desqueyroux* (1962, based on François Mauriac) and *Thomas l'imposteur/Thomas the Imposter* (1965, based on Jean Cocteau*). He also worked in television.

FRENCH AVANT-GARDE

Film movement(s) of the 1920s. From World War I to the coming of sound, Paris witnessed an extraordinary explosion of artistic and intellectual interest in the cinema, constituting a series of 'avant-gardes' which, following the pioneering work of Georges Sadoul*, it is customary to divide into three waves. First, the 'impressionist school' around Germaine Dulac* (*La Fête espagnole*, 1920), Louis Delluc* (*Fièvre*, 1921), Jean Epstein* (*Cœur fidèle*, 1923), Marcel L'Herbier* (*El Dorado*, 1921) and Abel Gance* (*La Roue*, 1921–23). Although these film-makers' formal concerns varied substantially, they shared a desire to develop a specific film language made of 'impressionist' or 'pointillist' notations to express subjectivity, using techniques such as slow motion and superimposition, but also, importantly, natural locations and natural light – a major difference from German expressionist film. The 'impressionists' were concerned with authorship, loved American cinema (and generally disliked French popular genres) and at the same time wanted to create a specifically French (art) cinema – thus anticipating the concerns of the French New Wave*. Their concentration on subjectivity gave rise to the accusation of 'navel-gazing' by the more cosmopolitan and iconoclastic members of what is regarded as the 'second' avant-garde, influenced by Cubism, Dadaism and Surrealism. These include Fernand Léger (*Ballet mécanique*, 1924), René Clair* (*Entr'acte*, 1924, in which artists Marcel Duchamp and Man Ray, among others, appear), Dulac with *La Coquille et le clergyman/The Seashell and the Clergyman* (1928), from a script by Antonin Artaud, Luis Buñuel* (*Un Chien andalou*, 1929, made with Salvador Dali, and *L'Age d'or*, 1930) and Jean Cocteau* (*Le Sang d'un poète*, 1930). The 'third' avant-garde had a more socially oriented agenda, making important use of documentary, and includes Alberto Cavalcanti's* *Rien que les heures* (1926), Marcel Carné's* *Nogent, Eldorado du dimanche* (1930) and Jean Vigo's* *A propos de Nice* (1930).

Neat as these distinctions are, they are complicated by several factors. First, these French developments took place within international movements [> AVANT-GARDE CINEMA IN EUROPE]. Secondly, film-makers such as Dulac moved between different 'waves'; in her case, as Sandy Flitterman-Lewis has shown, a commitment to feminism unites her work. Thirdly, as Richard Abel has pointed out, French avant-garde practitioners combined their experiments with narrative cinema, and many moved frequently between avant-garde and mainstream genres. Finally, there were many interconnections in the period's extraordinary cultural activities; the creation of film clubs, art cinemas, film theory, specialised film journals and regular film columns in the press truly elevated the cinema to the status of the 'seventh art' [> CANUDO], but also inscribed it firmly within a wider cultural field in France and outside.

Bib: Richard Abel, *French Cinema: The First Wave, 1915–1929* (1984).

FRENCH NEW WAVE – see NEW WAVE (FRANCE)

FRESNAY, Pierre

Pierre Laudenbach; Paris 1897 – Neuilly-sur-Seine 1975

French actor. Though Fresnay started in film as early as 1915, he made his mark when sound allowed his urbane and distinguished voice, polished at the Comédie Française, to be heard. Ironically, it was a put-on southern accent that made him famous. Though surrounded by real Provençal actors, Fresnay was credible as Marius in Marcel Pagnol's* Marseilles trilogy, *Marius* (1931), *Fanny* (1932) and *César* (1936). The films' triumph launched him on a career as a matinée idol, including in costume dramas with his wife, the singer Yvonne Printemps (*Trois valses* and *Adrienne Lecouvreur*, both 1938). The gentlemanly formality of Fresnay's acting was brilliantly used by Jean Renoir*, who cast him as the aristocrat de Boieldieu in *La Grande illusion* (1937). A versatile actor, Fresnay was excellent as a detective in *L'Assassin habite ... au 21/The Murderer Lives at Number 21* (1942) and as the cool doctor of *Le Corbeau/The Raven* (1943). He continued playing doctors and other figures of authority in less distinguished but popular films in the 1950s. Fresnay's (and Printemps') postwar career was increasingly slanted towards theatre. They acted on stage and co-managed a theatre.

FUNÈS, Louis de

Louis Germain de Funès de Galarza; Courbevoie 1914 – Nantes 1983

French actor. It may surprise many outside France who never got the chance to see his films that Louis de Funès was the biggest French box-office star of all time. He trained in music hall and appeared in small parts in over seventy films before his first leading roles. These came with *Ni vu, ni connu/Incognito* (1958), *Pouic-Pouic* (1963) and especially *Le Gendarme de Saint-Tropez* (1964) and its sequels, which made him the French king of comedy. Throughout the 1960s and 1970s, in contrast to Alain Delon's* and Jean-Paul Belmondo's* flatteringly virile heroes, de Funès, with his slight physique and ultra-mobile face, portrayed Frenchmen as irascible and bumbling petit-bourgeois. He was often paired with contrasting male stars like Yves Montand* and Bourvil*, with the latter in *Le Corniaud/The Sucker* (1965) and *La Grande vadrouille/Don't Look Now, We're Being Shot At* (1966), two of the biggest French box-office hits. His hallmark was barely contained rage – against authority, domineering wives, foreigners (his films were regrettably often sexist and racist). But overblown and incompetent as his characters were (the gendarme was the archetype), they still triumphed, and that is one secret of his immense popularity. The other was his great comic talent, unfortunately not always matched by his films.

Other Films Include: *Le Mouton à cinq pattes/The Sheep Has Five Legs* (1954); *La Traversée de Paris/A Pig Across Paris* (1956); *Oscar* (1967); *La Folie des grandeurs* (1971); *Les Aventures de Rabbi Jacob* (1973); *L'Aile ou la cuisse* (1976); *La Zizanie* (1978).

G

GABIN, Jean

Jean Alexis Moncorgé; Paris 1904–76

French actor. The greatest male star in classic French cinema, Gabin is known primarily as the embodiment of the 1930s proletarian hero in such classics as Julien Duvivier's* *La Belle équipe* (1936), Jean Renoir's* *La Bête humaine* (1938) and Marcel Carné's* *Le Jour se lève* (1939), although he had a long and prolific career until his death in 1976.

Gabin started out as a music-hall singer, and his early films – *Chacun sa chance* (1930), *Paris-Béguin* (1931), *Les Gaietés de l'escadron/The Joys of the Squadron* (1932) – deploy theatrical aesthetics. With *La*

Bandera (1935), which made him a star, he switched to (melo)dramatic roles, combining the signs of French working-class masculinity with those of a tragic, and often criminal, hero ('Oedipus in a cloth cap', as André Bazin* put it), epitomised in Duvivier's *Pépé le Moko* (1936). His minimalist, naturalistic acting and tremendous charisma smoothed over the contradictions inherent in this dual persona. Thus he symbolised both the hopes of the Popular Front* and the gloom of the approaching war, which he spent first in Hollywood (making *Moontide*, 1942, and *The Imposter*, 1944) and then in the Free French forces, earning a decoration. Gabin's postwar career was more uneven, films like *Martin Roumagnac* (1946, with Marlene Dietrich) and Carné's 1950 *La Marie du port* failing to achieve the expected success. But he resoundingly regained his prewar popularity in 1954 with Jacques Becker's* *Touchez pas au grisbi/Honour Among Thieves* (1954) and Renoir's *French Cancan* (1955). From then on he was a pillar of mainstream cinema, alternating between populist dramas (*L'Air de Paris*, 1954, *Rue des prairies*, 1959, *Le Chat*, 1971), comedies (*Le Baron de l'écluse*, 1960) and thrillers (three Maigret films, *Mélodie en sous-sol/The Big Snatch*, 1963, and others). Often accused of betraying his prewar proletarian image in his roles, Gabin in the 1960s and 1970s nevertheless retained his popular audience, who identified with both his social rise and his enduring working-class identity. A Gabin museum opened in September 1992 in his childhood village of Mériel, north of Paris.

Bib: Claude Gauteur and Ginette Vincendeau, *Jean Gabin, Anatomie d'un mythe* (1993).

Other Films Include: *Cœur de Lilas* (1931); *Du haut en bas* (1933); *Zouzou* (1934); *Les Bas-fonds/The Lower Depths* (1936); *La Grande illusion, Gueule d'amour* (1937); *Quai des brumes* (1938); *Remorques/Stormy Waters* (1939–41); *Au-delà des grilles* (1949); *Le Plaisir, La Vérité sur Bébé Donge* (1952); *Razzia sur la chnouf, Chiens perdus sans collier, Gas-oil* (1955); *Des gens sans importance, Voici le temps des assassins, La Traversée de Paris/A Pig Across Paris* (1956); *Le Rouge est mis* (1957); *Les Misérables, Maigret tend un piège/Maigret Sets a Trap, En cas de malheur/Love is My Profession, Les Grandes familles* (1958); *Le Président* (1961); *Un singe en hiver/A Monkey in Winter* (1962); *Monsieur* (1964); *Le Tonnerre de Dieu* (1965); *Le Pacha* (1968); *Sous le signe du taureau, Le Clan des Siciliens/The Sicilian Clan* (1969); *La Horse* (1970); *Le Tueur* (1972); *L'Affaire Dominici* (1972); *Deux hommes dans la ville* (1974).

GANCE, Abel — Paris 1889–1981

French director, who worked as a scriptwriter (notably for Gaumont*) and actor before directing his first film in 1915. Many of his early works were war propaganda. With *Mater dolorosa* (1917) and especially *La Dixième symphonie* (1918), *J'Accuse* (1919) and *La Roue* (1921–23), Gance became a leading member of the French avant-garde*. His work was characterised by melodramatic excess (*La Dixième symphonie*), formal inventiveness (*La Roue*), and technical innovation (split screens, complex camera movements, experiments with sound), all trends which find their apotheosis in *Napoléon vu par Abel Gance/Napoléon* (1927), a five-hour epic comparable to Griffith's *The Birth of a Nation* (1915) in its combination of reactionary ideology and formal brilliance. *Napoléon* became an international art-house success in the early 1980s thanks to a restored version by British film historian Kevin Brownlow (shown with live music), which also helped revive early cinema studies.

Film history loses interest in Gance after the coming of sound, as he seemed to content himself with making sound versions of his earlier films (*Mater dolorosa*, 1932, *Napoléon Bonaparte*, 1934, and *J'accuse*, 1937) and directing Georges Milton* in the reactionary *Jérôme Perreau, héros des barricades* (1935). Yet he also made sumptuous melodramas, including the remarkable *Paradis perdu* (1939) and *La Vénus aveugle* (1943), whose qualities have been overshadowed by the fact that Gance was an avowed admirer of Pétain. In the 1950s, Gance turned to epics and swashbucklers, with *La Tour de Nesle* (1955), *Austerlitz* (1960) and *Cyrano et d'Artagnan* (1964). He also made historical epics for television. The importance of Gance, as Norman King put it, is not just as an innovator, but as a film-maker 'who blurred the distinction between the "artistic" and the "popular" '.

Bib: Norman King, *Abel Gance: A Politics of Spectacle* (1984).

Other Films Include: *La Folie du Docteur Tube* (1915); *Au secours!* (1923, with Max Linder*); *Le Roman d'un jeune homme pauvre* (1935); *Un grand amour de Beethoven/The Life and Loves of Beethoven* (1936); *Louise* (1939); *Le Capitaine Fracasse* (1943); *Magirama* (1956, short); *Bonaparte et la Révolution* (1971).

GARAT, Henri Henri Garascu; Paris 1902 – Hyères 1959

French actor and singer. Garat's immense popularity in the early 1930s is matched only by the critical contempt in which he was held (Henri Jeanson* called him 'the suburbs of Maurice Chevalier'*). After a spell as Mistinguett's partner in the 1920s Parisian music halls, Garat starred in French versions of German-filmed operettas (notably *Le Chemin du paradis* [*Die Drei von der Tankstelle*], 1930, dir. Wilhelm Thiele, and *Le Congrès s'amuse* [*Der Kongreß tanzt*], 1931, dir. Erik Charell, both co-starring Lilian Harvey). With his athletic matinée-idol looks, Garat became the new sentimental hero; women threw themselves at him, his kisses were auctioned for charity. A Hollywood-style French star whose life mirrored the fantasy world of his films, he failed in the US. As the popularity of filmed operettas declined, so did his. Apart from the amusing *Un mauvais garçon* (1936, with Darrieux*), his career petered out. Garat slid into drugs, serial marriages and gambling; he died poor and forgotten.

GAUMONT, Léon Paris 1864 – Sainte-Maxime 1946

French pioneer. Léon Gaumont founded the Comptoir Général de la Photographie – later Gaumont et Cie – in 1895 to market equipment. His company, which he ran with an iron hand, expanded spectacularly until World War I, forming the other French 'empire' (symbolised by a daisy logo) to rival Pathé*. Gaumont's success was based on the successful development and marketing of others' inventions. With the backing of major financiers (including Gustave Eiffel), Gaumont developed the camera-projector Chronophotographe and in 1897 an improved version for 35mm film, the Chronographe. He experimented with sound (Chronophone), showing synchronised sound films as early as 1902. His sound experiments included a system used for *L'Eau du Nil* (1928), but all eventually failed. In 1905 Gaumont built the then largest studio in the world, a 'glass cathedral' with the most advanced technology of the time. From 1907, Gaumont worked on colour and expanded into distribution and exhibition, building a chain of Parisian and provincial cinemas; its jewel in the crown was the Gaumont-Palace in Paris (opened in 1911, demolished in 1972) which, with at one point over 6,000 seats, was the largest in the world. By 1914 Gaumont had 2,100 employees and its capital was FF4m, both large figures by French standards (although Pathé employed 5,000). A studio was built in Nice (La Victorine), and subsidiaries established in Britain, eastern Europe and the US. Legend has it that Léon Gaumont was uninterested in films (there is some dispute over this) and delegated film production to his secretary Alice Guy*. As well as making her own films, Guy hired and trained a team of film-makers – including Louis Feuillade*, Victorin Jasset, Emile Cohl* and Léonce Perret, joined later by Jacques Feyder*, Marcel L'Herbier*, Henri Fescourt and Léon Poirier – who developed realist and crime series (especially Feuillade's), biblical scenes and comic series such as *Calino*, *Léonce* (Perret), *Zigoto* and *Onésime*. In addition, Gaumont shot newsreels (Gaumont-actualités) and educational films (Encyclopédie Gaumont).

Like Pathé, Gaumont suffered a crisis provoked by World War I and competition from Hollywood, although for a time it was supported by foreign capital. Foreign subsidiaries such as Gaumont-British maintained an independent existence. Gaumont retired in 1929; the firm merged with two others to form Gaumont-Franco-Film-Aubert (GFFA), which went bankrupt in 1938. A new injection of funds revived the firm during World War II, and Gaumont has been producing and distributing films since. Today Gaumont is still one of the most powerful names in French cinema.

GIRARDOT, Annie

Paris 1931

French actress. Girardot trained for the stage and worked for three years at the Comédie française. After a few small parts in plays, cabarets and films such as *L'Homme aux clés d'or* (1956), co-starring Pierre Fresnay* and for which she gained a prize as most promising young actress, she started appearing in mainstream French films, playing sexy, waspish young *garces* ('bitches'), for instance in thrillers like *Le Rouge est mis* (1957) and *Maigret tend un piège/Maigret Sets a Trap* (1958), both co-starring Jean Gabin*. Luchino Visconti cast her, with Jean Marais* in a play he staged in Paris in 1958, and then in his film *Rocco e i suoi fratelli/Rocco and His Brothers* (1960, with Alain Delon*, and Renato Salvatori whom she married), bringing her international fame. Throughout the 1960s, she led a Franco-Italian career, alternating films by prominent directors such as Marco Ferreri, Marcel Carné* (*Trois chambres à Manhattan*, 1965, best actress prize at Venice) and Claude Lelouch* (*Vivre pour vivre*, 1967) with popular comedies such as *Erotissimo* (1967) and *La Zizanie*, (1978, co-starring Louis de Funès*). A major turning point came with *Mourir d'aimer* (1970, directed by André Cayatte), a film based on the true story of a female teacher hounded for her affair with a teenage male pupil, and who committed suicide. This turned her for several years into the top box-office French actress, playing strong though vulnerable female characters in populist melodramas. Her toughness and aura of authenticity fitted well these 'positive heroines', in the heyday of feminism; other such films include *Docteur Françoise Gailland* (1976, for which she won a César*) and *La Clé sur la porte* (1978). As she put it, 'I think I'm the only one in France who played roles that could help women. I played tough parts, masculine parts.' With the vanishing of feminist issues from the mainstream agenda, her popularity waned. She successfully went back to the stage, however, and made a 'come back' with an astonishing performance as a rapacious yet compassionate farmer in Lelouch's *Les Misérables du XXe siècle* (1995).

GODARD, Jean-Luc

Paris 1930

French director. Originally a film critic at *Cahiers du cinéma**, Godard was the most radical director of the New Wave*; his body of work is central to modern *auteur* cinema. The son of a Franco-Swiss bourgeois family, Godard briefly studied anthropology before he began writing on film. His first feature, *A bout de souffle/Breathless* (1960), with its jagged editing, references to American cinema and casual male lead

(Jean-Paul Belmondo*), was an instant success. It initiated Godard's lifelong reflection on the image, which in his 'first period' combined a search for modernist cinema with romanticism and cinephilia, most lyrically in *Le Mépris/Contempt* (1963, starring Brigitte Bardot*) and *Pierrot le fou* (1965, with Anna Karina*, Godard's first wife). Godard's 1960s work scrutinised France in the grip of the consumer boom, with its spreading housing estates, computers and advertisements, as in *Alphaville* (1965) and *Masculin féminin* (1966). It also posited prostitution as the – literal and metaphorical – condition of women (*Vivre sa vie/My Life to Live*, 1962, *Une femme mariée/The Married Woman*, 1964, *2 ou 3 choses que je sais d'elle/Two or Three Things I Know About Her*, 1967) and, by extension, of the human condition under capitalism. Anticipating the events of May 1968, *La Chinoise* and *Week-end* (1967) launched Godard's 'second period' of increasingly experimental work. With Jean-Pierre Gorin he founded the 'Dziga Vertov* group', making films (*Le Gai savoir*, 1968, *Pravda*, 1969, *Vent d'Est/Wind from the East*, 1970) aimed at smaller, militant audiences. Most starred Anne Wiazemsky, his second wife. Godard now developed an extreme counter-cinema informed by Marxist/Maoist ideology. His aim, as he famously put it, was not to make 'political films' but to 'make films politically'. *Tout va bien* (1972), starring Yves Montand* and Jane Fonda, angled these concerns towards a more accessible format. Godard subsequently worked in video with his third partner, Anne-Marie Miéville (a photographer and film-maker), most powerfully in *Numéro Deux* (1975), returning to film with *Sauve qui peut (la vie)/Slow Motion* (1980), a pessimistic self-reflexive account of male-female collaboration, again crossed with questions of prostitution. This film marked Godard's return to Switzerland, where he has since lived. In this 'third period', Godard has pursued narrative film – *Prénom Carmen* (1983), *Je vous salue, Marie/Hail Mary!* (1984), *Détective* (1984), and video/documentary work, for instance the idiosyncratic *Histoire(s) du cinéma* (1989, made for television). Godard's later films have often disappointed, with the exception of *Passion* (1982), a reflection on the specificity of the cinematic image. The ironically titled *Nouvelle vague* (1990), while continuing such investigation, is typical of the pared-down narratives and desultory melancholy of his late work.

Godard's films have been a site of contradictions. While regularly predicting the 'end of cinema', they are romantically cinephile. His use of women is both critical of and complicit with patriarchal representations: evidence, in Laura Mulvey's words, of his 'deep-seated but interesting misogyny'. Godard's cinema, while politically motivated, has alienated audiences; his relationship with Hollywood has moved from adoration to rejection to collaboration (*King Lear*, 1987). At the same time, the tensions have been productive and are transcended by the brilliance of Godard's use of image and sound. Godard's key role in developing modernist and post-modernist cinema can be felt not only directly in the work of such film-makers as Chantal Akerman* and

Leos Carax*, but throughout postwar world cinema. He was awarded a César* for life achievement in 1986.

Bib: Raymond Bellour and Mary Lea Bandy (eds.), *Jean-Luc Godard, Son + Image* (1992).

Other Films Include: *Le Petit soldat* (1960, rel. 63), *Une Femme est une femme/A Woman is a Woman* (1961); *Les Carabiniers* (1963); *Bande à part/Band of Outsiders* (1964); *Made in USA* (1967); *One Plus One (Sympathy for the Devil), British Sounds (See You at Mao), Luttes en Italie/Lotte in Italia/Struggle in Italy* (1969); *Vladimir et Rosa* (1971); *A Letter to Jane* (1972); *J.L.G. J.L.G.* (1995). **With Anne-Marie Miéville**: *Ici et ailleurs* (1974–76), *France/tour/détour/deux/enfants* (1979, TV); *Soft and Hard* (1985); *Soigne ta droite, Aria* [ep.] (1987); *2 × 50 years of French Cinema: The Century of Cinema* (1995, UK).

GRÉMILLON, Jean — Bayeux 1901 – Paris 1959

French director. One of the least known of the great French directors of the 1930s, Grémillon is possibly the most 'classic' in his combination of realism and popular genres. While studying music, Grémillon played the violin in cinemas. His first films were documentaries, and his first features, *Maldone* (1928) and *Gardiens de phare* (1929), critical successes. The popular success of the latter led to a contract with Pathé*-Natan, but *La Petite Lise* (1930), judged too black, displeased the company and Grémillon was fired; *Daïnah la métisse* (1931) was mutilated by its producer, GFFA. After a fallow period, success returned with *Gueule d'amour* (1937, one of Jean Gabin's* best films), lasting until *Le Ciel est à vous* (1943–44), and including *L'Etrange Monsieur Victor* (1938), *Remorques/Stormy Waters* (1939–41) and *Lumière d'été* (1943). His postwar career was chequered. But among documentaries and aborted projects the excellent *Pattes blanches* (1948) and *L'Amour d'une femme* (1954) stand out.

Grémillon's atmospheric realism, especially his depictions of social milieux (typographers, seamen, the provincial bourgeoisie), echoed his definition that 'it is a question not of mechanical naturalism, but, rather, of the beauty in achieving the maximum of expression within the maximum of order.' He also, unusually, offered portraits of remarkably strong and complex women in *Le Ciel est à vous* and *L'Amour d'une femme*, feminist heroines *avant la lettre* (respectively Madeleine Renaud* and Micheline Presle*), struggling equally with work and love. There as in *Gueule d'amour*, Grémillon made explosive use of melodrama, subverting (as Geneviève Sellier has noted) dominant cinema from inside, reaching a wide audience without compromising his own ideas.

Bib: Geneviève Sellier, *Jean Grémillon, Le Cinéma est à vous* (1989).

Other Features: *Pour un sou d'amour* (1931, uncredited); *La Dolorosa* (1934, Sp.); *La Valse royale* [French version of *Koenigswalzer*, Ger.], *Pattes de mouche* (1936); *L'Etrange Madame X* (1951).

GRIMAULT, Paul

Neuilly-sur-Seine 1905 – Yvelines 1994

French animation director. A draughtsman and designer, Grimault was close to the Surrealists and a friend of Jacques Prévert*, with whom he later collaborated; he appeared briefly in *L'Atalante* (1934) and *Le Crime de Monsieur Lange* (1935). Learning animation techniques, he made *Phénomènes électriques* for the 1937 Paris Exhibition, using the French Hypergonar system (a precursor of CinemaScope) and Technicolor. Subsequently, Grimault made poetic and humorous animated shorts, including *Le Petit soldat* (1947) with Prévert. In the same year he began the first French animated feature, *La Bergère et le ramoneur/The Shepherdess and the Sweep*, a libertarian fairy tale from a Prévert script. Grimault disowned the butchered version released in 1953 but bought the negative in 1967 and reworked it with Prévert. The beautiful final version, mixing old and new footage, was released in 1980 as *Le Roi et l'Oiseau/The King and Mister Bird* (awarded the Prix Louis Delluc*). Grimault's last film, *La Table tournante* (1989), combines old animated films and live action by Jacques Demy*. Along with Emile Cohl*, Grimault was the key figure in French animation film and a great influence on younger generations.

GUITRY, Sacha

Alexandre Guitry; St Petersburg, Russia 1885 – Paris 1957

French director, actor and playwright, son of stage star Lucien Guitry. Sacha spent his youth among artistic celebrities (Cézanne, Auguste Renoir, Sarah Bernhardt, etc.), who feature in his documentary *Ceux de chez nous* (1915). He became one of the acclaimed playwrights and actors of the *boulevard* theatre, creating a glittering and frivolous world in which he and his successive wives figured prominently (he married five actresses). Guitry's main assets were his wit and his voice; after much publicised contempt for the cinema, he began filming his own plays in record time and with huge success. Films like *Désiré* and *Quadrille* (both 1937) attracted critical scorn, but recent writers, following François Truffaut*, have re-evaluated Guitry's work precisely because its distanced theatricality was so *modern*. Frivolous, misogynist and reactionary, Guitry's films are saved by his humour and his devastating verbal flow, as in the famous seventeen-minute telephone monologue of *Faisons un rêve* and his voice-over in the brilliant *Le Roman d'un tricheur/The Story of a Cheat* (both 1936). He created his own humorous historical genre, a unique amalgam of history textbook and music-hall revue, in *Les Perles de la couronne/The Pearls of the Crown* (1937) and *Remontons les Champs-Elysées* (1938). As collaborator and writer of the chauvinistic *De Jeanne d'Arc à Philippe Pétain* (published 1944), Guitry was jailed in August 1944. He continued making idiosyncratic historical films, such as *Si Versailles m'était conté/Royal Affairs in Versailles* (1953) and *Napoléon* (1955), and comedies, notably the vicious *La Poison* (1951, starring Michel Simon*). Guitry's populist spectacles had a modernist edge. Before Orson Welles, he invented the narrated credit sequence, parading the cinematic apparatus. He was a model for New Wave* *auteurs*; as Truffaut observed, 'he was always Sacha Guitry; that is, he embroidered on themes that were personal to him.'

GUY [GUY-BLACHÉ], Alice

Saint-Mandé 1873[5?] – Mahwah, New Jersey 1968

French director, arguably the world's first fiction film-maker. As a secretary fascinated by the Lumière* cameras, she sought her boss Léon Gaumont's* permission to direct her own sketches. The earliest (arguably the first fiction film ever, now lost), *La Fée aux choux/The Cabbage Fairy* (1896), was a comic fairy tale; a later version, *Sage-femme de première classe/First Class Midwife* (1902), still exists. Gaumont delegated his growing production department to Guy, and there followed intense activity until 1906, during which she directed about 200 one-reelers, acting also as scriptwriter, producer and wardrobe assistant. This heady, anarchic period gave Guy great scope and power: she experimented with photography, sound and tinting, and spanned the spectrum of popular genres from slapstick and melodrama to historical epics. Ferdinand Zecca, Victorin Jasset and Louis Feuillade* – France's future leading directors – were all her apprentices. In 1907 she married Herbert Blaché and emigrated to the US. After the birth of her first child in 1909, Guy founded the Solax film company, releasing over 300 titles, up to fifty of them directed by herself. Solax became Blaché Features, specialising in four-reelers; later the Guy-Blachés founded various short-lived companies before being driven out of business in 1917. Guy stopped making films after *Tarnished Reputation* (1920), her seventieth American picture. Divorced, she returned to France with her two children, unsuccessfully trying to revive her film career and struggling (with equally little success) to correct histories which regularly attributed her French films to male directors such as Jasset and Emile Cohl*.

Alice Guy was belatedly celebrated by the Cinémathèque Française* and awarded the Legion of Honour in 1953, but her pioneering role was only widely recognised in the 1970s. She gave credence to her own statement that 'there is nothing connected with the staging of a motion picture that a woman cannot do as easily as a man.'

Bib: Anthony Slide (ed.), *The Memoirs of Alice Guy-Blaché* (1986).

HOLLAND, Agnieszka – see 'French Cinema in Europe', page 156

HUILLET, Danièle and STRAUB, Jean-Marie – see 'French Cinema in Europe', page 156

HUPPERT, Isabelle — Paris 1955

French actress. One of the most prominent French art cinema actresses since the late 1970s, Huppert trained for the stage. One of her early film parts was as a rebellious teenager in Bertrand Blier's* *Les Valseuses/Going Places* (1973); her first success was in Claude Goretta's *La Dentellière/The Lacemaker* (1977). These two films established the dual features of her persona: sexual intensity on the one hand, victimised innocence on the other. This duality is epitomised in Claude Chabrol's* *Violette Nozière* (1978), the story of a real-life patricide, for which she won a Best Actress award at Cannes. Huppert's most interesting parts express resistance through sexuality, as in Maurice Pialat's* *Loulou*, Jean-Luc Godard's* *Sauve qui peut (la vie)/Slow Motion* (1980) and Diane Kurys'* *Coup de foudre/Entre nous/At First Sight* (1983). In others, she embodies a more conventional coolness: Bertrand Tavernier's* *Coup de torchon/Clean Slate* (1981), Joseph Losey's *La Truite/The Trout* (1982), Blier's *La Femme de mon pote/My Best Friend's Girl* (1983). This last film, like Josiane Balasko's* *Sac de noeuds/All Mixed Up*, extended her range to comedy, though her register is predominantly dramatic. As in France, Huppert's international films have been more critically than commercially successful (Michael Cimino's *Heaven's Gate*, 1980, Werner Schroeter's *Malina*, 1990). She has been supportive of women *auteurs* such as Kurys, Balasko and others, including her sister Caroline Huppert. Her performance as Emma in Chabrol's *Madame Bovary* (1991) may signal a move towards more popular, melodramatic, parts, although her intense performance in Christian Vincent's *La*

Séparation recalled her earlier work in smaller-scale art film. She was awarded the acting prize, jointly with Sandrine Bonnaire* for her part in Chabrol's *La Cérémonie/Judgement in Stone* (1995).

Other Films Include: *Aloïse* (1974); *Le Juge et l'assassin* (1976); *Les Soeurs Brontë/The Brontë Sisters* (1979); *Passion* (1982); *La Garce* (1984); *Cactus* [Australia], *The Bedroom Window* [US] (1986); *Les Possédés* (1987); *Une affaire de femmes* (1988); *La Vengeance d'une femme* (1989); *Après l'amour* (1992); *Amateur* (1994, US); *L'Inondation* (1995).

I

IDHEC – see FEMIS

J

JAQUE-CATELAIN

Jacques Guerin-Castelain; Saint-Germain-en-Laye 1897 – Paris 1965

French actor, star of the late silent cinema. Jaque-Catelain's career is closely linked to that of his favourite director and mentor Marcel L'Herbier*. He appeared in many of the director's classics – *Rose-France* (1919), *El Dorado* (1921), *L'Inhumaine* (1924) – and in films by other directors, such as Léonce Perret's *Koenigsmark* (1923). A delicately handsome young man, fabulously attired amid L'Herbier's art deco sets, he was France's first *jeune premier*, anticipating stars such as Pierre Richard-Willm*, Charles Boyer*, Gérard Philipe* and Vincent Perez. Despite parts in further films by L'Herbier, he was not favoured by the transition to sound. He devoted much of his subsequent career to the stage.

Bib: Pierre Cadars, *Les Séducteurs du cinéma français (1928–1958)* (1982).

JAUBERT, Maurice

Nice 1900 – Azerailles 1940

French composer. Jaubert wrote music criticism and was director of music at Pathé*-Natan (1930–34). As a composer he wrote the scores (songs and music) of some of the greatest French films of the 1930s, among them René Clair's* *Quatorze juillet* (1932), Jean Vigo's* *Zéro de conduite* and *L'Atalante* (both 1934) and Marcel Carné's* *Drôle de drame* (1937), *Quai des brumes* (1938) and *Le Jour se lève* (1939), perhaps his most affecting of all. As his biographer François Porcile put it, Jaubert always refused 'illustrative redundancy'. Jaubert himself remarked, 'Three notes on the accordion, if they are what a particular image demands, will always be more stirring than the Good Friday music from *Parsifal.*'

JEANSON, Henri

Paris 1900 – Honfleur 1970

French scriptwriter. From the early 1930s to the late 1960s, Jeanson wrote some of the wittiest lines in French cinema. Like many French film writers, including Jacques Prévert* and Michel Audiard*, he was particularly good at dialogue, the withering joke or aphorism his trademark, especially on the lips of the top stars of the time. Unlike Prévert, who developed a coherent universe, but like Audiard, Jeanson did not pursue particular themes in his films. A glance at his filmography, however, reveals many popular classics, from *Pépé le Moko* (1936) to *Fanfan la Tulipe* (1952) and *La Vache et le prisonnier/The Cow and I* (1959). Jeanson also wrote plays, scripts, film reviews, and journalism, notably for the satirical weekly *Le Canard enchaîné,* where his wit could be vitriolic (he was involved in a number of controversies and occasionally in court cases). He directed one film, *Lady Paname* (1950).

JOUVET, Louis

Crozon 1887 – Paris 1951

French actor. When Jouvet first appeared in Marcel Pagnol's* *Topaze* in 1932, well into his forties, the press remarked that 'such a complete artist, first-rate stage director, highly cultured theatre manager and scintillating actor is for the cinema a precious conquest'. Although for Jouvet the cinema was mainly a way of supporting his theatrical ventures, he gave memorable performances in such classics as *La Kermesse héroïque/Carnival in Flanders* (1935), *Entrée des artistes/The Curtain Rises* (1938, where he plays himself as Paris Conservatoire teacher), *La Marseillaise* (1937), *Un carnet de bal* (1937) and *Quai des orfèvres* (1947). Tall and elegant, Jouvet exuded phlegmatic distinction bordering on insolence and occasionally menace. His main feature was an inimitable voice, a syncopated diction, as Robert Brasillach* put it, 'at once aristocratic and sly, moving and funny'. In one of his best pre-war films, *Les Bas-fonds/The Lower Depths* (1936), he condensed these qualities as the destitute 'Russian' baron; in *Hôtel du Nord* (1938), he and Arletty*, as pimp and prostitute, stole the film from the romantic leads. Jouvet endures in French popular memory in his mockingly threatening 'bizarre, bizarre', uttered in dark tones to Michel Simon* in the surreal *Drôle de drame* (1937).

KAPLAN, Nelly

Buenos Aires, Argentina 1934

French director. Kaplan was a journalist and assistant to Abel Gance* before starting to make her own films, including several shorts on painters. She has also written Surrealist/erotic novels under the name of Belen, and worked for television. Her claim to fame is her first feature, *La Fiancée du pirate/Dirty Mary* (1969), a key film in early feminist film debates. The 'fiancée' is a young woman (the sensual and impertinent Bernadette Lafont*) who takes her revenge on a whole village by selling herself to the men who maltreated her mother and then ruining their reputation. Harshly criticised for its politically incorrect use of prostitution and humiliation of other female characters, the film is nevertheless a joyful attack on misogyny, seen by Lafont as 'a libertarian act'. Kaplan's subsequent films have been less successful, perhaps because her libertarian sensitivity became outmoded, but they have been consistently interesting if controversial: for instance *Néa* (1976), an attempt at soft porn from a woman's point of view, and *Plaisir d'amour* (1991), a tale of three women (grandmother, mother and daughter) who exhaust a man sexually.

Other Films Include: *Abel Gance: hier et demain* (1963, short); *Papa les petits bateaux...* (1971); *Charles et Lucie* (1979); *Patte de Velours* (1987, TV).

KARINA, Anna

Hanne Karin Blarke Bayer; Copenhagen, Denmark 1940

French actress of Danish origin. A former model, Karina appeared in commercials and a short film in Denmark before moving to Paris in 1959. Her meeting with Jean-Luc Godard* was decisive for both. Godard's 'Karina years' (during most of which they were married) include seven features: *Le Petit soldat* (1960, rel. 1963), *Une femme est une femme/A Woman is a Woman* (1961), *Vivre sa vie/My Life to Live* (1962), *Bande à part/Band of Outsiders* (1964), *Alphaville*, *Pierrot le fou* (1965) and *Made in USA* (1967). The stunningly beautiful Karina was central to Godard's (and the New Wave's*) vision of a 'new' femininity: sensual, but also sensitive and intellectual, epitomised in the dreamy close-ups of Karina in *Vivre sa vie*: smoking, reading, talking philosophy in cafés, crying at the cinema (Jeanne Moreau* embodied another version of the New Wave woman). Karina starred in a few other *auteur* films, such as Michel Deville's *Ce soir ou jamais* (1961) and Jacques Rivette's* *La Religieuse* (1965, rel. 1967). Her career lost momentum after the split with Godard, although she directed *Vivre ensemble* in 1973, a telling document on the libertarian ethos of the 1960s and early 1970s.

KARMITZ, Marin

Bucharest, Romania 1938

Romanian-born French producer, distributor and director. After studying at IDHEC* (1957–59) and working as an assistant director, he made a few shorts and features, of which the most interesting is *Coup pour coup* (1972), part of the militant cinema of the 1970s. After 1973, Karmitz switched to production and distribution through his company MK2. A passionate defender of *auteur* cinema, he also controls a cinema chain, which is still expanding. His production credits include films by Marco Bellocchio, Jean-Luc Godard*, Louis Malle*, Lucian Pintilie and Claude Chabrol*, as well as Krzysztof Kieślowski's* high-profile pan-European venture *Trois couleurs Bleu/Three Colours Blue* (1993), *Trois couleurs Blanc/Three Colours White* (1993) and *Trois couleurs Rouge/Three Colours Red* (1994), a great success which seems to support Karmitz's claim that 'though financial conditions for production are better than they used to be, political conditions are not. We live in a world of slogans, appearances, stereotypes. [...] It is possible to do it differently, as I proved with Kieślowski's's trilogy.' He produced many successful films of the mid-1990s, among them Claude Chabrol's* *L'Enfer* (1994) and *La Cérémonie/Judgement in Stone* (1995).

KIEŚLOWSKI, Krzysztof – see 'French Cinema in Europe', page 157

KOSMA, Joseph

Budapest, Hungary 1905 – Paris 1969

French composer of Hungarian origin. Kosma trained and worked in Budapest and Berlin, where he was influenced by Bertolt Brecht,

Hanns Eisler and Kurt Weill, before moving to Paris in 1933. His meeting with Jacques Prévert* was decisive. Together they produced a huge number of songs, some of them for the films of Jean Renoir* (*Le Crime de Monsieur Lange*, 1935) and Marcel Carné* (*Les Portes de la nuit*, 1946), Kosma working in hiding during the war. He said, 'I put Jacques Prévert's poems to music without changing a comma – it was not easy but my enthusiasm for his poetry helped me surmount many technical obstacles.' Kosma's music contributed greatly to the identity and popularity of Poetic Realism*. He also composed scores for many films by Renoir, Carné and others, and wrote ballets, oratorios and an opera.

KURYS, Diane — Lyons 1948

French director. Kurys was a stage and film actress before directing her first film, *Diabolo menthe/Peppermint Soda* (1977), an account of her adolescence in Paris in the late 1960s. A great popular and critical success, it contained the major elements of her work to come: naturalistic style, light humour based on social observation, an eye for period detail and the ability to rework aspects of her own life for a wide audience. However, *Cocktail Molotov* (1980), *Un homme amoureux/A Man in Love* (1987; an international production with Claudia Cardinale) and *Après l'amour* (1992), though also reflecting personal concerns, did less well. Kurys' most successful films have been those which returned to her childhood: *Coup de foudre/Entre Nous/At First Sight* (1983) and *La Baule-les-Pins/C'est la vie* (1990). *Coup de foudre*, with Isabelle Huppert* and Miou-Miou*, found a wide international audience for its seductive treatment of a close female friendship. Although Kurys refuses the label 'woman director', finding it 'negative, dangerous and reductive', the strength of her work is in exploring the family and emotions from a female-centred perspective. *A la folie* (1994), also about female friendship and starring the explosive duo of Anne Parillaud and Béatrice Dalle*, is a surprising and not altogether satisfying foray into a darker mood.

L

LAFONT, Bernadette — Nîmes, 1938

French actress. Like Jeanne Moreau*, Stéphane Audran*, Anna Karina*, Anouk Aimée* and others such as Emmanuelle Riva, Lafont is internationally renowned as a star of the New Wave*, especially for her performances in François Truffaut's* early short *Les Mistons* (1957) and in Claude Chabrol's* *Le Beau Serge* (1959) and *Les Bonnes femmes* (1960). But where the other actresses evoked a cerebral, bourgeois or neurotic type of femininity, Lafont's was more joyful and carnal. This was the basis for the second phase of her career, as a rebellious heroine, especially in Nelly Kaplan's* seminal *La Fiancée du pirate/Dirty Mary* (1969), Moshe Mizrahi's *Les Stances à Sophie* (1970), an unjustly unknown feminist comedy, based on Christiane Rochefort's novel, and Truffaut's vehicle for her, *Une belle fille comme moi/A Gorgeous Bird Like Me* (1972). The rest of Lafont's career has been prolific and eclectic, alternating popular comedies and auteur films. Among the latter, the most important is undoubtedly Jean Eustache's* *La Maman et la putain/The Mother and the Whore* (1973), a brilliant if misogynist disquisition on the 1970s, in which she is paired with Jean-Pierre Léaud*; twenty years later, the young director Marion Vernoux paid tribute to the film and its leading couple by casting Lafont and Léaud in *Personne ne m'aime* (1994). Also notable in her later filmography are Claude Miller's *L'Effrontée* (1985) and Chabrol's comic thrillers *Inspecteur Lavardin* (1986) and *Masques* (1987).

LANGLOIS, Henri

Smyrna [now Izmir], Turkey
1914 – Paris 1977

French film archivist. Although Georges Franju*, Jean Mitry and P. A. Harlé co-founded the Cinémathèque Française* (on 12 September 1936) with Langlois, it is the latter's personality which for better or worse was imprinted on the institution. Langlois' passion for the cinema and his catholic tastes created a collection of truly world dimensions. He collected everything – initially thanks to personal means – and in the early days notoriously stocked it anywhere he could (including, legend has it, in his bath). His priority of showing as many films as possible turned the Cinémathèque into a university for generations of film buffs and future film-makers, notably those of the New Wave*. But Langlois' lack of concern for administration and for conserving his prints clashed with the increasing professionalism of the Cinémathèque: when André Malraux, the Minister for Culture, tried to impose a new administrator in 1968 and film personalities flew to Langlois' defence, they were defending a romantic notion of cinephilia rather than a valid concept of film archiving. Nevertheless, Langlois' Cinémathèque was a central pillar of French film culture. Though his personality was dominant, his team of (often voluntary, usually female) helpers should be acknowledged, including Lotte Eisner*, Mary Meerson and Marie Epstein*.

Bib: Richard Roud, *A Passion for Films: Henri Langlois and the Cinémathèque Française* (1983).

LE VIGAN, Robert

Robert Coquillaud; Paris 1900 – Tandil, Argentina 1972

French actor, who left a vivid mark on French cinema, despite rarely rating top billing in his sixty-odd films between 1931 and 1943. A brilliant, extravagant actor, Le Vigan specialised in louche, menacing or diabolical characters. He worked frequently with Julien Duvivier* (*Golgotha*, as Christ, and *La Bandera*, both 1935), and appeared in classics such as *Les Bas-fonds/The Lower Depths* (1936), *Quai des brumes* (1938) and *Goupi Mains-rouges/It Happened at the Inn* (1943). His career was curtailed at the Liberation because of his overt fascism. Condemned to forced labour, he escaped to Spain and then Argentina, abandoning his part (Jéricho) in *Les Enfants du paradis* (1943–45); he was replaced by Pierre Renoir*.

LÉAUD, Jean-Pierre

Paris 1944

French actor, linked to the New Wave* and especially François Truffaut*. In their first film, *Les Quatre cents coups/The 400 Blows* (1959), the fourteen-year-old Léaud gave a remarkable performance as Antoine Doinel, his engaging spontaneity convincingly suggesting both the streetwise young Parisian and the lonely unloved child. The product of a close relationship with Truffaut was a Doinel saga (*L'Amour à 20 ans*, 1962, *Baisers volés/Stolen Kisses*, 1968, *Domicile conjugal/Bed and Board*, 1970, *L'Amour en fuite/Love on the Run*, 1978) in which he fell in love, got married and divorced. The candidness gave way to a mannered performance style, the adult personality a self-absorbed romantic, in love with 'magic' women but irresponsible with real ones (charming or exasperating depending on one's point of view). He successfully transferred this persona to non-Doinel Truffaut films (such as *La Nuit américaine/Day for Night*, 1973), several films by Jean-Luc Godard* (including *Masculin féminin*, 1966, *Made in USA*, 1967), and Jean Eustache's* extraordinary *La Maman et la putain/The Mother and the Whore* (1973). Léaud was badly affected by Truffaut's death in 1984. His later parts – small roles in films by, among others, Godard, Agnès Varda*, Catherine Breillat and Aki Kaurismäki – have tended to refer back to his earlier image, especially Marion Vernoux's *Personne ne m'aime* (1994), in which he is paired with Bernadette Lafont*, his partner in *La Maman et la putain*.

LECLERC, Ginette   Geneviève Menut; Paris 1912–92

French actress, typecast as an erotic vamp from the 1930s to the 1950s. She started in music hall and played in many light films of the 1930s which exploited her voluptuous physique rather than her talent. She was cast by Marcel Pagnol* in *La Femme du boulanger/The Baker's Wife* (1938) in a part allegedly intended for Joan Crawford, as the sultry wife who elopes but is eventually reconciled with her older husband (Raimu*) in a memorable scene in which he insults the cat instead. Leclerc enjoyed her greatest popularity in the 1940s, especially for her part in Henri-Georges Clouzot's* *Le Corbeau/The Raven* (1943), although the film, deemed 'anti-French', cost her a jail sentence in 1944. She resumed her career, but never really found the parts she deserved. Though Leclerc's talent and humour sometimes transcended the sluts and schemers she played, she was ultimately limited by sexist typecasting.

LEGRAND, Michel   Paris 1932

French composer and singer, the son of popular musician Raymond Legrand. Like his father, who had studied with Paul Whiteman in the US, Legrand specialised in fusing popular French *chanson* with jazz. A prolific composer and singer, he is particularly known for his work on New Wave* films, working with Jean-Luc Godard* and with Agnès Varda*, in whose *Cléo de 5 à 7/Cleo from 5 to 7* (1962) he appears – composing a song. Legrand also wrote the music for Jacques Demy's* *Lola* (1961) and his musicals *Les Parapluies de Cherbourg/The Umbrellas of Cherbourg* (1964) and *Les Demoiselles de Rochefort* (1967); his melancholy tunes contributed much to the bitter-sweet image of Demy's films. He has also had a successful international career, composing music for such diverse films as Robert Altman's *Prêt-à-porter* (1994, US) and Claude Lelouch's* *Les Misérables du XXe siècle* (1995) and directed one film.

LELOUCH, Claude   Paris 1937

French director. Lelouch started his career as a film reporter, which explains his presence along with Godard*, Resnais* and Varda* (among others) as one of the directors of *Loin du Viêt-Nam/Far from Vietnam* (1967). The tone of his work, however, was set by *Un homme et une femme/A Man and a Woman* (1966), a glossy melodrama with a famous theme tune, one of the most successful and prize-bedecked French films ever, starring Anouk Aimée and Jean-Louis Trintignant*. Lelouch has made some thirty popular and populist films, 'naive stories' as he puts it, overblown epics according to others, typically intercutting storylines from antiquity to the present day, and with programmatic titles such as *La Vie, l'amour, la mort/Life, Love, Death* (1968). His *Les Misérables du XXe siècle* (1995, with Jean-Paul Belmondo*) characteristically alternates the nineteenth-century setting of Victor Hugo's novel with World War II. Some of his most interesting films are smaller in scale: *La Bonne année* (1973, with Lino Ventura* and Françoise Fabian) and *Edith et Marcel* (1983), a biopic of singer Edith Piaf.

L'HERBIER, Marcel — Paris 1890–1979

French director (also novelist, scriptwriter poet and composer), whose career, like that of Abel Gance*, is split between a highly regarded silent phase and a neglected sound one. L'Herbier worked for the French army's film unit during the war and in 1919 made the patriotic *Rose France.* He shared the formal concerns of the French avant-garde*, deploying technical virtuosity (such as superimpositions) to express his characters' psychology, as in *El Dorado* (1921), considered by many his masterpiece. He published an early essay on film language, *Hermès et le silence* (1918), worked for Gaumont*, and set up his own production company, Cinégraphic, in 1923. *Feu Mathias Pascal/The Late Mathias Pascal* (1925), praised by Georges Sadoul* for its use of Italian locations, starred Ivan Mosjoukine*. L'Herbier's largest projects, *L'Inhumaine* (1924) and the brilliant *L'Argent* (1929, with Brigitte Helm), display modernist architecture and production values lavish enough to compete with Hollywood while reflecting an image of European sophistication. L'Herbier worked successfully through the 1930s and 1940s, directing opulent melodramas such as *Le Bonheur* (1935), *Nuits de feu* (1937) and *Adrienne Lecouvreur* (1938), the wartime 'fantastic' costume drama *La Nuit fantastique* (1942) and the delightful Edwige Feuillère* comedy *L'Honorable Catherine* (1943); he also made pompous military dramas such as *La Porte du large* and *Les Hommes nouveaux* (both 1936), the latter an apology for French colonisation of Morocco. L'Herbier was an active participant in French film industry affairs, heading several professional associations throughout his career and co-founding IDHEC* in 1943. He published a collection of film essays, *L'Intelligence du cinématographe* in 1947 (revised 1977), and his autobiography *La Tête qui tourne* in 1979; he also worked for television.

Bib: Noël Burch, *Marcel L'Herbier* (1973).

LINDER, Max

Gabriel Maximilien Leuvielle; Saint-Loubès 1883 – Paris 1925

French actor and director, the greatest comic genius of the French silent cinema. After theatre work in Bordeaux and Paris, Linder joined Pathé* in 1905 and acted in comic shorts, creating the character of 'Max' in 1907. When his rival André Deed* left for Italy, Linder's career took off in 1909 thanks to a prolific series with such titles as *Max aéronaute*, *Max toréador* and *Max virtuose*, many of which he himself directed after 1911. Linder's humour was theatrical, elegant and ironic, foreshadowing René Clair*. He created much-imitated gags, such as the 'fake mirror' (with someone else pretending to be him on the other side), and was a major influence on Chaplin, Harold Lloyd and others. Linder's handsome dandy – frock coat, striped trousers, spats, top hat and cane – courting women in Parisian salons, 'epitomised the leisured French bourgeois rentier [...] pursuing a life of "decadence"', as Richard Abel put it. His success was phenomenal and international, as he discovered on a tour of Europe. He obliged Pathé to raise his salary to FF1m in 1912, making him the world's highest-paid film star. He travelled to the USA in 1917 and 1922, on his second trip making successful films such as the parodic *The Three-Must-Get-Theres* (1922). Although shrouded in mystery, Linder's dramatic suicide (with his wife) may be traced to recurring illness and depression, war wounds and, arguably, the rising popularity of Hollywood comics. His reputation and some of his work survive, partly thanks to his daughter Maud Linder's documentaries, especially *L'Homme au chapeau de soie/The Man in the Silk Hat* (1983). His Paris cinema, the 'Max Linder' (built in 1924), was recently renovated.

Bib: Richard Abel, *The Ciné Goes to Town: French Cinema, 1896–1914* (1994).

LITVAK, Anatole – see 'French Cinema in Europe', page 158

LUMIÈRE, Louis

Besançon 1864 – Bandol 1948

and

LUMIÈRE, Auguste

Besançon 1862 – Lyons 1954

French pioneers. Louis and Auguste Lumière ran their father Antoine's photographic business in Lyons. Louis was the brilliant inventor of the Cinematograph (meaning 'writing in movement', later shortened to 'cinema'). He built on previous inventions such as Edison's Kinetoscope, but with the key addition of a mechanism allowing the intermittent motion of the film in the camera, based on the sewing machine. The Cinematograph was both camera and projector. The invention was patented in February 1895, first demonstrated on 22 March 1895 and then through the summer at various learned societies and congresses. Its hugely successful public screening on 28 December 1895 in Paris constitutes the official 'birth' of the cinema. The uncannily aptly-named Lumières (as Jean-Luc Godard* pointed out) were canny businessmen. To demonstrate their apparatus, they recorded trains entering stations (*L'Arrivée d'un train en gare de La Ciotat*), workers leaving (their) factories (*La Sortie des usines Lumière*), participants at conferences, etc. They showed a fascination for the trappings of modernity as well as idyllic views of bourgeois domesticity in sunlit gardens such as *Le Déjeuner de bébé*, and little comic scenes (*L'Arroseur arrosé*) [all films, 1895]. Meanwhile, their cinematographers travelled all over the world shooting *actualités*, world events and the European colonial expansion, building a catalogue of over a thousand films over the next two years. The Lumière documentary approach is often simplistically contrasted with the fantasy and invention of Georges Méliès*. But while even these earliest films show an attention to framing and narrative organisation, Lumière cameramen also produced religious scenes, such as the thirteen-tableau *La Vie et la passion de Jésus-Christ* (1897). The films having achieved their purpose, the Lumières stopped production to concentrate on technical developments such as wide-screen, colour and 3-D cinema.

The Lumière home in Lyons is now a museum at the splendid address of 1, rue du Premier Film.

MALLE, Louis

Thumeries 1932 – Beverley Hills, California 1995

French director. A graduate of IDHEC*, Malle co-directed with Jean-Yves Cousteau the prize-winning documentary *Le Monde du silence/ The Silent World* (1956). His subsequent work is characterised by classicism, versatility and international success. Malle's early features place him in an odd position vis-à-vis the New Wave*; he was a precursor to it with *Ascenseur pour l'échafaud/Lift to the Scaffold* (1957), with his use of locations, Jeanne Moreau* and a Miles Davis score, and *Les Amants* (1958), and already marginal to it with the zany comedy *Zazie dans le métro* (1960, based on Raymond Queneau's novel). Malle's subsequent work combined classic *mise-en-scène* with 'risky' topics: suicide in *Le Feu follet/A Time to Live and a Time to Die* (1963), mother-son incest in *Le Souffle au coeur/Dearest Love* (1971), child sexuality in *Pretty Baby* (1978, US) and, most incisively, French collaboration during the Occupation in *Lacombe, Lucien* (1974). Unusually for a French director, Malle made a successful transition to the US with such films as *Atlantic City, U.S.A.* (1980, Can./Fr.) and *My Dinner with André* (1981), returning to France for his moving autobiographical wartime drama *Au revoir les enfants* (1987) and the Renoiresque *Milou en Mai* (1989). He made the glossy *Fatale/Damage* (1992) with Juliette Binoche* and Jeremy Irons, shot in England and (controversially for the French) in English, and ironically returned to a more modest type of European art cinema* with the American *Vanya on 42nd Street* (1994). Malle has directed many documentaries on subjects ranging from the American Bible belt to the Tour de France.

Other Films Include: *Vie privée/A Very Private Affair* (1962); *Viva Maria!* (1965); *Le Voleur/The Thief of Paris* (1967); *Black Moon* (1975).

MARAIS, Jean

Jean Alfred Villain-Marais; Cherbourg 1913

French actor. There are two aspects to the career of the extravagantly good-looking Jean Marais: the critically acclaimed films he made as Jean Cocteau's* personal and professional partner, and the popular swashbucklers of the 1950s and 1960s. Marais trained for the stage and had small parts in films by Marcel L'Herbier*. In 1937 he met Cocteau, who propelled him into the limelight of Paris artistic circles, which led to a long and successful stage and film career. Cocteau used Marais' beautifully chiselled face and athletic body in his poetic-mythical fantasies, especially in *L'Éternel retour* (1943, scripted by Cocteau, directed by Jean Delannoy*), a reworking of the Tristan and Iseult legend, the fairy tale *La Belle et la bête* (1946), and *Orphée* (1950). Narratives, lighting and costumes turned on Marais' eroticism; he became one of France's top heart-throbs. When his partnership with Cocteau loosened (they remained friends), Marais starred in popular genre films of the 1950s, melodramas such as *Le Château de verre/The Glass Castle* (1950, with Michèle Morgan*), and costume dramas such as Jean Renoir's *Eléna et les hommes/Paris Does Strange Things* (1956). He found his niche in swashbucklers, the perfect setting for his dashing, muscular performances: *Nez de cuir* (1952), *Le Comte de Monte-Cristo* (1954), *Le Capitaine Fracasse* (1961), and many others, including a *Fantômas* series. These films, though critically scorned, made Marais one of the top ten stars of the French postwar box office. Alongside Gérard Philipe*, Marais represented an ambivalent masculinity which, as with Rudolf Valentino in Hollywood, combined the pleasures of feminine identification with 'male' narrative mastery. Marais' film career came to an end in the early 1970s. A prominent media personality in France, he has kept active in theatre, as well as painting and sculpture (he sculpted the head of Jean Gabin* displayed at the Gabin museum).

Other Films Include: *Carmen (*1943–45); *L'Aigle à deux têtes* (1948); *Les Parents terribles* (1948); *Dortoir des Grandes* (1953); *Napoléon* (1955); *La Princesse de Clèves*, *Le Miracle des loups* (1961); *Les Mystères de Paris, Le Masque de fer* (1963); *Peau d'Ane* (1970); *Parking* (1985); *Johanna d'Arc of Mongolia* (1988); *Stealing Beauty* [US], *Les Misérables du XXe siècle* (1995).

MARCEAU, Sophie

Paris 1966

French actress, who emerged as a cute adolescent in Claude Pinoteau's family comedy *La Boum* (1980), when she was barely fifteen. The phenomenal success of the film prompted *La Boum 2* (1982) and other comedies. Marceau was part of the 1980s fashion for pairing very young women with mature men such as Jean-Paul Belmondo* (*Joyeuses Pâques*, 1984). As she matured, her looks evolved into sultry sexiness, adorning for instance the historical epics *Fort Saganne* (1984, with Gérard Depardieu*), *Chouans!* (1988) and *La Fille de d'Artagnan/D'Artagnan's Daughter* (1994). Marceau has tried to move into *auteur* cinema, notably with Pialat's* *Police* (1985), but without much success so far. Her next career move has taken her in the direction of international productions; in 1995 she appeared in Michelangeo Antonioni's *Beyond the Clouds* [It.] and the Mel Gibson historical epic, *Braveheart* [US].

MARIANO, Luis

Mariano Eusebio González; Irun, Spain 1920 – Paris 1970

French singer and actor of Spanish origin. Mariano, a remarkable singer, started as an operetta star. Although his film persona was a continuation of his stage one, his phenomenal success was characteristic of popular French film genres of the 1940s and 1950s. In filmed operettas (*Violettes impériales/Violetas Imperiales/Imperial Violets*, 1952), or in musical comedies (*Le Chanteur de Mexico*, 1956), Mariano, his dark good looks enhanced by colourful costumes, epitomised the Latin lover. His huge popular appeal (especially to women) was matched by critical disdain.

MARKER, Chris

Christian François Bouche-Villeneuve; Neuilly-sur-Seine 1921

French director and photographer. Marker, who has been making documentaries since 1952, is considered a member of the 'Left Bank' of the New Wave* for his left-wing politics and the way his work combines social issues with formal experiment. He has shot films in many countries, but perhaps his most famous film, *Le Joli mai* (1963), is a portrait of Parisians in May 1962, a classic of *cinéma-vérité** in its blend of ethnographic interviews with auteurist self-portrait. For Marker as for Jean-Luc Godard*, 1968 marked a turning point; Marker turned to collective film-making with the founding of SLON. In the 1980s and 1990s, his films, especially *Sans soleil/Sunless* (1983) and *L'Héritage de la chouette/The Legacy of the Owl* (1988), were complex reflections on image culture (film, video, photography) in the post-modern era. Among his numerous films as director are *Lettre de Sibérie/Letter from Siberia* (1958), *Cuba Si!* (1961), *La Jetée/The Pier* (1964, composed mostly of still photographs), *Le Train en marche/The Train Rolls On* (1973, on Alexander Medvedkin), *La Solitude du chanteur de fond/The Loneliness of the Long-distance Singer* (1975, on Yves Montand*), *Le Fond de l'air est rouge/The Air is Red* (1977), and *Le Tombeau d'Alexandre/The Last Bolshevik* (1993, also on Medvedkin). Versatile and cultured, Marker is also a writer and has worked at various times as editor, cameraman and producer.

MEERSON, Lazare

Polish/Russian border 1900 – London 1938

French set designer of Russian origin, highly influential in French cinema. Meerson emigrated to Germany in 1917 and to France in 1924, where he joined the Russian personnel at the Albatros studios in Paris [> EMIGRATION AND EUROPEAN CINEMA]. In 1930 he worked for Tobis and began his celebrated collaboration with René Clair*, designing the sets of *Sous les toits de Paris* (1930) and creating an enduring image of popular Paris. Meerson designed Clair's other French films of the 1930s and many others, including Jacques Feyder's* *La Kermesse héroïque/Carnival in Flanders* (1935). His sets were characterised by a dialectic between stylisation and accurate naturalistic details; his assistants and disciples included Alexander Trauner* and Jean d'Eaubonne.

MÉLIÈS, Georges

Paris 1861–1938

French film pioneer. Georges Méliès was the inventor and populariser of the 'trick film' and one of the first all-round entrepreneurs of the cinema, heading his own 'empire' from 1896 to 1919. He learnt conjuring and worked as a magician and puppeteer at the Musée Grévin (a wax museum) in Paris before taking over the Théâtre Robert-Houdin in 1888, where he presented spectacles of magic, fantasy and acrobatics. An enthusiastic spectator at Lumière's* first screening, he quickly acquired film and machinery from R. W. Paul* and began making films. After some Lumière-inspired documentaries, he moved on to the trick film in which the gimmicks of the theatre were supplemented by cinematic ones (jump cuts, double exposures, etc.), leading to an array of spectacular genres, from reconstructed current events to *féeries* (fantasies). Méliès founded his production company, Star-Film, in 1896, built a studio in Montreuil-sous-bois in 1897 and played all parts in the production process: make-up artist, actor, scriptwriter, director, editor, exhibitor and exporter (he opened a subsidiary in New York in 1902), producing over 500 films which he developed in his own laboratory. Among his best-known titles are *Le Voyage dans la lune/A Trip to the Moon* (1902) and *Voyage à travers l'impossible* (1904), drawing on the science fiction of Jules Verne; he also made a film about a Channel tunnel, *Le Tunnel sous la Manche/ Tunnelling the English Channel* (1907). Méliès' decline was as swift as his rise. Changes in distribution patterns and the fading novelty of trick films caused him to lose control to Pathé* and eventually to stop producing in 1919. Star-Film went bankrupt and Méliès opened a kiosk at the Gare Montparnasse, where he was discovered in the late 1920s. Georges Sadoul* organised a gala evening in his honour in 1929.

In Méliès' films, the powers of imagination and humour were given full scope. As Claude Beylie put it, 'With Lumière, trains entered stations, with Méliès they got off the rails and flew into the clouds.' Theatrically inspired as they were, his films formed the basis of what early film historians call the 'cinema of attractions', a cinema of spectacle in which the spectator marvels at the possibilities of the medium itself.

Bib: Madeleine Malthête-Méliès (ed.), *Méliès et la naissance du spectacle cinématographique* (1984).

MELVILLE, Jean-Pierre

Jean-Pierre Grumbach; Paris 1917–73

French director, one of the most important independent film-makers to emerge in the immediate postwar period and a great admirer of American culture, from which he derived his name, his sartorial style (Stetson hat, dark glasses) and his films, especially his *policiers**. Melville founded his production company (OGC) in 1945 and built a studio in Rue Jenner, Paris, in 1949. His first feature, *Le Silence de la* *mer* (1949, based on Vercors' novel), was an Occupation drama made on the margins of the French film industry; in 1950 he collaborated with Jean Cocteau*, filming the latter's *Les Enfants terribles/The Strange Ones* (1950). *Bob le flambeur* (1956) set the agenda for the rest of his career. It is a seductive, good-humoured tale of loyalty among male gangster clans, shot partly in the streets and cafés of Montmartre and Pigalle to a cool jazz score. Melville's subsequent work took the *policier* in the direction of increased abstraction and bleaker masculinity: *Le Doulos* (1963), *Le Deuxième souffle/The Second Breath* (1966), and especially the remarkable *Le Samouraï* (1967), with its subtle colour range, pared-down decor and a laconic Alain Delon*. Melville used the thriller format for his Gaullist account of the Resistance, *L'Armée des ombres/Army in the Shadows* (1969). His work combined popular appeal (using stars like Delon, Jean-Paul Belmondo*, Serge Reggiani, Lino Ventura*) with formal images of modernity, one reason he is so admired by the American director Quentin Tarantino. Melville acted in a few films, notably as the 'novelist' Parvulesco in Jean-Luc Godard's* *A bout de souffle/Breathless* (1960).

Bib: Rui Nogueira (ed.), *Melville on Melville* (1971).

Other Feature Films: *Quand tu liras cette lettre...* (1953); *Deux hommes dans Manhattan* (1959); *Léon Morin, prêtre* (1961); *L'Aîné des Ferchaux* (1963); *Le Cercle rouge/The Red Circle* (1970); *Un flic* (1972).

MIÉVILLE, Anne-Marie – see GODARD, Jean-Luc

MILTON, Georges

Georges Michaud;
Puteaux 1888 – Juan-les-Pins 1970

French actor and singer. Unknown outside France, Milton was an enormously popular comedian, first in the *café-concert* before and after World War I, and then in the cinema of the 1930s. His screen character, known as 'Bouboule', built on his stage work and his small, round physique. He was the *resquilleur* (eternal cheat), jovial and bawdy, who got the better of his social superiors through clowning and cunning in a series of hits, especially *Le Roi des resquilleurs/King of Cheats* (1930) and *La Bande à Bouboule/Bouboule's Gang* (1931). His only foray into *auteur* cinema was as the hero of Abel Gance's* politically ambiguous *Jérôme Perreau, héros des barricades* (1935), in which he plays the eponymous populist hero who befriends the great and the good and saves the country.

MIOU-MIOU

Sylvette Héry; Paris 1950

French actress, who rose to prominence alongside Gérard Depardieu* and Patrick Dewaere in Bertrand Blier's* *Les Valseuses/Going Places* (1973). Her first acting experience was in the *café-théâtre* [> COMEDY IN FRANCE]. From this libertarian tradition, she emerged as the strong but vulnerable independent woman of Yves Boisset's* *La Femme flic/Female Cop* (1980), Diane Kurys'* *Coup de foudre/Entre Nous/At First Sight* (1983) and Jacques Renard's *Blanche et Marie* (1985, a wartime story). It is a measure of her talent that she overcame the limitations of the comic nickname provided by Coluche to play moving dramatic parts, often using her erotic potential, as in Daniel Duval's *La Dérobade* (1979), Michel Deville's* *La Lectrice*, 1988, and Louis Malle's* *Milou en Mai*, 1989. She has also appeared in many comedies, such as those of Georges Lautner and Patrice Leconte. Miou-Miou has supported feminist projects like Claire Simon's *Scènes de ménage* (1991) but her limited room for manoeuvre in French popular cinema is illustrated by her humiliatingly misogynist role in Blier's successful *Tenue de soirée/Menage/Evening Dress* (1986). One of her latest roles is as the heroic mother of *Germinal* (1993).

MOCKY, Jean-Pierre

Jean-Paul Mokiejewski, Nice 1929

French director and actor. An iconoclastic and original filmmaker, Mocky started as an actor on stage and in film, his first part an extra in Marcel Carné's* *Les Visiteurs du soir* (1942). He began directing films in 1959, with *Les Dragueurs*, though his first project, the same year, was *La Tête contre les murs*, eventually directed by Georges Franju* (Mocky is the lead actor in it). Despite starting at the same time as François Truffaut*, Claude Chabrol* and other directors of the New Wave*, and despite pursuing a chiefly independent career, he has remained marginal to the movement and in fact to French cinema in general. Equally, despite a long and distinguished filmography and work with major stars such as Bourvil*, Fernandel* and many others, he is a relatively unknown figure outside France. His films have been poorly distributed, chiefly because of their 'untranslatable' black and often radical humour and denunciation of institutions such as the police and the political class. Mocky himself gives an accurate flavour of his work, when he describes it as characterised by 'freedom, lust, satisfied desire, bad taste, extravagance, and derision'. His most prominent features are *Un drôle de paroissien* (1963), *La Grande lessive* (1968), *A mort l'arbitre* (1984), *Snobs* (1962), *Solo* (1970), *Y-a-t-il un Français dans la salle?* (1982, based on the comic thriller writer Frédéric Dard), *Agent trouble* (1987), and *Une nuit à l'Assemblée Nationale* (1988). He has also made short films and worked for radio and commercials.

MODOT, Gaston

Paris 1887–1970

French actor. Though never a star, Modot has one of the most distinguished filmographies in French cinema. After many popular silent films, including French 'Westerns', Modot, who trained as a painter, was attracted to the avant-garde, notably the films of Germaine Dulac* and Louis Delluc*. His part in Luis Buñuel's* *L'Age d'or* (1930) brought him international notoriety (although the film was quickly banned). Modot then started a long collaboration with directors like Jean Renoir*, René Clair*, Marcel Carné* and Jacques Becker* which lasted until the 1960s. His most memorable parts are the engineer in *La Grande illusion* (1937) and the game-keeper in *La Règle du jeu/Rules of the Game* (1939), where he was characteristically laconic and reserved.

MONTAND, Yves

Ivo Livi; Monsummano Alto, Italy 1921 – Senlis 1991

French actor and singer. The son of poor Italian immigrants, Montand started his singing and film careers under the wing of the great singer Edith Piaf, with whom he co-starred in *Étoile sans lumière* in 1945. Replacing Jean Gabin* in *Les Portes de la nuit* (1946) brought him notoriety though not success; this came with Henri-Georges Clouzot's* *Le Salaire de la peur/The Wages of Fear* (1953), now a cult classic, which launched Montand's brand of tough virility. To this he later added the aura of his left-wing commitment, which found cinematic expression in Alain Resnais'* *La Guerre est finie/The War is Over* (1966), Jean-Luc Godard's* *Tout va bien* (1972) and a series of films directed by Costa-Gavras* (*Z*, 1969, *L'Aveu/The Confession*, 1970, *État de siège/State of Siege*, 1973). Montand achieved worldwide fame in George Cukor's *Let's Make Love* (1960, US), largely because of his relationship with co-star Marilyn Monroe. In the 1970s and 1980s, Montand's screen identity matured into a more melancholy masculinity; he widened his range, from thrillers like *Le Cercle rouge/The Red Circle* (1970) to comedy (*Le Sauvage*, 1975), to the intimate realist films of Claude Sautet* (*César et Rosalie*, 1972, *Garçon!*, 1983). Always a popular star, he crowned his career with huge success as the patriarch of *Jean de Florette* and *Manon des sources* (1986). Montand's overt political positions, increasingly anti-communist, made him one of France's most famous personalities; there was even talk of Montand for President. But he was equally popular as a singer (the subject of Chris Marker's* *La Solitude du chanteur de fond/The Loneliness of the Long-distance Singer* in 1974), and as Simone Signoret's* lifelong partner. He died while making his last film, Jean-Jacques Beineix's* *IP5* (released 1992).

Other Films Include: *Marguerite de la nuit* (1956); *Les Sorcières de Salem/The Crucible* (1957); *Compartiment tueurs/The Sleeping Car Murders* (1965); *Un soir, un train, On a Clear Day You Can See Forever* [US] (1970); *La Folie des grandeurs* (1971); *Vincent, François, Paul ... et les autres* (1974); *Police Python 357* (1975); *Le Choix des armes* (1981); *Trois places pour le 26* (1988).

MOREAU, Jeanne Paris 1928

French actress and director. A key actress of the French New Wave*, Moreau had a solid training in the theatre (including the Comédie Française) and the popular French cinema of the 1950s, starring for example in *La Reine Margot* (1954). Her leading parts in Louis Malle's* *Ascenseur pour l'échafaud/Lift to the Scaffold* (1957) and *Les Amants* (1958) made her a focus of the emerging *auteur* cinema, a position confirmed by François Truffaut's *Jules et Jim* (1962). As the mesmerising Catherine in the latter, but also as Mme de Merteuil in Roger Vadim's* *Les Liaisons dangereuses* (1959), she crystallised the paradox of New Wave femininity: both cerebral and erotic, an authentically modern heroine who asserts her desire yet whose identity is ultimately confined to sexual icon. Moreau exported well and in the 1960s she became a fixture of international art cinema, playing in such films as Michelangelo Antonioni's *La notte* (1960) and Orson Welles' *Le Procès/The Trial* (1962). Where Brigitte Bardot* was sex and Catherine Deneuve* elegance, Moreau incarnated 'intellectual' French femininity, with her lived-in looks and husky voice. Since the 1970s her star has waned, but her aura and talent have continued to fascinate film-makers, who tend to cast her in tragic cameo parts which she invests with more weight than they sometimes deserve, from Bertrand Blier's* *Les Valseuses/Going Places* (1973) to Luc Besson's* *Nikita* (1990). Lately, Moreau has developed the character of the scandalously sexy older woman, as in the delightful British television film *The Clothes in the Wardrobe* (1993), and the disappointing *La Vieille qui marchait dans la mer/The Old Lady who Walked on the Sea* (1991), an adaptation from the popular French writer San Antonio. Moreau has continued to work on stage and has directed four films, *Lumière* (1976), *L'Adolescente* (1979, starring Simone Signoret*), *Lillian Gish* (1984) and *Adieu Bonjour* (1994).

Bib: Marianne Gray, *La Moreau* (1994).

Other Films Include: *Moderato Cantabile* (1960); *Eva/Eve* [It.], *La Baie des anges* (1962); *Le Feu follet/A Time to Live and a Time to Die* (1963); *Le Journal d'une femme de chambre/Diary of a Chambermaid* (1964); *Viva Maria!* (1965); *La Mariée était en noir/The Bride Wore Black* (1968); *Mr Klein* (1976); *Querelle* (1982, Ger.); *Le Paltoquet* (1986).

MORGAN, Michèle

Simone Roussel; Neuilly-sur-Seine 1920

French actress. With little training but an immensely photogenic face, the very young Morgan started with bit parts in the mid-1930s and the lead in Marc Allégret's* *Gribouille* and *Orage* (both 1937). It is as Jean Gabin's* partner in *Quai des brumes* (1938, Marcel Carné*), however, that her cool beauty entered film history. Wearing a shiny raincoat and a beret, she was the mythical 'lost girl', a persona carried over to Albert Valentin's* *L'Entraîneuse* (1938) and Jean Grémillon's* *Remorques/Stormy Waters* (1939–41). Contracted by RKO, she went to Hollywood in 1940, married actor William Marshall, had a son, took American citizenship and, in her own words, made five unmemorable films (with the honourable exception of Michael Curtiz's *Passage to Marseille*, 1944, a substitute for *Casablanca* which she had lost to Ingrid Bergman). Back in France, Jean Delannoy's* *La Symphonie pastorale* (1946) inaugurated her second career as a leading star of the 'tradition of quality'*. Co-starring with Gabin, Gérard Philipe*, Jean Marais* and her then husband Henri Vidal, she graced costume dramas such as *Les Grandes manoeuvres* (1955) and *Marie-Antoinette* (1956), and psychological dramas such as *Les Orgueilleux/The Proud Ones* (1953), always the elegant, restrained and tragic Parisienne. Ignored by the New Wave* (except for Claude Chabrol's* *Landru/Bluebeard*, 1963) and by now handicapped by her age, she phased out her film career in the 1960s but successfully transferred to theatre. She has been awarded the Legion of Honour and many prizes, is a painter, and has written two volumes of memoirs.

MORLAY, Gaby

Blanche Fumoleau; Angers 1893 – Nice 1964

French actress. Primarily a stage actress, Morlay was a popular star of the French classical cinema. Equally talented in comedy (she started with Max Linder* in 1914) and drama (starring in Jacques Feyder's* *Les Nouveaux Messieurs* in 1929), she was a quintessential *boulevard* actress; most of her films were play adaptations. In comedies, like *Le Roi* (1936) and Sacha Guitry's* breathtaking *Quadrille* (1937), she bubbled (and sang too). However, one of her greatest successes was the tearfully patriotic wartime melodrama *Le Voile bleu* (1942, directed by Jean Stelli).

MOSJOUKINE [MOZZHUKHIN], Ivan – see 'French Cinema in Europe', page 158

MUSIDORA Jeanne Roques; 1889–1957

French actress and director, one of silent cinema's greatest stars. Musidora owes her reputation to the part of Irma Vep (an anagram of vampire) in Louis Feuillade's* adventure serial *Les Vampires* (episodes 3–10, 1915–16), though she acted in more than sixty films up to 1926. She was France's first vamp, a sexy villainess in black leotards, a persona she carried (without the leotards) into Feuillade's *Judex* (1917) and exploited in contemporary stage acts. The Surrealists worshipped her 'subversive' eroticism and flamboyant life; she was a close friend of Colette*, Germaine Dulac*, Louis Delluc* and Marcel L'Herbier*. Musidora wrote a novel at fifteen, was a painter, dancer, songwriter and playwright, and a film-maker with her own production company. After adaptations of Colette's *Minne* (1916) and *La Vagabonde* (1917), and a film based on a Colette script (*La Flamme cachée*, 1920), she directed four films which showed her taste for real locations and stylistic experimentation; they rarely met with popular success. She was crowned 'queen of the cinema' in 1926, but her film career ended with sound (save for a short compilation film in 1951). She went on writing and from 1946 worked at the Cinémathèque Française*. Musidora's legend as sexual muse has endured, but her importance as a pioneer was recognised when her name was adopted by the women's group who organised the first women's film festival in Paris in 1974.

Other Films (as director) Include: *Vicenta* (1920); *Pour Don Carlos* (1921); *Sol y Sombra* (1922); *La Tierra de los Toros* (1924); *La Magique Image* (1951).

N

NEW WAVE

French film movement. While other European countries such as Britain and Czechoslovakia saw important changes in film-making practices and styles in the late 1950s and early 1960s, it was in France that the *Nouvelle Vague* (New Wave) challenged most profoundly the established cinematic order and had the biggest international impact. The expression designates a 'freer' approach to film, outside traditional production and stylistic norms (professionalism, studios, literary sources, large budgets, stars), an approach which privileges spontaneity and the individual expression of the *auteur*-director. A number of factors account for the emergence of the New Wave: lighter and cheaper equipment allowed for location shooting, while the advent of television introduced new concepts of realism. Concurrently, the demise of the Hollywood studio system created opportunities to promote European national film styles on the world market. On a wider social front, the new regime of the Fifth Republic demanded 'new blood', while the rise of youth power helped shake older values and promote a younger generation of film-makers, as well as the increased presence of youth on screen.

In France, the New Wave was also preceded by a critical onslaught on classical French cinema – especially the 'tradition of quality'* – and by the development of the '*politique des auteurs*'* by the young critics at *Cahiers du cinéma**, under the sometimes reluctant aegis of André Bazin*. François Truffaut*, Jean-Luc Godard*, Eric Rohmer*, Jacques Rivette* and Claude Chabrol* were passionate *cinéphiles* who had learned their cinema history at the Cinémathèque Française*, a knowledge which would be seen in the high degree of self-reflexivity of their films. They championed their own pantheon of film-makers (Jean Renoir*, Alfred Hitchcock, Howard Hawks) and posited the importance of a director's personal vision and of *mise-en-scène* over content and theme, paving the way for their own future practice.

The New Wave was neither a truly revolutionary nor a cohesive 'movement'. To opponents such as Bernard Chardère of *Cahiers'* rival *Positif**, it was 'rather vague and not that new'. There were antecedents in French silent cinema and in Renoir; closer in time there was Italian neo-realism*, the ethnographic cinema of Jean Rouch*, and the films of Agnès Varda*, Robert Bresson* and Jean-Pierre Melville*. Of the hundred first films made in France between 1958 and 1962, however, the central ones are clearly the *Cahiers* critics' own: Truffaut's *Les Quatre cents coups/The 400 Blows* (1959), Chabrol's *Le Beau Serge* (1957), Rohmer's *Le Signe du lion* (1959, rel. 1962), Rivette's *Paris nous appartient/Paris Belongs to Us* (1958–60) and Godard's *A Bout de souffle/Breathless* (1960) – the Godard film a virtual manifesto with its location shooting, rule-breaking editing, casual acting and references to US *film noir*. While aesthetically innovative and exhilarating, these films generally lacked an interest in political or social issues, concentrating on personal angst among the (male) Parisian middle class (although another less media-prominent band of film-makers known as the 'Left Bank' group – Chris Marker*, Alain Resnais*, and Varda – showed greater political awareness). On the whole, the New Wave did not significantly challenge traditional representations of women. Although some films presented 'unconventional' heroines, mainly through the more spontaneous performances of a new breed of star (Jeanne Moreau*, Stéphane Audran*, Anna Karina*, Bernadette Lafont*), others were downright misogynist (like Chabrol's *Les Bonnes femmes/The Girls*, 1960) or showed women as traditional muses or alluring temptresses, accessories to the tribulations of the young heroes.

The New Wave by no means achieved its aim of a complete revolution in French cinema; indeed Truffaut and Chabrol, while pursuing recognisable personal themes, soon joined the mainstream. However, the promotion of the director as *auteur*/artist, as well as the creation of a new audience attuned to this type of cinema, greatly helped institutionalise *auteur* cinema and make it a lasting force in the French film industry.

Bib: Peter Graham (ed.), *The New Wave* (1968).

NOIRET, Philippe — Lille 1930

French actor. Neither a character actor nor a 'star', Noiret is one of the most popular male figures in French cinema. A stage and cabaret actor, Noiret's first notable films were Agnès Varda's* *La Pointe courte* (1956), Louis Malle's* *Zazie dans le métro* (1960) and Georges Franju's* *Thérèse Desqueyroux* (1962). His eclectic filmography of over a hundred titles includes films by French and Italian *auteurs* – among them Bertrand Tavernier's* *L'Horloger de Saint-Paul/The Watchmaker of Saint-Paul* (1973), *Coup de torchon/Clean Slate* (1981), and *La Vie et rien d'autre/Life and Nothing But* (1989), for which he won a César*; Marco Ferreri's* *La Grande bouffe/Blow Out* (1973); Francesco Rosi's *Tre fratelli/Three Brothers* (1981, Italy) – and popular cinema, including Claude Zidi's* *Les Ripoux/Le Cop* (1984) and Giuseppe Tornatore's *Nuovo Cinema Paradiso* (1988, It.). With his heavy-set figure and unctuous voice, Noiret incarnates middle-aged patriarchal figures, ranging from the reassuringly avuncular to the deeply misogynist. He embodied two fine versions of the former in Bertrand Tavernier's *La Fille de D'Artagnan/D'Artagnan's Daughter* (1994) and Michael Radford's *Il Postino* (1995, UK/It.), in which he plays the writer Pablo Neruda.

NOUVELLE VAGUE – see NEW WAVE

OPHULS, Max and OTSEP, Fyodor A. [OZEP, Fédor] – see 'French Cinema in Europe', pages 159–60

P

PAGNOL, Marcel

Aubagne 1895 – Paris 1974

French director, writer and producer, who contributed more than anyone to the promotion of Provençal culture. A young English teacher from Marseilles, he wrote successful plays and novels in the 1920s and launched his own short-lived magazine, *Les Cahiers du film*, to disseminate his enthusiasm for sound cinema. His first film, *Marius* (1931, based on his own play and directed by Alexander Korda), was a triumph; *Fanny* (1932, directed by Marc Allégret*) and *César* (1936) likewise. The universe of this 'Pagnol trilogy', as it became known, was steeped in the humorous folklore of the 'little people' of Marseilles; the key to its success was nostalgia, but also wonderful performances by Raimu*, Pierre Fresnay*, Charpin and Orane Demazis, coupled with the primacy of dialogue and the southern accent. A darker side to Pagnol's work drew on an older Mediterranean culture, that of the rural drama reflected in *Jofroi* (1933), *Angèle* (1934) and *Regain/Harvest* (1937). These melodramas were grounded in the same archaic patriarchal values as the trilogy, but they swapped theatricality for location shooting and have been recognised as influential on neo-realism*. Pagnol's activities were awesome: not content with being a film-maker, writer and journalist, he was also a producer, studio and cinema owner. The populist universe of the trilogy was seen again in *La Femme du boulanger/The Baker's Wife* (1938) and *La Fille du puisatier/The Well-Digger's Daughter* (1940). There was a musical with Tino Rossi (*La Belle meunière*, 1948), but Pagnol's activities then slowed down. His penultimate rural drama, *Manon des sources* (1953), was remade by Claude Berri* in 1986.

Pagnol's work has often been criticised as 'filmed theatre'; in fact, like Sacha Guitry's*, it shows a sophisticated awareness of the relation between film and the stage. Pagnol received the highest cultural accolade of membership of the Académie Française in 1946, but his epitaph as popular entertainer comes from his own *Le Schpountz* (1937): 'The man who amuses those who have so many reasons to cry [...] is loved like a benefactor.'

PATHÉ, Charles

Chevry-Cossigny 1863 – Monaco 1957

French pioneer, arguably the world's first 'movie mogul', who became the head of the most powerful film company in France. The son of modest parents, Charles Pathé was a brilliant entrepreneur who exploited Edison's phonograph and Kinetoscope by selling counterfeit copies of the latter made in Britain by R. W. Paul. With his associate Henri Joly, Pathé produced a film in October 1895. He then switched to marketing the Lumière* Cinematograph and founded Pathé Frères with his brother Emile in September 1896. The company prospered as Pathé applied modern business principles to the emerging entertainment form. It expanded vertically – into equipment, film stock manufacture and processing, exhibition and film-making, with factories, laboratories and studios near Paris – and internationally, from 1902 taking its Gallic cockerel logo to the far corners of the earth. In 1907 it switched from sale to rental, inaugurating modern film distribution.

Charles Pathé's reputation is that of a businessman with little interest in films. However, like his rival Léon Gaumont*, he shaped French and world cinema. Through his team of film-makers (Ferdinand Zecca, Alfred Machin, Louis Gasnier, René Leprince, Albert Capellani, Segundo de Chomón* and many others) Pathé codified early film genres: burlesque chase films – precursors of Mack Sennett – and comic series with Prince-Rigadin* and André Deed*, and created the first major international star of French cinema, Max Linder*. He commissioned scientific films, produced newsreels, serials and melodramas, trick films and *féeries* (fantasies), and the literary adaptations of the Film d'Art*. Pathé produced newsreels (Pathé-News) and shot serials in America during World War I, but the war damaged the Pathé empire. Branches closed down from 1920, and French operations were reduced to film stock and equipment. The diminished company was taken over by Bernard Natan in 1929, a year before Pathé retired. Natan, a Romanian émigré involved in pornographic film, created Pathé-Natan, which until 1935 was a relatively successful mainstream production outfit. Recession and fraud brought the company down, however. (Natan was tried for fraud and later died in a concentration camp; it has recently been suggested that he may have been a scapegoat for politicians who had covertly enjoyed his pornographic movies). Pathé-Cinéma was bailed out during the war, and the name Pathé survives to this day in production, newsreels and exhibition, though with only distant links to the original company.

Charles Pathé said, 'I did not invent the cinema, I industrialised it'; his genius was precisely to understand the industrial dimension without which it could not have become the art or educational form he also predicted: 'Cinema will be the theatre, the newspaper and the school of tomorrow.'

Bib: Jacques Kermabon (ed.), *Pathé, premier empire du cinéma* (1995).

PHILIPE, Gérard — Cannes 1922 – Paris 1959

French actor. Philipe's wonderful looks, his elevated status as one of the great classical stage actors of his time, and his untimely death all contributed to his mythic position in French cinema. His film portrayal of the deranged Prince Myshkin in *L'Idiot* (1946) and the fragile, boyish hero of *Le Diable au corps/Devil in the Flesh* (1947) set his early persona as the tortured young romantic, in evidence also in Yves Allégret's* *noir* drama *Une si jolie petite plage/Riptide* (1949). Rising quickly to the top of the box-office rankings, Philipe became the sophisticated male star of the 'tradition of quality'* costume film, in comedies such as the successful *Fanfan la Tulipe* and *Les Belles de nuit* (both 1952), and, more frequently, in prestigious literary adaptations such as Stendhal's *La Chartreuse de Parme/La certosa di Parma* (1948) and *Le Rouge et le noir/Scarlet and Black* (1954), and Zola's *Pot-bouille/The House of Lovers* (1957). By contrast with the rugged Jean Gabin* and action man Eddie Constantine*, his equally famous rivals, Philipe was very much a star of 'women's films'. French critic Claude Beylie sees his image as split between the 'smooth fashion plate' of many films, and the 'perverse dandy' of others, notably René Clair's* *Les Grandes manoeuvres/Summer Manoeuvres* (1955), in which he is caught in his own love games, and in the contemporary settings of Roger Vadim's* *Les Liaisons dangereuses* (1959), where he is a brilliant Valmont. In fact, the power of Philipe's on-screen masculinity was that he incorporated elements of both aspects of his image, subtly commenting on the cynical and predatory nature of the male hero of romance while at the same time giving a beguiling portrait of just such a man.

Other Films Include: *La Beauté du diable/Beauty and the Devil* (1949); *La Ronde* (1950); *Juliette ou la clé des songes* (1951); *Les Orgueilleux/The Proud Ones*, *Monsieur Ripois/Knave of Hearts* (1953); *Les Aventures de Till L'Espiègle/The Adventures of Till Eulenspiegel* (1956; co-dir); *Montparnasse 19/Modigliani of Montparnasse* (1958); *La Fièvre monte à El Pao/Republic of Sin* (1960).

PIALAT, Maurice — Cunlhat 1925

French director, one of the most important *auteurs* to emerge since the New Wave*. Originally a painter, Pialat worked for the stage and television, acted, and shot documentaries. He made his first cinema feature, *L'Enfance nue*, in 1968. This examination of deprived childhood heralded Pialat's most original period in which, in such films as *La Gueule ouverte* (1974), *Loulou* (1979) and *A nos amours/To Our Loves* (1983), he revealed an ethnographic concern with unglamorous aspects of French society. Pialat's potent, bleak realism combines a demanding, quasi-*cinéma-vérité** approach – some non-professional actors, very long takes, improvisation, colloquial language – with the reworking of personal issues such as marital breakdown. *Police* (1985), like *Loulou* starring Gérard Depardieu*, was a departure towards genre, here the thriller, though sociological interest was in evidence in the (problematic) portrayal of the immigrant milieu. Subsequently,

Ginette Leclerc, 'vamp' of the 1940s.

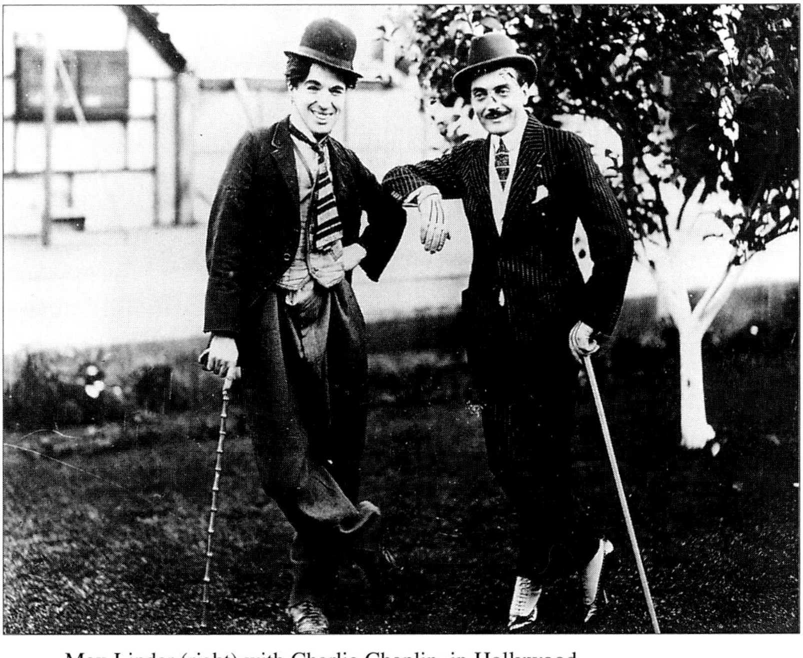

Max Linder (right) with Charlie Chaplin, in Hollywood.

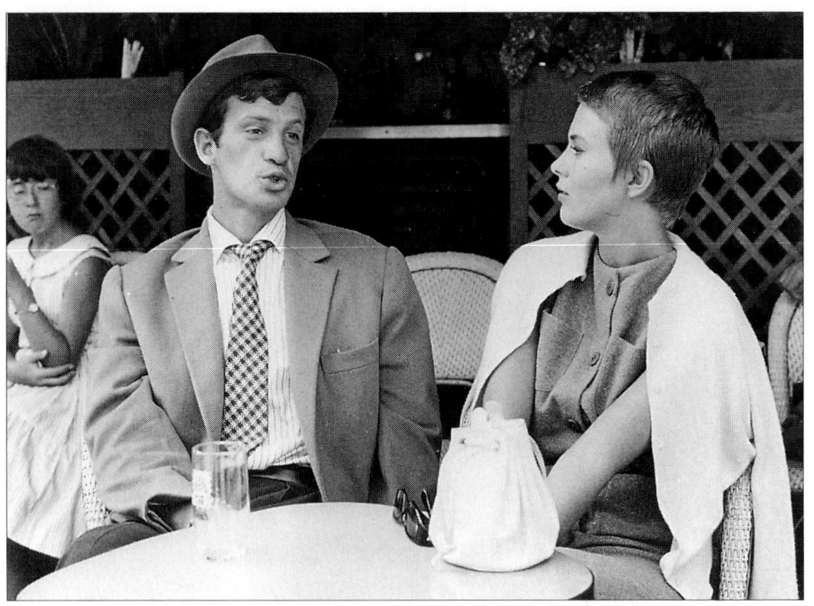

Jean-Paul Belmondo and Jean Seberg in *A bout de souffle/Breathless* (Jean-Luc Godard, 1960).

Brigitte Helm in *L'Argent* (Marcel L'Herbier, 1929).

Jeanne Moreau in *Ascenseur pour l'échafaud/ Lift to the Scaffold* (Louis Malle, 1957).

The young heroes of *Au revoir les enfants* (Louis Malle, 1987).

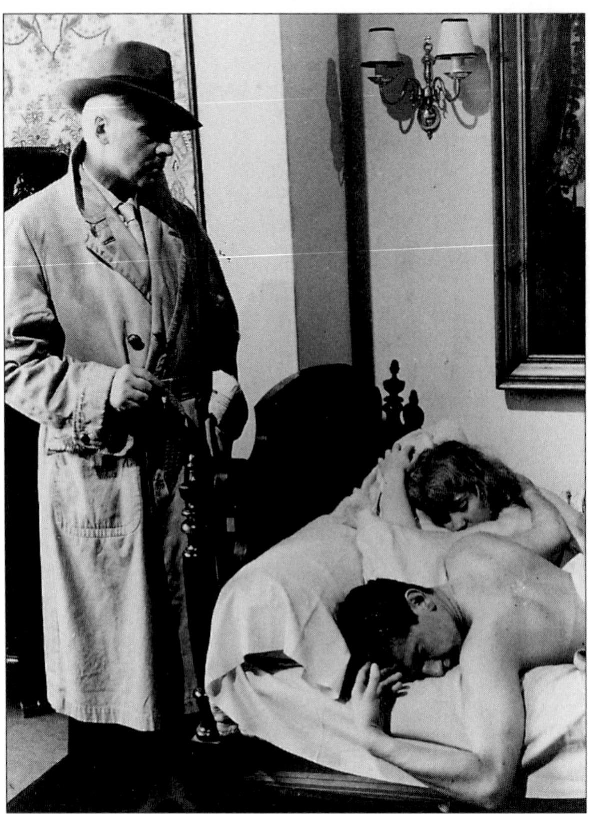

Roger Duchesne as 'Bob' (standing), Daniel Cauchy and Isabelle Corey, in *Bob le flambeur* (Jean-Pierre Melville, 1956).

Isabelle Huppert (left) and Miou-Miou in *Coup de foudre/ Entre nous/At First Sight* (Diane Kurys, 1983).

Florelle and Jules Berry in *Le Crime de Monsieur Lange* (Jean Renoir, 1935).

Véra Clouzot (left), Simone Signoret and Paul Meurisse in *Les Diaboliques* (Henri-Georges Clouzot, 1955).

Pierre Richard-Willm and Françoise Rosay in *Le Grand jeu* (Jacques Feyder, 1933).

Yves Montand (left) and Gérard Depardieu in *Jean de Florette* (Claude Berri, 1986).

Georges Poujouly and Brigitte Fossey in *Jeux interdits/Forbidden Games* (René Clément, 1952).

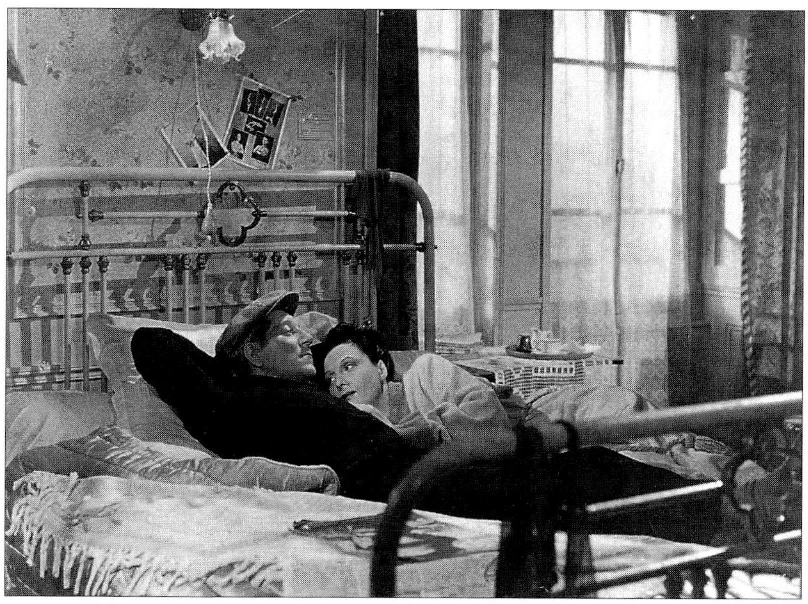

Jean Gabin and Arletty in *Le Jour se lève* (Marcel Carné, 1939).

Gérard Philipe and Jeanne Moreau in *Les Liaisons dangereuses* (Roger Vadim, 1959).

Raimu kisses Pierre Fresnay in *Marius* (Marcel Pagnol and Alexander Korda,

Pialat moved to literary adaptation (*Sous le soleil de Satan/Under Satan's Sun*, 1987) and period drama (*Van Gogh*, 1991). Both films, though, are consistent with his focus on tortured individuals, *Van Gogh* especially a reflection on the 'difficult' artist, a description comprehensively earned by Pialat himself. Pialat returned to personal issues with the autobiographical *Le Garçu* (starring Depardieu), a reflection on the torments of modern fatherhood. But it is in his earlier work that Pialat's cinematic power is most in evidence.

Other Films Include: *L'Amour existe* (1960, short); *Janine* (1961, TV); *La Maison des bois* (1971, TV); *Nous ne vieillirons pas ensemble* (1972); *Passe ton bac d'abord*... (1979).

PICCOLI, Michel

Jean Daniel Michel Piccoli; Paris 1925

French actor of Italian origins. A classically trained stage actor, Piccoli moved from dependable character actor, with small parts in such classics as Jean Renoir's* *French Cancan* (1955) and Jean-Pierre Melville's* *Le Doulos* (1963), to major figure of European art cinema*. In his immense filmography, titles such as *Le Mépris/Contempt* (1963), *Belle de jour* (1967), *Themroc* (1973), *Le Charme discret de la bourgeoisie/The Discreet Charm of the Bourgeoisie* (1972) and *La Grande bouffe/Blow Out* (1973) stand out, as well as his work with Claude Sautet*. A consummate and subtle actor, Piccoli emerged as the sexually opportunistic middle-class intellectual with a hint of the perverse libertine (he starred in a French television version of *Don Juan* in 1965), a character usually mobilised to serve 'progressive' themes. Piccoli unusually combined *auteur* credibility with box-office success throughout the 1970s. Since then his career has fluctuated, though he has continued to support French *auteur* films, appearing memorably in Leos Carax's* *Mauvais Sang/The Night is Young* (1986) and Jacques Rivette's* *La Belle Noiseuse* (1991). He plays the role of 'Monsieur Cinéma' in Agnès Varda's* centenary film, *Les Cent et une nuits du cinéma* (1995). He has also returned successfully to the stage.

POETIC REALISM

French stylistic trend of the 1930s. The term 'Poetic Realism' was originally applied to literature; in the cinema it was first used in relation to Pierre Chenal's* *La Rue sans nom* (1933). It is a critical construction with blurred edges – terms such as 'populist melodrama', 'the social fantastic', '*noir* realism' and 'magic realism' can also apply. However, 'Poetic Realism' designates pessimistic urban dramas, usually set in Paris (though there were colonial examples) in working-class settings, with doomed romantic narratives often tinged with criminality. The supreme examples are the films of Marcel Carné* and Jacques Prévert* – *Quai des brumes* (1938), *Le Jour se lève* (1939) – but the canon also includes Jean Vigo's* *L'Atalante* (1934), Jean Renoir's* *La Bête humaine* (1938), Jacques Feyder's* *Le Grand jeu* (1933), Julien Duvivier's* *La Belle équipe* (1936) and Jean Grémillon's* *Gueule d'amour* (1937); to which could be added Marie Epstein's* *La Maternelle* (1933), Raymond Bernard's* *Faubourg-Montmartre* (1931) and several films by Chenal. As its name indicates, Poetic Realism proposes a duality between the everyday and the lyrical/emotional, the poetry arising precisely *from* the everyday, from a world created – beyond individual directors – by an exceptional ensemble of craftsmen and artists: the decors of Alexandre Trauner*, the dialogues of Prévert, Charles Spaak and Henri Jeanson*, the photography of Jules Kruger, Eugen Schüfftan*, Curt Courant*, the music of Maurice Jaubert* and Joseph Kosma*; and of course the stars: Jean Gabin*, but also Arletty*, Jules Berry*, Charles Vanel* and others. It was a highly stylised world, both in its *mise-en-scène* and in its 'mythical' characters, yet the box-office success of the films shows that they 'spoke' to their popular audience.

Often – superficially – seen as a reflection of the collapse of the Popular Front* and of the gloomy prewar years, Poetic Realism was rather the product of a long French cultural tradition, which went back to nineteenth-century classic (Balzac, Eugène Sue, Zola) and crime literature (including Georges Simenon*), to the populist novels of the 1920s and 1930s (Eugène Dabit and Pierre MacOrlan), and to popular songs, magazines and photography. Cinematically, antecedents can be found in both French and German cinema, especially the *Kammerspielfilm** and the *Straßenfilme**. Although only one important trend among many in French 1930s cinema, Poetic Realism caught historians' attention not only for its formal beauty and cultural prestige, but also because it formed such a strong contrast to Hollywood. While Carné and Prévert's *Les Enfants du paradis* (1943–45) and *Les Portes de la nuit* (1946) are considered respectively the culmination and the swan-song of Poetic Realism, by the mid-1940s it had become, as Dudley Andrew put it, 'codified and citable'.

Bib: Dudley Andrew, *Mists of Regret: Culture and Sensibility in Classic French Film* (1995).

POIRÉ, Jean-Marie — Paris 1945

French director. A successful director of comedies since 1977, Poiré is the film-maker of the *café-théâtre* generation [> COMEDY IN FRANCE] which includes Christian Clavier, Gérard Jugnot, Thierry Lhermitte and Josiane Balasko*, producing irreverently funny comedies whose titles are an art form in themselves – *Les Hommes préfèrent les grosses/*

Men Prefer Fat Girls (1981), *Le Père Noël est une ordure/Santa Claus is a Louse* (1982, recently remade in Hollywood as *Mixed Nuts*, 1994), *Opération Corned Beef* (1991). But none of this could have suggested the extraordinary success of *Les Visiteurs* (1993), starring Clavier, Valérie Lemercier and Jean Reno, in which present-day middle-class characters meet their medieval equivalent. As in Poiré's previous films, linguistic puns and social ridicule are the key, but clearly the film hit a nerve in France, where it has become the most popular film ever at the box office, an astonishing achievement considering that the audience is considerably smaller than in the mid-1960s, when Louis de Funès* and Bourvil* were the box-office champions. Poiré's next blockbuster comedy, *Les Anges gardiens* (1995), starring Clavier and Gérard Depardieu*, was something of a disappointment, but nevertheless topped the French box-office of that year.

POLANSKI, Roman – see 'French Cinema in Europe', page 160

POLICIER

French genre, embracing any crime film (whether the police appear or not). France is the only country outside the US to have built up a large and consistent body of thrillers. Although considered a 'bread-and-butter' genre (virtually all French directors have made at least one such film), unlike comedy* the *policier* often combines critical status with popular appeal. This has undoubtedly to do with its literary origins in the nineteenth-century *noir* novels of Eugène Sue and the realism of Balzac, Victor Hugo and Zola; and later, crime literature proper – Marcel Allain and Pierre Souvestre (*Fantômas*), Maurice Leblanc (*Arsène Lupin*), Georges Simenon*. After the war, interest was renewed by Marcel Duhamel's famous *Série noire* imprint which translated US and British writers and published French ones; English-language crime literature always enjoyed great popularity and intellectual credence in France, from Edgar Allan Poe to Jim Thompson.

In films, the popularity of the *policier* sprang instantly from silent crime series and the serials of Louis Feuillade* – *Fantômas* (1913–14) and *Les Vampires* (1915–16). It continued through the 1930s with Simenon adaptations (*La Nuit du carrefour/Night at the Crossroads*, *La Tête d'un homme*, both 1932), with Duvivier's* *Pépé le Moko* (1936), Pierre Chenal's* *Le Dernier tournant* (1939, the earliest film version of James M. Cain's *The Postman Always Rings Twice*), and the work of émigré directors such as Kurt Bernhardt and Robert Siodmak*. Simenon adaptations were popular during the war and after, and directors such as Henri-Georges Clouzot* bent the *policier* to the extreme *noir* trend in France at the time. But the greatest burst of energy was triggered by Jacques Becker's* immensely popular *Touchez pas au grisbi/Honour Among Thieves* (1954), which relaunched Jean Gabin's* postwar career, followed by Jean-Pierre Melville's* *Bob le flambeur* (1956) and Jules Dassin's *Du Rififi chez les hommes/Rififi* (1955). These films gave rise to countless derivations and established the genre as a kind of professional test paper for directors and male stars (some critics argue that the 1950s *policier* obliquely evokes the trauma of the German occupation). The 1960s saw the *policier* evolve either along comic lines (the films of Georges Lautner) or towards abstraction (those of Melville), and in the 1970s it moved in the direction of political critique (directors Yves Boisset*, Alain Corneau*, Costa-Gavras*). It also served as a regular format for the star vehicles of Alain Delon* and Jean-Paul Belmondo*. In the 1980s and 1990s the genre was revisited by *auteurs* as disparate as Maurice Pialat*, Bertrand Tavernier* and Claude Chabrol*, by the post-modern films of the *cinéma du look** (*Subway*, 1985, *Nikita*, 1990), and again by comedy (Claude Zidi's* *Les Ripoux/Le Cop*, 1984), taking stock of social changes (the presence of immigrant communities, the breakdown of families).

Through this huge corpus common motifs recur, helping to define a specifically French thriller, quite different from the Hollywood version: the centrality of Paris (*qua* Paris, not just 'the city'), the consistent weight placed on social observation, and the blurring of law and lawlessness within more ambiguous moral codes (the French *policier* never showed much interest in the social origins of crime).

Bib: François Guérif, *Le Cinéma policier français* (1981).

POLITIQUE DES AUTEURS

French critical concept, evolved by critics at *Cahiers du cinéma** in the 1950s, especially François Truffaut*, Jean-Luc Godard*, Jacques Rivette* and Eric Rohmer*. Building on the work of André Bazin* and Alexandre Astruc's notion of *caméra-stylo* ('camera pen'), but also distantly on the debates of the 1920s [> FRENCH AVANT-GARDE], the *politique des auteurs* was both a romantic notion and a polemic designed to promote personal film-making and establish the director-*auteur* as artist in charge. The professionally organised, polished cinema of the French 'tradition of quality'* was the *politique*'s main target (Truffaut said: 'I do not believe in the peaceful co-existence of the Tradition of Quality and an *auteur*'s cinema'), but it also championed American directors such as Howard Hawks and Alfred Hitchcock as true *auteurs* (as opposed to mere *metteurs-en-scène*) struggling against the Hollywood studio system and therefore responding *personally* to constraints. This was possible through the assertion of *mise-en-scène* as the primary indicator of a director's personality, although thematic continuity was also valued. As John Hess put it, this concentration on the personal could be read at the time as 'a justification, couched in aesthetic terms, of a culturally conservative, politically reactionary attempt to remove film from the realm of social and political concern'. The *politique* has been enormously influential on film criticism, from Andrew Sarris in the US to film journals such as *Movie* and *Sight and Sound* and even the mainstream press, and continues to shape film history – sometimes beneficially, as in the defence of independent small-scale films, especially in Europe, sometimes less so (the ignorance of or contempt for popular genres outside Hollywood).

POPULAR FRONT CINEMA

French film movement of the late 1930s, embracing a body of films made at the time of, and engaging with, the Popular Front, the historic left political alliance which ruled from May 1936 to October 1938. As well as introducing significant social changes (paid holidays, trade union rights, a health service), the Popular Front unleashed a ferment of cultural experiment as intellectuals and artists poured into the political arena. Newsreels, documentaries and propaganda films were made in an extraordinary burst of activity and enthusiasm, especially at the cooperative Ciné-Liberté, of which Jean Renoir* was a member. With others, including Jacques Becker* and Jean-Paul Dreyfus (Le Chanois), Renoir directed the Communist propaganda film *La Vie est à nous* (1936) and then (on his own) the epic *La Marseillaise* (1937), financed by public subscription. Renoir's marvellous *Le Crime de Monsieur Lange* (1935, script by Jacques Prévert*) is the story of a workers' cooperative, symptomatic in its exuberant celebration of the power of popular culture and imagination. Julien Duvivier's* *La Belle équipe* (1936) is also about a cooperative, although its use of star Jean Gabin* and particularly its original bleakly pessimistic ending inflect it towards Poetic Realism*. Other films directly dealing with Popular Front themes include Le Chanois' *Le Temps des cerises* (1937), Georges Monca's *Choc en retour* (1937) and the documentary *Les Bâtisseurs* (1938, dir. Jean Epstein*). Some films outside this canon dealt with contemporary social trends, such as *Club de femmes*, *Avec le sourire/With a Smile* (1936), *L'Entraîneuse/Night Club Hostess*, *Eusèbe député/Eusèbe MP*, *Altitude 3200* (1938); many others, in their avoidance of the subject, may be just as characteristic of the period.

Bib: Ginette Vincendeau and Keith Reader (eds.), *La Vie est à nous, French Cinema of the Popular Front 1935–1938* (1986).

POSITIF

French film journal. Founded in 1952 in Lyons by Bernard Chardère (and based in Paris since 1954), *Positif* has long been the rival of *Cahiers du cinéma**, although sharing with it fundamental values such as the promotion of *auteur* cinema (albeit different *auteurs*). *Positif* was initially the more politicised journal, taking up virulent anti-New Wave* positions and showing concern for political events (such as the Algerian war). Its libertarian attitude, inherited from Surrealism, made it champion, for instance, Jerry Lewis and Italian comedy. In the early 1980s it took part in debates on 'American imperialism'. The fact that *Positif* writers did not become film-makers, and that it did not specifically champion any theory, explains the absence of translations of its texts in English. Nearly fifty years on, *Positif* and *Cahiers* remain the two quality French magazines of film criticism.

PRÉJEAN, Albert — Paris 1893–1979

French actor and singer. Préjean emerged internationally as the singing hero of René Clair's* *Sous les toits de Paris* (1930), one of the most important early French sound films, and in the French version of G. W. Pabst's *L'Opéra de quat' sous/Die Dreigroschenoper/The Threepenny Opera* (1930). He was already well established in French silent films, including Clair's *Paris qui dort* (1924) and *Un chapeau de paille d'Italie/An Italian Straw Hat* (1928); he directed a short, *L'Aventure de Luna Park*, in 1929. Sound cinema suited his Parisian accent and brand of popular *chanson*. A substantial career followed, embracing over forty films in the 1930s, among them Robert Siodmak's* *La Crise est finie* (1934, co-starring Danielle Darrieux*) and *Mollenard* (1937), Edmond T. Gréville's *Princesse Tam-Tam* (1935, co-starring Josephine Baker*), Marcel Carné's* *Jenny* (1936), and Pierre Chenal's* *L'Alibi* (1937). Préjean played a theatrical and optimistic version of Jean Gabin's* tragic proletarian hero. He was very active during the war, notably incarnating Inspector Maigret in a series of adaptations of Simenon's* novels. As a prominent personality during the war, he attended social occasions with Germans and visited Germany for film premieres; he was briefly arrested at the Liberation. His postwar career was lacklustre, but thanks to his 1930s films and his song recordings, his place as one of the best-liked actors of the *'cinéma du sam'di soir'* is secure.

PRESLE, Micheline

Micheline Chassagne; Paris 1922

French actress. Although less famous internationally than her contemporaries Michèle Morgan* and Danielle Darrieux*, the beautiful Presle was a top box-office star from the late 1930s to the early 1950s. Her first important roles were in G. W. Pabst's* *Jeunes filles en détresse/Young Ladies in Distress*, and the dual lead – as mother and daughter – in Abel Gance's melodrama *Paradis perdu* (both 1939). She emerged as a major star during the German occupation, in comedies and costume dramas like *Félicie Nanteuil* (1942–45), and contemporary dramas such as Jacques Becker's* *Falbalas* (1945). At the Liberation she starred in Christian-Jaque's* *Boule de suif/Angel and Sinner* (1945). Her star persona combined elegance, effervescence, energy and modernity and she acquired a reputation for sophisticated comedy. Her best-known film, Claude Autant-Lara's* *Le Diable au corps/Devil in the Flesh* (1947, co-starring Gérard Philipe*), was a return to melodrama. A first trip to Hollywood in 1948 produced disappointing films and a brief marriage to Morgan's ex-husband, William Marshall (Marshall and Presle's daughter, Tonie Marshall, is an actress and successful director; her second film, *Pas très catholique*, 1994, starring Anémone, is an excellent comedy).

Presle's subsequent French career in costume dramas (Sacha Guitry's* *Napoléon*, 1955) and comedies (*La Mariée est trop belle/The Bride is Too Beautiful*, 1956, with Brigitte Bardot*) was mixed, though she starred in Jean Grémillon's* remarkable *L'Amour d'une femme* (1954), one of the few 'feminist' films of the time. Presle has since alternated mainstream films, *auteur* work (Jacques Rivette's* *La Religieuse*, 1965, rel. 1967), television series and theatre. She generously supports young *auteur* cinema, notably by women – for instance Marie-Claude Treilhou's *Le Jour des rois* (1991), co-starring Darrieux and Paulette Dubost. She appears in Claude Lelouch's* *Les Misérables du XXe siècle* (1995).

PRÉVERT, Jacques

Neuilly-sur-Seine 1900 – Omonville-la-Rogue 1977

and

PRÉVERT, Pierre

Neuilly-sur-Seine 1906 – Paris 1988

French scriptwriters and directors. The Prévert brothers were at the centre of the Surrealist group in Paris in the early 1920s. Pierre became assistant to Alberto Cavalcanti* and later Jean Renoir*, while Jacques worked for an advertising agency and began writing poetry. Both appeared in minor film parts (including Jean Vigo's* *L'Atalante*, 1934). In 1932, Jacques joined the agit-prop 'Groupe Octobre', many of whose members appeared in Pierre's medium-length film *L'Affaire est* *dans le sac* (1932), a witty Surrealist fantasy but a commercial flop. Pierre's career as a director was sketchy (two features – *Adieu Léonard*, 1943, *Voyage-surprise*, 1947 – and some shorts, including *Paris La Belle*, 1959, with scenes shot in 1928 with Jacques, and several unrealised projects). His work for television included a film about his brother (1961).

Jacques meanwhile was for almost thirty years one of the most important script and dialogue writers in French cinema, beginning with the 1933 *Ciboulette*; his last film was *Les Amours célèbres* (1961). He worked with Renoir on *Le Crime de Monsieur Lange* (1935) [> POPULAR FRONT CINEMA] and Jean Grémillon* on *Remorques/Stormy Waters* (1939–41) and *Lumière d'été* (1943), among others, but is best known for his collaboration with Marcel Carné, with whom he formed the central team of Poetic Realism* on films such as *Jenny* (1936), *Drôle de drame* (1937), *Quai des brumes* (1938), *Le Jour se lève* (1939) and *Les Enfants du paradis* (1943–45). The publication of *Paroles* in 1946 made him the best-selling French poet ever, and Joseph Kosma's* music turned some of his poems into songs that became international hits; one such was 'Les Feuilles mortes', sung by Yves Montand* in *Les Portes de la nuit* (1946). The latter film neatly encapsulates the dominant Prévertian theme of 'pure' young love struggling against a corrupt and cynical world. Although Prévert's texts for Carné were sometimes overladen with doom, the abiding characteristic of his work is wit; his dialogues, poems and songs sparkle with humour, erudition, romanticism and genuinely popular language.

PRINCE-RIGADIN

Charles Petit-Demange; Maisons-Laffitte 1872 – Paris 1933

French actor. With Max Linder*, one of the two first comic stars of French cinema. Both were dubbed 'the kings of the cinematograph' and reaped unprecedented benefits of stardom, fame and large salaries. 'Prince', as he was known on stage, became 'Rigadin' in a series of successful and influential early French comedies, many directed by Georges Monca for Pathé*, although he himself helped develop the stories. Raymond Chirat describes the Rigadin persona as 'lumpish and bewildered, with a clowning routine inherited from vaudeville'. Before World War I, Prince-Rigadin (like Linder) was, in his own words, 'the international ambassador of Gallic humour in all the countries where cinema penetrated. I had a different surname in each country: *Whiffles* in England and the Commonwealth, *Moritz* in Germany, *Maurice* in Romania, *Salustiano* in Spain, *Tartufini* in Italy, *Prenz* in Scandinavian and Slav countries, *Rigadin* everywhere else. In the Orient, if you please, I was *the prince Rigadin* !' Though he appeared in a couple of sound films, his career belongs to the early, exuberant phase of French silent cinema.

RAIMU

Jules Muraire; Toulon 1883 – Neuilly-sur-Seine 1946

French actor. Originally a comic actor, Raimu also imposed a magisterially humane presence in some key French films of the 1930s and 1940s, for which Orson Welles called him 'the greatest actor in the world'. Raimu, then 'Rallum', started as a *comique troupier** in the music halls of his native town before moving on to Paris in 1910, where he quickly became one of the most popular *boulevard* stage actors. Although he made two silent films, it was sound cinema's ability to exploit his formidable voice and picturesque Midi accent which made him a star (after which, except for a brief spell at the Comédie Française, he abandoned the stage). After two comedies, *Le Blanc et le noir* (1930, based on Sacha Guitry*), and *Mam'zelle Nitouche* (1931, directed by Marc Allégret*), the adaptation of Marcel Pagnol's* *Marius* (1931), for which he had already played the lead on stage, shot him to fame. *Marius* was followed by *Fanny* (1932) and *César* (1936), consolidating Raimu's image as the authoritarian yet vulnerable patriarch, deeply believable despite the obvious theatricality of the films. He played similar roles in two other Pagnol films, *La Femme du boulanger/The Baker's Wife* (1938) and *La Fille du puisatier/The Well-Digger's Daughter* (1940), and, in a darker register, in films such as Marc Allégret's* *Gribouille* (1937) and Jeff Musso's *Dernière jeunesse* (1939). But while such films, as well as Jean Grémillon's* *L'Etrange Monsieur Victor* (1937) and Henri Decoin's* *Les Inconnus dans la maison/Strangers in the House* (1942), confirmed him as the formidable dramatic actor admired by Welles, Raimu continued to act in many comedies based on vaudeville or *boulevard* plays, such as the hilarious *Ces Messieurs de la Santé* (1933) and *Le Roi* (1936), which were equally responsible for his popularity at the time. Pagnol's work, however, gave Raimu the scope to combine both comic and dramatic registers, making *Marius* one of the best-loved French films, now officially declared an inalienable part of the French cultural patrimony.

RAPPENEAU, Jean-Paul

Auxerre 1932

French director and scriptwriter. After serving as an assistant to Raymond Bernard* among others, Rappeneau worked as a scriptwriter, collaborating with such directors as Jacques Becker* and Louis Malle*. Two strands emerge in this early career – comedy and costume film – which also inform Rappeneau's later directorial work. His first feature, *La Vie de château* (1966), was a light comedy set during the German occupation, starring Catherine Deneuve* and Philippe Noiret*, and a critical and popular success. Other successful comedies followed, including *Les Mariés de l'an II* (1971) and *Le Sauvage* (1975). These were nothing, however, compared with the worldwide triumph of *Cyrano de Bergerac* in 1990, winner of ten Césars* and one of the most popular French films ever outside France. *Cyrano* reclaimed both a popular-classic literary heritage – Edmond Rostand's play, with English subtitles in verse by Anthony Burgess [> HERITAGE CINEMA IN EUROPE] – and the epic tradition, with swirling camerawork, dynamic editing and sumptuous sets and costumes. As a character, Cyrano also perfectly fitted Gérard Depardieu's* dual star persona, both larger than life national hero and vulnerable romantic. Rappeneau subsequently made the costume epic *Le Hussard sur le toit* (1995).

RENAUD, Madeleine

Paris 1903–94

French actress. Like Jean-Louis Barrault* (whom she met in 1936 and married in 1940), Renaud, one of the most important French theatrical personalities, worked primarily on stage. However, she also made her mark on French cinema of the 1930s and 1940s in play adaptations and in dramas, especially Marie Epstein* and Jean Benoît-Lévy's remarkable *La Maternelle* (1933) and *Hélène* (1936), and four films directed by Jean Grémillon*: *L'Etrange Monsieur Victor* (1937), *Remorques/Stormy Waters* (1939–41), *Lumière d'été* (1943) and *Le Ciel est à vous* (1943–44). A brilliant actress, her performances were always devoid of theatricality. She often played unusually modern heroines. Her postwar career was mostly devoted to the theatre, with a few exceptions such as Max Ophuls'* *Le Plaisir* (1951) and Marguerite Duras'* *Des journées entières dans les arbres/Whole Days in the Trees* (1976).

RENOIR, Jean

Paris 1894 – Beverly Hills, California 1979

French director, also actor, scriptwriter and producer. François Truffaut* and Orson Welles described Renoir as 'the greatest filmmaker in the world'. There is no doubt that Renoir has dominated both the French cinema of the classical period and the international pantheon of great *auteurs*.

The second son of Impressionist painter Auguste Renoir, Jean grew up in the artistic milieu of turn-of-the-century Paris. Much – too much – has been made of this legacy, though it was of consequence for Renoir's realist aesthetics and financial independence. Following World War I, in which he was wounded, and an attempt at ceramics,

Renoir's film career began when he scripted *Catherine* (or *Une Vie sans joie*, 1924, directed by Albert Dieudonné), prompted by his admiration for Stroheim and Chaplin and the desire to promote his wife Catherine Hessling, a former model of his father. Renoir then directed his first film, *La Fille de l'eau* (1925), followed by several more, notably *Nana* (1926) and *La Petite marchande d'allumettes/The Little Match Girl* (1928, with Jean Tedesco), all displaying Hessling's expressionist performances, in contrast to Renoir's naturalistic use of actors in his later films. The coming of sound propelled him on to a higher plane – commercially with *On purge Bébé* (1931), and artistically with the remarkable *La Chienne* (1931). This story of a petit-bourgeois' obsession with a prostitute (remade as *Scarlet Street* by Fritz Lang* in 1945) introduced cardinal Renoir features. He not only directed, but helped script, produce and edit. Thematically, it signalled his fascination with popular milieux (shared by other French film-makers) and his disregard of conventional morality: 'respectable' Legrand (Michel Simon*) kills Lulu (Janie Marèse) and ends up unpunished as a tramp (a very Renoirian figure, reprised in *Boudu sauvé des eaux/Boudu Saved from Drowning*, 1932), although the price of male anarchic freedom is female punishment or repression. *La Chienne* also exemplifies Renoir's *mise-en-scène*. An exceptional sense of space is created by complex, though unobtrusive, staging in depth, long takes (even by French standards), and the use of sound counterpoint. The overall effect is a dynamic linking of characters to their environment. Casual acting, sometimes by non-professionals (here Georges Flamant, later Renoir and his friends), is also a hallmark. Yet Renoir's realism goes hand in hand with the theatrical, most of his films alluding to, or staging, spectacles.

Renoir's 1930s films offer a Zolaesque panorama of French society: petit-bourgeois shop-keepers (*Boudu*, *Partie de campagne*, 1936, rel. 1946), Provençal farm and immigrant workers (*Toni*, 1935, hailed as a precursor of Italian neo-realism), railway workers (*La Bête humaine*, 1938), the aristocracy (*La Règle du jeu/Rules of the Game*, 1939). Across this diversity, however, a benevolent Renoirian humanism has been identified ('Everyone has their reasons', says Octave/Renoir in *La Règle du jeu*), made up of easy-going sensuality and a feeling that human beings transcend national or class divisions, as in the pacifist *La Grande illusion* (1937). But some important Renoir films of the 1930s were not only aware of class divisions, they analysed them. Sympathy for the anti-fascist Popular Front* informs the working-class solidarity of *Le Crime de Monsieur Lange* (1935), as well as *La Vie est à nous* (1936, a collectively directed Communist manifesto) and *La Marseillaise* (1937), a chronicle of the French Revolution. Renoir's populism, later increasingly backward-looking, was (in the 1930s) sharpened by left politics; it produced a sensual and generous yet ideologically incisive universe, epitomised by *Le Crime de Monsieur Lange* (scripted by Jacques Prévert*). Because several Renoir films found little commercial success and *La Règle du jeu*, considered his masterpiece, was a resounding failure, he is often regarded as a misunderstood genius. But Renoir was also supremely capable of addressing popular tastes: *Les Bas-fonds/The Lower Depths* (1936), *La Grande illusion* and *La Bête humaine*, with melodramatic plots and major stars like Jean Gabin*, were box-office triumphs.

The war was a decisive break in Renoir's life and career. He left France for Italy to work on *La Tosca* (1940 , completed by Carl Koch), and then went to Hollywood, accompanied by Dido Freire, who became his second wife. A classic European in Hollywood, Renoir made six American films with limited success, including, for the war effort, *This Land is Mine* (1943) and *Salute to France* (1944). Renoir became a US citizen in 1944 (keeping French nationality) and lived on and off in California, travelling to India to make *The River* (1951), Italy for *Le Carrosse d'or/The Golden Coach* (1953), and France where he shot five more films. With the exception of *French Cancan* (1955), a dazzling tribute to the music hall, these never matched his 1930s successes. Nor, despite the backing of *Cahiers du cinéma**, did these films benefit from the critical standing of his prewar work. As his film career stalled, he turned to writing (novels and autobiographies), to the theatre, and to television. Renoir liked to say that an artist must keep his cultural roots. He was right, not only because his great works were made when his virtuosity and emotions were engaged with French subjects, but less obviously because he was nourished by the French prewar industrial context, when it was possible to combine a craft-based, informal way of filming with reaching a popular audience. This is no doubt why he became such a role model for the directors of the New Wave*. Renoir was awarded an Oscar for life achievement in 1975 and the French *légion d'honneur* in 1977.

Jean Renoir's brother Pierre Renoir (Paris 1885–1952) was a distinguished stage and film actor, who played in several of Jean's films, notably *La Nuit du carrefour/Night at the Crossroads* (1932, as Inspector Maigret) and *La Marseillaise* (1937, as Louis XVI). Pierre's son Claude Renoir (born Paris 1914) became a prominent cinematographer, starting with some of his uncle's 1930s films and working on numerous postwar French films. Jean's great-niece Sophie Renoir (Claude's daughter) has appeared in some of Eric Rohmer's* films. Special mention should be made of Marguerite Houllé (sometimes Houllé-Renoir, sometimes Renoir), Jean Renoir's editor and partner in the 1930s. Though they never married, she took his name and pursued a brilliant career as an editor in France after Renoir left for the US.

Bib: André Bazin, *Jean Renoir* (1971); Alexander Sesonske, *Jean Renoir, The French Films 1924–1939* (1980).

Other Films: *Charleston/Sur un air de Charleston* (1926); *Marquitta* (1927); *Tire-au-flanc* (1928); *Le Tournoi dans la cité/Le Tournoi, Le Bled* (1929); *La Nuit du carrefour/Night at the Crossroads, Chotard et*

Cie (1932); *Madame Bovary* (1933); *Swamp Water* (1941, US); *The Southerner* (1945, US); *The Diary of a Chambermaid* (1946, US); *The Woman on the Beach* (1947, US); *Eléna et les hommes/Elena and Men/Paris Does Strange Things* (1956); *Le Déjeuner sur l'herbe* (1959); *Le Testament du Dr Cordelier* (1961); *Le Caporal épinglé/The Elusive Corporal* (1962); *La Direction d'acteurs par Jean Renoir/Jean Renoir Directing Actors* (1969, short); *Le Petit Théâtre de Jean Renoir/Jean Renoir's Little Theatre* (1970).

RESNAIS, Alain Vannes 1922

French director. One of the most consistently interesting *auteurs* of French cinema, Resnais was making short silent films as early as 1936. A graduate of IDHEC*, he started shooting documentaries on art in 1948 with *Van Gogh*. Many other documentaries followed, including *Gauguin* and *Guernica* (both 1950), *Toute la mémoire du monde* (1956) and the celebrated *Nuit et brouillard/Night and Fog* (1955), a testimony to the Holocaust alternating archive documents with long tracking shots (in colour) of the empty concentration camps. Resnais' interest in social and political issues, his modernist concerns and drawing on serious literature (rather than pulp fiction) set him apart from other New Wave* directors right from his first feature, *Hiroshima mon amour* (1959, with a script by Marguerite Duras*), in which the catastrophe of the atomic bomb is juxtaposed with the personal tragedy of a French woman. Resnais' modernism came to the fore in his stunning though controversial collaboration with Alain Robbe-Grillet, *L'Année dernière à Marienbad/Last Year at Marienbad* (1961), in which the camera glides along the corridors of a baroque palace, revealing seemingly frozen characters who may or may not remember 'last year at Marienbad' – the greatest art film for some, pretentious nonsense for others. What unites both the social and the formal strands of Resnais' work is the theme of time and memory, of how to retrieve traces of the past, as well as complex work on narrative structure, especially evident in *Muriel ou le temps d'un retour/Muriel* (1963), *La Guerre est finie/The War is Over* (1966), *Mon oncle d'Amérique/My American Uncle* (1980) and *La Vie est un roman/Life is a Bed of Roses* (1982). He has also experimented with the theatrical style, with *Mélo* (1986) and the two-part *Smoking/No Smoking* (1993).

Other Feature Films: *Loin du Viêt-Nam/Far from Vietnam* (1967, ep.); *Je t'aime, je t'aime* (1968); *L'An 01* (1973, ep. 'Wall Street'); *Stavisky…* (1974); *Providence* (1977); *L'Amour à mort* (1984); *I Want to Go Home* (1989).

RICHARD-WILLM, Pierre

Pierre Richard; Bayonne 1895 – Paris 1983

French actor. With a few exceptions such as Jacques Feyder's* *Le Grand jeu* (1933) and Julien Duvivier's* *Un carnet de bal* (1937), Richard-Willm was not a star of classic films, which explains his present obscurity. Yet in the 1930s and 1940s he was extremely popular, presenting a romantic alternative to the proletarian heroes embodied by the likes of Jean Gabin*. His blond good looks made him ideal for costume dramas such as *Le Roman de Werther/Werther* (1938) and *Le Comte de Monte-Cristo* (1943). Very much a 'women's star', he anticipated the Gérard Philipe* of the 1950s.

RIVETTE, Jacques

Rouen 1928

French director. With his first feature, *Paris nous appartient/Paris Belongs to Us* (1958–60), and his critical work, Rivette was a central figure in the New Wave*. The banning of *La Religieuse/The Nun* in 1965 (the film was released in 1967) also made him a *cause célèbre*. Along with Jean-Luc Godard* Rivette was also its most experimental member (because of their unconventional narratives and length – some exceed four hours – Rivette's films are rarely shown). The dual motif of plot (as conspiracy and narrative) and performance (often improvised) provides a complex reflection on narrative, fiction and imagination in, for instance, *L'Amour fou*, 1967–69, and *L'Amour par terre/Love on the Ground*, 1984.

Rivette frequently focuses on women. The celebrated *Céline et Julie vont en bateau/Céline and Julie Go Boating* (1974) remains a brilliant challenge to narrative and patriarchal structures: Céline and Julie control their destiny (actresses Juliet Berto and Dominique Labourier contributed to the script), live by their wits and reject men and marriage. *Le Pont du Nord* (1981) and *L'Amour par terre* also centred on two women and involved the actresses in the writing process. On the other hand, *La Belle Noiseuse* (1991, based on a Balzac short story), while a profound reflection on the nature of artistic creation and the relationship between painting and the cinema, endorsed a conventional patriarchal vision of a male painter and his female model. It has been Rivette's most successful film. *Jeanne la pucelle* (1994, starring Sandrine Bonnaire*) was a rare incursion, since *La Religieuse*, in the historical film. The film's combination of austere mise-en-scène and epic sweep produced a most original and moving portrait of one of the most frequently filmed heroines (Joan of Arc).

Other Films: *Le Coup du Berger* (short, 1956); *Jean Renoir, le Patron* (1966, TV); *Out 1: Noli Me Tangere* (1971, TV); *Out 1: spectre* (1973); *Duelle/Twilight, Noroît/Nor'west* (1976); *Merry-go-round* (1978–83); *Hurlevent/Wuthering Heights* (1985); *Haut, bas, fragile* (1995).

ROHMER, Eric

Jean-Marie Maurice Schérer;
Nancy 1920

French director, former academic and film critic. Like other French New Wave* directors, Rohmer began working in the 1950s, but it was not until *Ma nuit chez Maud/My Night with Maud* (1969) that he became internationally recognised. His films, most of them divided into 'moral tales' (1962–72) and 'comedies and proverbs' (1980–87), are chamber pieces, focusing on the moral, intellectual and romantic dilemmas of highly articulate characters. This has led to Rohmer's characterisation as a 'literary' film-maker. But while in the tradition of psychological French literature, Rohmer's work is eminently cinematic – in its mastery of a classical economical style, and in its recourse to *cinéma-vérité** techniques.

Even when focusing on the dilemmas of male protagonists, Rohmer's films give women a prominent place. The title character in *Maud* is the prototypical 'moral tales' heroine: sensually and intellectually superior to the prim and rather dull hero. With the 'comedies and proverbs' Rohmer increasingly became a 'woman's director', and his semi-artisanal methods often closely involve his actresses, for instance Marie Rivière for *Le Rayon vert/The Green Ray* (1986). In these later films, it is the women's desire which drives the narrative, even if often thwarted, as in the powerful *Les Nuits de la pleine lune/Full Moon in Paris*, 1984. Still made with small budgets and crews, and shot on location, Rohmer's latest films, *L'Arbre, le maire et la médiathèque* (1993, a brilliant combination of *vérité* documentary and frivolous *marivaudage*), and the new series, 'Tales of the Four Seasons', show his continuing commitment to the aesthetics as well as the methods of the New Wave.

Bib: Pascal Bonitzer, *Eric Rohmer* (1992).

Other Films Include: *La Collectionneuse* (1967); *Le Genou de Claire/Claire's Knee* (1970); *L'Amour l'après-midi/Love in the Afternoon* (1972); *Die Marquise von O.../La Marquise d'O* (1976, Ger./Fr.); *La Femme de l'aviateur/The Aviator's Wife* (1980); *Le Beau mariage/A Good Marriage, Pauline à la plage* (1982); *Quatre aventures de Reinette et Mirabelle/Four Adventures of Reinette and Mirabelle, L'Ami de mon amie/My Best Friend's Boyfriend* (1987); *Conte de printemps/A Tale of Springtime* (1989); *Conte d'hiver/A Winter's Tale* (1992); *Les Rendez-vous de Paris* (1995).

ROMANCE, Viviane

Pauline Ortmans; Roubaix 1909 [1912?] – Nice 1991

French actress. Viviane Romance came to prominence in the mid-1930s in roles that repeatedly cast her as the 'bitch', notably in Julien Duvivier's* *La Belle équipe* (1936) and Augusto Genina's *Naples au baiser de feu* (1937). A beautiful and talented actress, she was limited by this typecasting (which was reinforced by her scandalous private life) and the fact that in her populist register the leading parts went to male stars such as Jean Gabin*, Charles Vanel* or Michel Simon*. The war provided an interesting break by offering her leads in melodramas, including the unusual *Vénus aveugle* directed by Abel Gance* in 1941 (rel. 1943). In the conservative climate of Vichy, her 'bitch' persona underwent a dramatic change, too dramatic perhaps for her audience. In 1947, Duvivier's *Panique* again cast her as a malevolent seductress, but such characters do not age well and her subsequent career never regained its prewar momentum; she appeared fleetingly in *Mélodie en sous-sol/The Big Snatch* (1963) and *Nada* (1973). She will remain, however, the memorable 'number one French vamp' of the 1930s, her sensual performances often transcending her limiting roles.

Other Films Include: *L'Etrange Monsieur Victor* (1937); *Le Puritain, La Maison du Maltais, Prisons de femmes* (1938); *La Boîte aux rêves, Carmen* (both 1943–45); *L'Affaire du collier de la reine* (1946).

ROSAY, Françoise

Françoise Bandy de Nalèche; Paris 1891–1974

French actress. Françoise Rosay's long career is closely linked to that of her husband, the director Jacques Feyder*, with whom she started her film career proper (after parts on stage and a few in films) in *Gribiche* (1926). While in Hollywood with Feyder, she appeared in French versions of multi-language films. Back in France, she co-starred with Fernandel* in the scandalous *Le Rosier de Madame Husson/The Virtuous Isidore* (1931), based on Maupassant. Her greatest performances were still to come: in Feyder's *Le Grand jeu* (1933), *Pension Mimosas* (1934), and *La Kermesse héroïque/Carnival in Flanders* (1935), and in Marcel Carné's* *Jenny* (1936) and the surrealist *Drôle de drame* (1937). During and after World War II she pursued a prolific European career, her films including the British resistance drama *Johnny Frenchman* (1945) and Claude Autant-Lara's* comedy *L'Auberge rouge/The Red Inn* (1951). As shown by her classic 1930s parts, Rosay had the talent to impose herself as a humorous and seductive presence while already in her forties, like Arletty*, with whom she shared the ability to be both world-weary and touching.

ROUCH, Jean
Paris 1917

French ethnographer and director. Rouch studied ethnography in Paris and became interested in Africa in the early 1940s, making his first documentaries there in 1947. He transformed the practice of ethnographic film-making by using light, portable cameras and direct sound, heavily influencing the New Wave*, but also – more controversially – by increasingly implicating himself and the subjects of his films in the film-making process. His best-known documentaries are *Initiation à la danse des possédés/Initiation to Possession Dancing* (1949), *Les Maîtres fous/The Manic Priests* (1955) and *Moi, un Noir* (1958). He later turned his camera on Parisians, producing (with Edgar Morin) *Chronique d'un été/Chronicle of a Summer* (1961), a key work of *cinéma-vérité**. The marriage of *cinéma-vérité* and the New Wave is best seen in Rouch's 'Gare du Nord' episode for *Paris vu par...* (1965), a virtuoso twenty-minute sequence shot entirely in two takes, where the camera follows two characters in a flat, and then one of them in the street. Rouch has made over ninety films; he was president of the Cinémathèque Française* from 1987 to 1991.

RUIZ, Raúl – see 'French Cinema in Europe', page 161

S

SADOUL, Georges
Nancy 1904 – Paris 1967

French film historian. A Surrealist, then a Communist and a member of the Resistance during World War II, Sadoul was a journalist, lecturer (including at IDHEC*) and passionate *cinéphile* who in 1936 conceived his ambitious *Histoire générale du cinéma.* Volume I was published in 1945, volume II in 1947, volume III in 1951 and volume IV in 1952 – and they still only reached 1920. An isolated volume on the 1939–45 period was published in 1954, but Sadoul never finished his project, although he published numerous articles and other books, including two dictionaries (of films and of directors, both 1965), a history of French cinema (1962) and many monographs on film-makers. Sadoul's political convictions (like those of his ideological opposites Maurice Bardèche* and Robert Brasillach*) structured his work; his general history, building on Marxist principles, attempts to place the cinema within an industrial and social context; he championed Soviet cinema and criticised Hollywood entertainment; at the same time he shared some of the aesthetic values of his time, for instance for *auteur* cinema over popular genres. Although they can be criticised for factual errors and obvious *parti pris*, Sadoul's works were central to the development and popularisation of film culture in France.

SAUTET, Claude — Montrouge 1924

French director. A graduate of IDHEC*, Sautet worked as a scriptwriter and assistant to, among others, Jacques Becker*; his own films can indeed be seen in the Becker tradition of 'French-style' intimate realism and classic *mise-en-scène*, although his early features were thrillers – the excellent *Classe tous risques/The Big Risk* (1960) and *L'Arme à gauche/Guns for the Dictator* (1965). His major work came in the 1970s, with an impressive body of intimist romantic stories in a carefully depicted middle-class setting: *Les Choses de la vie/The Things of Life* (1970) was a critical and popular success, as were *César et Rosalie* (1972), *Vincent, François, Paul ... et les autres* (1974), *Mado* (1976) and *Garçon!* (1983). Sautet's work has been little known outside France, until his *Un coeur en hiver/A Heart in Winter* (1993), with Emmanuelle Béart* and Daniel Auteuil*, a major international arthouse hit. This was followed by the successful *Nelly et M. Arnaud* (1995), also starring Béart.

SCHNEIDER, Romy – see 'French Cinema in Europe', page 162

SCHROEDER, Barbet — Teheran, Iran, 1941

French producer, director and actor of Swiss origins whose varied and prolific career may be divided into three phases. Schroeder is first of all associated with the New Wave* as the creator of the production company Les Films du Losange, which produced such films as Eric Rohmer's* Moral tales, the episode film *Paris vu par...* (1965) and Jacques Rivette's* landmark *Céline et Julie vont en bateau/Céline and Julie Go Boating* (1974). He appeared as an actor in a number of these films, notably in the 'Gare du Nord' episode of *Paris vu par...* (directed by Jean Rouch*) and in the film-within-the-film of *Céline et Julie vont en bateau*. Secondly, his role as producer acted, as he wished, as a stepping stone to his career as a filmmaker. His first film, *More* (1969, with dialogue in English), a commentary on the 1960s, with scenes of hedonism and drugs, was a success. His other features also explored similar areas of searches for personal fulfillment, whether through a trip to New Guinea (*La Vallée/The Valley Obscured by*

Clouds, 1972), deviant sexual practices (*Maîtresse/Mistress*, 1976), and gambling (*Tricheurs/The Cheaters*, 1984) as well as to documentaries (*Général Idi Amin Dada Autoportrait/General Amin* (1974), and *Koko le gorille qui parle/Koko the Gorilla* (1978). In turn, this led to the third, internationally famous, phase of Schroeder's career, as one of the very few French directors (with perhaps Louis Malle*) to have made a successful career in America. *Barfly* (1987, starring Mickey Rourke) was followed by *Reversal of Fortune* (1990, with Jeremy Irons and Glenn Close) and *Single White Female* (1992, with Bridget Fonda and Jennifer Jason Leigh).

SERREAU, Coline — Paris 1947

French director, who trained as a stage actress and trapeze artist before acting in films from 1970. Her coming of age in the 1968/early feminist era determined the first direction of her career. In 1975 she made an acclaimed feminist documentary, *Mais qu'est-ce qu'elles veulent?/What Do They Want?* (rel. 1977), a series of interviews with women from all backgrounds. This was followed by a fiction film, *Pourquoi pas!*, a libertarian vision of a *ménage à trois*, which demonstrated Serreau's utopian streak, strong in all her subsequent films. With *Qu'est-ce qu'on attend pour être heureux?/Why Wait to Be Happy?* (1982), and more spectacularly *Trois hommes et un couffin/Three Men and a Cradle*, she moved into mainstream comedy. The box-office triumph of the latter (1985 César for best film, remade in Hollywood as *Three Men and a Baby*) derived from Serreau's meticulous social observation, the excellent performances she elicited, and her knack for choosing topical issues, here the 'new fathers'. *Romuald et Juliette* (1989, about a white company executive and his black cleaning lady) and *La Crise* (1992, on the tribulations of an executive who loses wife and job) have done well without being quite so successful. Serreau's comic universe is bourgeois, affectionate and soft-centred; her essentialist view of femininity makes her a controversial figure for feminists. Nevertheless, she has importantly changed French comedy, making possible a woman-oriented exploration of masculinity and other issues unimaginable before feminism.

SEYRIG, Delphine — Beirut, Lebanon 1932 – Paris 1990

French actress. Two films – Alain Resnais'* *L'Année dernière à Marienbad/Last Year at Marienbad* (1961) and *Muriel ou le temps d'un retour/Muriel* (1963, Best Actress at Venice) – made Seyrig an icon of European art cinema (she also appeared in American underground films). Seyrig's blonde, ethereal beauty and upper-class yet seductive voice graced other art film classics: *Accident* (1967, UK), *Baisers volés/Stolen Kisses* (1968), *Le Charme discret de la bourgeoisie/The Discreet Charm of the Bourgeoisie* (1972), as well as the cult vampire film *Le Rouge aux lèvres/Les Lèvres rouges/Daughters of Darkness* (Harry Kümel, 1971). A committed feminist, Seyrig also supported women's cinema – Marguerite Duras'* *India Song* (1975), Chantal Akerman's* *Jeanne Dielman, 23 Quai du Commerce 1080 Bruxelles* (1975) and *Golden Eighties* (1985), and Ulrike Ottinger's *Freak Orlando* (1981), among others. She co-founded the audio-visual Centre Simone de Beauvoir in Paris in 1982, and directed two videos.

SIGNORET, Simone

Simone Kaminker; Wiesbaden, Germany 1921 – Autheuil 1985

French actress and novelist. The glowing sensual beauty of the young Signoret, as seen in her most famous film, Jacques Becker's* *Casque d'or/Golden Marie* (1952), is a familiar icon of French cinema. But Signoret signified more for her French audience. One of the rare female stars (a term she rejected) who aged on screen as 'an act of defiance', she also made a mark through her strong left-wing views, as well as her tumultuous marriage to Yves Montand*. Signoret's 'prostitute with a heart of gold' in Yves Allégret's* *Dédée d'Anvers* (1948) set the tone for a number of similar roles in the popular French cinema of the late 1940s and early 1950s. A more misogynistic variant was the schemer, as in Allégret's *Manèges/The Cheat* (1950) and Henri-Georges Clouzot's* *Les Diaboliques* (1955). *Casque d'or* stands as an exception in both her career and in French cinema, in allowing her character (a prostitute again) to assert her desire and independence. Despite an Oscar for *Room at the Top* (1958, UK), Signoret's acting was perhaps not fully recognised, and in the early 1960s her notoriety came more from the fracas around Montand's affair with Marilyn Monroe. The maturing Signoret embodied strong heroines in thrillers and psychological dramas such as Jean-Pierre Melville's* *L'Armée des ombres/The Army in the Shadows* (1969), which while (again) not devoid of misogyny, projected her powerful personality. Her role opposite Jean Gabin* in *Le Chat* (1971) is emblematic of such parts. Later in her life, Signoret took up writing and produced a successful autobiography and two novels. Her daughter Catherine Allégret is a film and television actress.

Bib: Catherine David, *Simone Signoret* (1990, trans. 1992).

Other Films Include: *La Ronde* (1950); *Thérèse Raquin* (1953); *Compartiment Tueurs/The Sleeping Car Murders* (1965); *La Veuve Couderc* (1971); *Police Python 357* (1975); *L'Adolescente* (1979); *L'Etoile du Nord* (1983).

SIMENON, Georges

Liège 1903 – Lausanne, Switzerland 1989

Belgian novelist, who worked in France, the US and Switzerland. The phenomenally successful and prolific Simenon wrote pulp novels, essays, memoirs and hundreds of crime stories, many featuring the character of Inspector Maigret. Simenon's brand of crime fiction was based on social observation and atmosphere rather than conventional detection, which perhaps explains why he has been one of the most adapted writers in French cinema.

The first Simenon adaptation was *La Nuit du carrefour/Night at the Crossroads* (1932), directed by Jean Renoir*. Over fifty, mostly French, films followed, and many great European actors have embodied the gruff, pipe-smoking Maigret: Pierre Renoir [> JEAN RENOIR], Harry Baur*, Gino Cervi*, Charles Laughton*, Albert Préjean* in the 1940s and Jean Gabin* in the 1950s and 1960s. Prominent French directors have successfully translated Simenon's misanthropic view of the world: from Renoir to Julien Duvivier* (*Panique*, 1946 – remade as *Monsieur Hire* by Patrice Leconte, 1989), Marcel Carné* (*La Marie du port*, 1950), Claude Autant-Lara* (*En cas de malheur/Love is My Profession*, 1958), Bertrand Tavernier* (*L'Horloger de Saint-Paul/The Watchmaker of Saint-Paul*, 1974) and Claude Chabrol* (*Les Fantômes du chapelier/The Hatter's Ghosts*, 1982; *Betty*, 1992). Though he professed to dislike most film adaptations of his novels, Simenon inspired some of France's best *noir* works, for instance *Panique* and *Les Inconnus dans la maison* (1942, scripted by Henri-Georges Clouzot* and directed by Henri Decoin*).

SIMON, Michel

Geneva, Switzerland 1895 – Bry-sur-Marne 1975

Swiss-born French actor. After stage roles in Geneva and Paris and a few bit parts in silent films, the screen adaptation of his stage success *Jean de la lune* (1931) launched Michel Simon on a career of some hundred films, establishing his reputation as one of the most gifted and versatile stars of French cinema. Like many actors of the 1930s, Simon appeared in numerous adapted plays, usually comedies (like *Fric-Frac*, 1939), in which he was gloriously funny. Film history, however, has preferred to concentrate on his roles in two films by Jean Renoir* – Legrand, the repressed petit-bourgeois of *La Chienne* (1931), and the anarchic tramp Boudu in *Boudu sauvé des eaux/Boudu Saved from Drowning* (1932) – and one by Jean Vigo* (*L'Atalante*, 1934). Simon's prematurely aged looks even in youth and his quaky, grating voice led to many parts trading on ambivalence, sexual or otherwise – for example as Molyneux in Marcel Carné's* *Drôle de drame* (1937), the repulsive father-figure in *Quai des brumes* (1938), the hero of Julien

Duvivier's* *Panique* (1947), both threatening and pathetic, and the dual protagonist of René Clair's* *La Beauté du diable/Beauty and the Devil* (1950).

Simon's presence in Swiss films is confined to an important role in *La Vocation d'André Carel* (1925) and appearances in *Es geschah am hellichten Tag/It Happened in Broad Daylight* (1958; dir. Ladislao Vajda*) and the short *Nicolas mon ami* (1961).

Bib: André Klopmann, *Michel Simon* (1993).

SIMON, Simone Béthune 1911

French actress. Though rarely given lead parts, the delicate, cat-like Simone Simon made a memorable mark on two classics: Jean Renoir's* *La Bête humaine* (1938) and Jacques Tourneur's cult horror movie *Cat People* (1942, US). A singer and model, she began her film career in 1931. Her role in Marc Allégret's* *Lac aux dames* (1934, scripted by Colette*) brought her fame in France and a contract in Hollywood. For a while she was a top French actress, and relatively successful in Hollywood. Her sex-kitten sensuality found an expression in *Cat People* but, to her dismay, was considerably toned down by US censorship in several other films, including the Maupassant adaptation *Mademoiselle Fifi* (1944, dir. Robert Wise). Back in France, however, it glowed in a more mature form in Jacqueline Audry's* *Olivia/The Pit of Loneliness* (1951, co-starring Edwige Feuillière*), and in two Max Ophuls* films, *La Ronde* (1950) and *Le Plaisir* (1951).

SIODMAK, Robert – see 'French Cinema in Europe', page 163

STRAUB, Jean-Marie and HUILLET, Danièle – see 'French Cinema in Europe', page 156

TATI, Jacques

Jacques Tatischeff; Le Pecq 1908 – Paris 1982

French director. For filmgoers throughout the world, Jacques Tati *is* French comedy. In France, his critical reputation is high, but after the immense popularity of his 1950s films his career was chequered. While acting in a few films and in music hall as a mime, he directed six shorts, drawing on silent comics Max Linder*, Chaplin and Keaton. Like them, he was an actor-*auteur*, and like them his comic style, based on sight gags, was universally exportable. His Monsieur Hulot, first seen in *Les Vacances de Monsieur Hulot/Monsieur Hulot's Holiday* (1953), derived from François the postman in *Jour de fête* (1947, rel. 1949) and resurfaced in *Mon Oncle* (1958), *Playtime* (1964, rel. 1967), *Trafic/Traffic* (1971) and *Parade* (1974). With his tall, ungainly figure, and his signature raincoat, hat and pipe, Tati made Hulot the universal childlike innocent who creates chaos by ignoring adult rules – breaking implements in his sister's kitchen in *Mon Oncle*, wrecking an entire restaurant in *Playtime*. But Tati's novelty was to combine slapstick with a modernist sensitivity. Formally, his films are extremely complex (and increasingly so, explaining his loss of popularity after *Mon Oncle*), exploiting to the full the possibilities of the frame and of sound. His soundtracks, mixing noises, grunts, expletives, advertisements, snatches of songs and different languages, are the aural equivalent of Jean-Luc Godard's* visual *bricolage*. From the start, too, Tati's films were a running commentary on the struggle between modernisation (or 'Americanisation') and tradition in France. An independent figure in the industry, he always had great difficulties raising finance (as well as satisfying the taxman); hence his small number of films.

Bib: Lucy Fischer, *Jacques Tati: A Guide to References and Resources* (1983).

TAVERNIER, Bertrand

Lyons 1941

French director, former press attaché (notably for Georges de Beauregard*) and *Positif** critic. From his *Positif* days, Tavernier inherited a distrust of New Wave* auteurism, but a love of cinema (American as well as French). While his work is indeed eclectic, his first feature, *L'Horloger de Saint-Paul/The Watchmaker of Saint-Paul* (1973), contains several characteristic motifs, combining thriller elements (from a Simenon* novel) with a naturalistic view of a popular milieu in old Lyons, his home town. Intimist realism also marks *Une semaine de vacances* (1980) and *Daddy nostalgie/These Foolish Things* (1990), while *L.627* (1992) further elaborates the thriller-naturalism combination. Written by ex-policeman Michel Alexandre, this bleak film follows a drugs squad ineffectually tracking down immigrant dealers in rundown areas of Paris. Though Tavernier has also ventured into the futuristic (*La Mort en direct/Deathwatch*, 1980), most of his other work is historical. Influenced by the 'new history' of the 1970s, *Que la fête commence* (1974) and *La Passion Béatrice* (1987) attempt a non-glamorous look at history, while *Coup de Torchon/Clean Slate* (1981, in which a Jim Thompson thriller is transposed to colonial Africa) started a more traditional type of period reconstruction: 1950s Paris (*Round Midnight/Autour de minuit*, 1986, US/Fr.) and pre-World War I France (*Un dimanche à la campagne/Sunday in the Country*, 1984), in the Heritage cinema* genre. *La Fille de d'Artagnan/ D'Artagnan's Daughter* (1994), a light swashbuckler, marks yet another departure. Tavernier has also made shorts and documentaries, including *Mississippi Blues* (1983, co-dir. Robert Parrish), and worked as a scriptwriter and producer. Tavernier's name has become synonymous with quality popular French cinema (solid scripts, classic performances, social issues, evoking the 'tradition of quality'*). During the 1993 GATT negotiations he was an ardent campaigner on behalf of European cinema. *L'Appât/The Bait* (1995) won the Silver Bear at the Berlin film festival. His son Nils Tavernier is an actor.

Other Films: *Le Juge et l'assassin* (1975); *Des enfants gâtés* (1977); *La Vie et rien d'autre/Life and Nothing But* (1988).

TÉCHINÉ, André — Valence d'Agen 1943

French director. A former film critic, Téchiné is one of the important post-New Wave* French directors. His *Souvenirs d'en France* (1975) explored the relation between history and personal 'histories' (the title contains a pun on 'en France' and 'enfance', childhood), focusing on a family from the 1930s to the 1970s. His subsequent work concentrated on the personal, couched in a spectacular, elegant though rather cold *mise-en-scène*: *Barocco* (1976), *Les Soeurs Brontë/The Brontë Sisters* (1979, with a distinguished cast including Isabelle Huppert*, Isabelle Adjani*, Marie-France Pisier and the writer Roland Barthes in a cameo part), *Hôtel des Amériques* (1981) with Catherine Deneuve*, and *Rendez-vous* (1985). Later films have narrowed the canvas to smaller-scale, intense family dramas such as *Le Lieu du crime* (1986), *Ma saison préférée* (1993) – both with Deneuve – and *Les Roseaux sauvages* (1994). One unusual characteristic of Téchiné's work is his unsensational evocation of homosexuality (*Les Innocents*, 1988, *J'embrasse pas*, 1991, *Les Roseaux sauvages*, 1994). Another is his use of his native south-west, acknowledging the beauty of the landscape while avoiding touristic cliché. His *L'Enfant de la nuit* (1995) repeated the successful casting of *Ma saison préférée* (Deneuve and Daniel Auteuil).

Bib: Jill Forbes, *The Cinema in France After the New Wave* (1992).

TOURNEUR, Maurice

Maurice Thomas; Paris 1876–1961

French director. An actor and then director at the Eclair studio, Tourneur had a successful career in Hollywood, where he was considered a great 'pictorialist', and came back to France in 1926. His thirty (mostly sound) French films show his skill with popular genres. *Les Gaietés de l'escadron/The Joys of the Squadron* (1932) is a classic *comique troupier** with a remarkable cast (Raimu*, Fernandel*, Jean Gabin*); *Justin de Marseille* (1934) a thriller set in Pagnol* territory; *Avec le sourire/With a Smile* (1936) a cynical comedy with – and to some extent about – Maurice Chevalier*. *Koenigsmark* (1935) and *Katia* (1938) are two melodramas of great visual beauty in the 'Slav' sub-genre; *Cécile est morte/Cécile is Dead* (1944) a Simenon* adaptation with Albert Préjean* as Inspector Maigret; and *Impasse des deux anges* (1948) a *noir* drama with Paul Meurisse and Simone Signoret*. Tourneur's son, Jacques Tourneur (Paris 1904 – Bergerac 1978), learnt his trade in Hollywood with his father and worked with him on some of his French films. In the US, he made the cult horror film *Cat People* (1942) and the *noir* thriller *Out of the Past/Build My Gallows High* (1947).

TRADITION OF QUALITY

French stylistic trend within mainstream French films made in the 1940s and 1950s. On the one hand, the term refers to a loose industry category, actively promoted (by financial aid and prizes) to project a 'quality' image of French film: expertly crafted pictures with high production values and often derived from literary sources. Psychological and/or costume dramas such as Jean Delannoy's* *La Symphonie pastorale* (1946), Claude Autant-Lara's* *Douce* (1943), René Clément's* *Jeux interdits/Forbidden Games* (1952), Max Ophuls'* *La Ronde* (1950), Jacqueline Audry's * *Minne, L'ingénue libertine/Minne* (1950), Jean Renoir's* *French Cancan* (1955), René Clair's* *Les Grandes manoeuvres* (1955), all projected an image of Frenchness tied to good taste and high culture. Many were co-productions, often with Italy, on account of cost, and most were box-office hits. On the other hand, the term was turned by François Truffaut* into one of abuse against what he labelled 'A certain tendency of French cinema' (*Cahiers du ciné-*

*ma**, January 1954). Truffaut's dislike of the 'quality' films rested on four notions antithetical to the future *auteur* cinema of the New Wave*. First, it was a 'cinema of scriptwriters' [> AURENCHE, JEAN AND BOST, PIERRE], as opposed to being made by 'men of the cinema'; second, its focus was on psychological realism– often pessimistic, anti-clerical and 'anti-bourgeois' rather than 'existential' romantic self-expression; third, the *mise-en-scène* was too polished (studio sets, scholarly framings, complicated lighting, classical editing), as against a more casual, improvised cinema of the 'open air'; fourth, it was mass-appeal cinema, relying on genres and especially stars, as opposed to the personality of the *auteur*. Truffaut's contempt was polemic and excessive (but has had a massive influence on the dominant historiography of French cinema ever since). If some of the 'quality' films are mannered and 'academic', others are sumptuous, lively or ironically distant. The costume dramas also presented to a mass audience subjects marginalised in other genres, such as women's desires – for instance Audry's *Olivia/The Pit of Loneliness* (1951) and Jacques Becker's* *Casque d'Or/Golden Marie* (1952).

TRAUNER, Alexandre

Sandor Trauner; Budapest, Hungary 1906 – Omonville-la-Petite 1993

Hungarian-born French set designer. Trauner studied painting in Budapest and moved to France in 1929, becoming assistant to Lazare Meerson*, then the greatest set designer in France. Trauner's name is closely connected with Poetic Realism*, a style of French film of the 1930s to which he contributed the most immediately recognisable element: a stylised yet minutely observed reconstruction of urban decors. Trauner's concern for accurate detail is well illustrated by his fight with the producer of *Le Jour se lève* (1939), who wanted to shorten the central building of the set by one storey to save money; understanding the close relationship between character and set in Poetic Realist films, Trauner insisted that the height of the building was crucial. He designed the sets of so many French films that one can pick almost at random: *Drôle de drame* (1936), *Quai des brumes* (1938), *Les Enfants du paradis* (1943–45), *Les Portes de la nuit* (1956), *Du rififi chez les hommes/Rififi* (1955), *Mr Klein* (1977), *Subway* (1985), *Round Midnight/Autour de minuit* (1986, US/Fr.). Trauner was also much in demand internationally, designing, among other films, Billy Wilder's *The Apartment* (1960), for which he won an Oscar, and Joseph Losey's *Don Giovanni* (1979).

TRINTIGNANT, Jean-Louis Pont Saint-Esprit 1930

French actor. An imposing presence rather than a 'star', the stage-trained Trintignant has acted in over 120 films since the mid-1950s, pursuing his prolific career in popular and art cinema in France and Italy (notably in Bernardo Bertolucci's *Il Conformista/The Conformist*, 1970). He came to public attention as Brigitte Bardot's* timid husband (and off-screen lover) in *Et Dieu ... créa la femme/And God Created Woman* (1956) and was the romantic hero of Claude Lelouch's* *Un homme et une femme/A Man and a Woman* (1966), racing from the Côte d'Azur to meet Anouk Aimée* on the beach at Deauville. Trintignant has played variations on the shy seducer, as in Eric Rohmer's* *Ma nuit chez Maud/My Night at Maud's* (1969), and repressed, sinister characters, for instance in Costa-Gavras'* *Compartiment Tueurs/The Sleeping Car Murders* (1965) and Alain Robbe-Grillet's *Trans-Europ-Express* (1966), evolving into an increasingly complex figure. A former student at IDHEC*, he has directed two films. He was married to director Nadine Trintignant (and starred in several of her films) and is the father of actress Marie Trintignant. His most affecting performance of the 1990s was as a solitary retired judge and 'aural voyeur' in Krzysztof Kieślowski's* *Trois couleurs: Rouge/Three Colours: Red* (1994).

TRUFFAUT, François Paris 1932–84

French director, with Jean-Luc Godard* the most famous director of the New Wave*. His first feature, *Les Quatre Cents Coups/The 400 Blows* (1959), was effectively one of the manifestos of the movement – the other was Godard's *A Bout de souffle/Breathless* (1960) – with its autobiographical focus, its independent production and its location shooting in the streets of Paris.

Truffaut had already made a name for himself as a critic at *Cahiers du cinéma**, where in 1954 he published 'A Certain Tendency of the French Cinema', a famously ferocious critique of the mainstream French cinema of the late 1940s and early 1950s [> TRADITION OF QUALITY]. Truffaut prized American cinema, especially Hitchcock, and Jean Renoir*. A Renoiresque realism informed *Les Quatre cents coups* and, after his pastiche of US *film noir*, *Tirez sur le pianiste/Shoot the Pianist* (1960), and his adaptation of Henri-Pierre Roché's novel *Jules et Jim* (1962), Truffaut moved increasingly in the direction of a classic-realist *mise-en-scène*. Notable in this respect is the Antoine Doinel saga, which follows the main character of *Les Quatre cents coups*, still played by Jean-Pierre Léaud*, through late adolescence and adult life, in *Baisers volés/Stolen Kisses* (1968), *Domicile conjugal/Bed and Board* (1970) and *L'Amour en fuite/Love on the Run* (1979). Even if the sentimentality can be irritating ('Are women magic?'), the

Doinel series is charming, funny and both accurate and evocative in its picture of middle-class Parisian life. Truffaut's other major strand was his love for popular entertainment, evidenced by his unfinished trilogy of films on film-making (*La Nuit américaine/Day for Night*, 1973) and the theatre (*Le Dernier métro/The Last Metro*, 1980, a major success); the third would have been on the music hall. Uniting all Truffaut's work, as Anne Gillain shows, is a deeply personal 'matrix' of Freudian motifs related to his childhood relationship to his mother, displayed by the emphasis on immature male characters (archetypally Léaud, but also Charles Denner in *L'Homme qui aimait les femmes/The Man Who Loved Women*, 1977) and cool mature women (Delphine Seyrig* in *Baisers volés*, Catherine Deneuve* in *Le Dernier métro*).

Truffaut wrote abundantly, including a book on *Hitchcock* (first published 1967), film reviews collected in *The Films in My Life* (1978) and *The Early Film Criticism of François Truffaut* (1993), and letters (1990) [all dates English translations]. He also acted, in his own *L'Enfant sauvage/The Wild Child* (1970) and *La Chambre verte/The Green Room* (1978) and in Steven Spielberg's *Close Encounters of the Third Kind* (1977, US).

Bib: Anne Gillain, *François Truffaut, Le Secret perdu* (1992).

Other Films: *Une visite* (1955, short); *Les Mistons* (1957, short); *Une histoire d'eau* (1958, short, co-dir. Godard); *L'Amour à vingt ans/Love at Twenty* (1962, ep. 'Antoine et Colette'); *La Peau douce/Silken Skin* (1964); *Fahrenheit 451* (1966, UK); *La Mariée était en noir/The Bride Wore Black* (1968); *La Sirène du Mississippi/The Mississipi Mermaid* (1969); *Les Deux Anglaises et le continent/Anne and Marie* (1971); *Une belle fille comme moi/A Gorgeous Bird Like Me* (1972); *L'Histoire d'Adèle H/The Story of Adèle H* (1975); *L'Argent de poche/Small Change/Pocket Money* (1976); *La Femme d'à côté/The Woman Next Door* (1981); *Vivement Dimanche!/Finally Sunday* (1983).

VADIM, Roger

Roger Vadim Plemiannikov; Paris 1928

French director. A former photographer, journalist and assistant to Marc Allégret*, Vadim is famous for directing his then wife Brigitte Bardot* in *Et Dieu ... créa la femme/And God Created Woman* (1956), a film often credited as a precursor of the New Wave* because of its small production team and location shooting in Saint-Tropez. Vadim's subsequent career blows this myth apart – instead he anticipated the erotic explosion of the late 1960s and 1970s – with films such as *Le Repos du guerrier/Warrior's Rest* (1962), *Le Vice et la vertu/Vice and Virtue* (1963) and *Barbarella* (1968). However, *Les Liaisons dangereuses* (1959), with Gérard Philipe* and Jeanne Moreau*, cleverly caught the fashionable edge of 'modern' life in France at the dawn of the Fifth Republic, with seductive black-and-white photography and a jazz score by Thelonius Monk and others, with a number of musicians playing, including Art Blakey's Jazz Messengers. He has been a prolific director and has also acted. In 1987 he directed a lacklustre remake of his early triumph, *And God Created Woman* (US), with Rebecca De Mornay in the lead.

VALENTIN, Albert

La Louvière, Belgium 1908 – Paris 1968

French director and scriptwriter. An underrated director of French classic cinema, Valentin was assistant to René Clair* and worked in German studios making French versions of German musicals such as Reinhold Schünzel's* *Amphitryon* (1935; French version: *Les Dieux s'amusent*). Despite the hit comedy *L'Héritier des Mondésir* (1939) with Fernandel*, Valentin's two most interesting films are sombre women's melodramas. *L'Entraîneuse* (1938) stars Michèle Morgan* as a young nightclub hostess who tries unsuccessfully to pass for a respectable woman, and *Marie-Martine* (1943) features Renée Saint-Cyr and Jules Berry* in another tale of a woman who tries and fails to escape her past. Valentin's emphasis on women and on clearly pointing the finger at oppressive patriarchal figures was unusual; he co-wrote another great woman's film of the Occupation period, *Le Ciel est à vous* (1943–44), directed by Jean Grémillon*.

VANEL, Charles

Charles-Marie Vanel; Rennes 1892 – Cannes 1989

French actor. Vanel's career was extremely long: born before the cinema, he allegedly made over 160 films, the last in 1987. Rugged and solid, Vanel embodied a variety of tough, taciturn and sometimes tragic male heroes, epitomised by the lorry driver of Henri-Georges Clouzot's* *Le Salaire de la peur/The Wages of Fear* (1953, which won him a prize at Cannes). Highlights of his lengthy filmography, which mixes mainstream and *auteur* films, include: Germaine Dulac's* *Ame d'artiste* (1923), Raymond Bernard's* *Les Misérables* (1933, as Javert), Marcel Carné's* *Jenny* (1936), Curt Bernhardt's* *Carrefour* (1938), Jean Grémillon's* *Le Ciel est à vous* (1943–44), and Clouzot's *Les*

Diaboliques (1955) and *La Vérité* (1960). He also appeared in Italian films, among them Francesco Rosi's *Cadaveri eccellenti/Illustrious Corpses* (1976) and *Tre fratelli/Three Brothers* (1981). In his own words, Vanel 'never was, nor claimed to be, a star', yet he was much more than a character actor and he retained a consistent image throughout his extremely varied roles.

VARDA, Agnès — Brussels, Belgium 1928

French director (of features and shorts) trained in art and photography. Her first feature, *La Pointe courte* (1956), anticipated the New Wave* in production methods and aesthetics. World recognition came with *Cléo de 5 à 7/Cleo from 5 to 7* (1962). *Sans toit ni loi/Vagabonde* (1985) was a universal success. Both films are powerful portraits of a female protagonist.

Varda's work manifests a central belief in film as personal expression, though she carefully places the inner world of her characters in a social context (her left-wing politics are explicit in *Black Panthers*, 1970 [US], and in her participation in *Loin du Viêt-Nam/Far from Vietnam*, 1967). She places equal emphasis on realism and symbolism, as in *Sans toit ni loi*, a statement on the disillusioned post-1968 generation combined with Christian and pagan myths. Varda's relationship to feminism is complex. Some of her work is avowedly feminist, for instance *L'Une chante, l'autre pas/One Sings, the Other Doesn't* (1977), a fictional rendering of the early French women's movement. However, in its celebration of biological femininity, it comes close to what feminist critic Claire Johnston saw, in the earlier *Le Bonheur* (1965), as endorsing patriarchal myths of women. On the other hand, in her search for a specific '*cinécriture*', Varda is seen by others as radical. *Jane B. par Agnès V.* and *Kung-Fu Master* (both 1988) – both starring Jane Birkin – continue her in-depth reflection on the representation of femininity and female desire. Varda has directed a documentary on her late husband Jacques Demy, *Jacquot de Nantes* (1991), and a feature on the centenary of the cinema, *Les Cent et une nuits du cinéma* (1995).

Bib: Agnès Varda, *Varda par Agnès* (1994).

Other Films: **Shorts**: *Ô saisons ô châteaux* (1958); *L'Opéra-Mouffe, Du côté de la côte* (1959); *Salut les Cubains*, *Les Enfants du musée* (1964); *Elsa la rose* (1966, TV); *Oncle Yanco* (1968, TV); *Réponse de femmes* (1975); *Plaisir d'amour en Iran* (1977); *Quelques femmes bulles* (1978); *Ulysse*, *Les Dites cariatides* (1984); *7 P., cuis., s. de b… (à saisir)*, *T'as de beaux escaliers… tu sais* (1986); *Une minute pour une image* (1990, TV, series of two-minute episodes). **Features**: *Les Créatures* (1966); *Lions Love* (1969, US); *Nausicaa* (1970, TV); *Daguerréotypes* (1975); *Mur murs, Documenteur* (1982); *Les Demoiselles ont eu 25 ans* (1993, TV); *L'Univers de Jacques Demy* (1994).

VENTURA, Lino

Angelo Borrini Ventura; Parma, Italy 1919 – Saint-Cloud 1987

French actor. As the gangster Angelo in Jacques Becker's* *Touchez pas au grisbi/Honour Among Thieves* (1954), newcomer Ventura impressed both the film's star Jean Gabin* (a determining influence) and the public with his muscular presence and laconic delivery. A former wrestler and salesman from a poor immigrant background, Ventura was catapulted overnight into the cinema limelight. *Grisbi* inaugurated a long series of *policiers** in which he excelled both as gangster and policeman: Claude Sautet's* *Classe tous risques/The Big Risk* (1960), Jean-Pierre Melville's* *Le Deuxième souffle/The Second Breath* (1966), Henri Verneuil's* *Le Clan des Siciliens/The Sicilian Clan* (1969) and many more, including comic pastiches of the genre. Parallel to this popular and commercially fruitful career, Ventura appeared in art films such as Melville's *L'Armée des ombres/The Army in the Shadows* (1969), Francesco Rosi's* *Cadaveri eccellenti/Illustrious Corpses* (1976) and Claude Miller's *Garde à vue* (1981); prestige productions like the 1982 version of *Les Misérables* (1982); and comedies such as *L'Emmerdeur* (1973). His minimalist acting in the thrillers evolved into a self-contained masculinity, which his lived-in face endowed with a combination of world-weariness, toughness and sensitivity. Popular in France for both his films and his charity work for handicapped children, Ventura, despite his Italian origins, came to represent a version of French masculinity in the Gabin and Yves Montand* lineage, deeply felt as 'authentic'.

VERNEUIL, Henri

Achod Malakian; Rodosto, Turkey 1920

French director. Verneuil's refugee Armenian family arrived in France in 1924. He studied engineering and came to the cinema through journalism at the Liberation, adopting his pseudonym then. After a spell as an assistant director, Verneuil was lucky to have Fernandel* – then one of the biggest French stars – appear (free) in his first short film, *Escale au soleil* (1949), which was selected for Cannes. This resulted in about thirty more shorts, and Fernandel also starred in Verneuil's first six features – including *Le Boulanger de Valorgue* (1953), *L'Ennemi public n° 1* (1954) and *Le Mouton à cinq pattes/The Sheep Has Five Legs* (1954) – with immense box-office success. Well established as a comedy director (*La Vache et le prisonnier/The Cow and I*, 1959, again with Fernandel, was one of the comic triumphs of the decade), Verneuil moved on to thrillers and psychological dramas, producing a number of hits, including *Mélodie en sous-sol/The Big Snatch* (1963) and *Le Clan des Siciliens/The Sicilian Clan* (1969, both co-starring Jean Gabin* and Alain Delon*) and a number of solid star vehicles for the likes of Yves Montand* and Jean-Paul Belmondo*. Ironically (and surprisingly), Verneuil was unsuccessful at the box office with his most personal projects, the melodramatic but moving *Mayrig* (1991) and *588, rue Paradis* (1992), based on his autobiography and starring Claudia Cardinale, Omar Sharif and Richard Berry.

VIGO, Jean Paris 1905–34

French director, one of the most talented romantic and tragic figures in French cinema. Vigo's father, an anarchist who died in jail in mysterious circumstances in 1917, came from an Andorran family. Jean Vigo was attracted to the avant-garde of the late 1920s [> FRENCH AVANT-GARDE; AVANT-GARDE CINEMA IN EUROPE]. After a brief spell in the Nice studios as an assistant cameraman, he made the iconoclastic short *A propos de Nice* (1930) with Boris Kaufman (one of Dziga Vertov's brothers) and a documentary on a swimmer, *Taris* (1931). He directed only two features before his untimely death from tuberculosis, but they remain two of the most beautiful French films ever made. The forty-five minute *Zéro de conduite* (1934), set in a boy's boarding school, is a powerful indictment of authoritarianism (partly based on Vigo's own school experience). The schoolmasters are portrayed as puppets and the children give the film a raw authenticity and energy, while some scenes, such as the pillow fight, are dreamily poetic. In *L'Atalante* (1934), an erotic romance set on a barge (starring Michel Simon*, Jean Dasté and Dita Parlo), Vigo made one of the key films of the 1930s, his own version of 'Poetic Realism'* *avant la lettre*; in the words of John Grierson*, 'At the base of it is a sense of documentary realism which makes the barge a real barge ... but on top of the realism is a crazy Vigo world of symbols and magic.' Vigo's films have a peculiar historical standing. *Zéro de conduite* was immediately banned and *L'Atalante* was briefly shown in various cut or altered versions, largely to indifferent audiences. But though they had little impact on contemporary audiences, his films were enormously influential on other film-makers, both in terms of his aesthetics and of Vigo's model of an *auteur* struggling against adversity; they now indelibly colour our vision of 1930s French cinema.

Bib: Marina Warner, *L'Atalante* (1993).

Z

ZIDI, Claude

Paris 1934

French director. A former assistant and cameraman, Zidi made his first films in what critics consider the *bas de gamme* (bottom drawer) of French comedy: the *comique troupier**, a genre which he updated with a then popular group of comic singers, Les Charlots – *Les Bidasses en folie* (1971), *Les Bidasses s'en vont en guerre* (1974) – and two Louis de Funès* vehicles, *L'Aile ou la cuisse* (1976) and *La Zizanie* (1978). He moved on to take in the *café-théâtre* generation [> COMEDY (FRANCE)] with *Inspecteur la bavure/Inspector Blunder* (1980, starring Coluche and Gérard Depardieu*), *Les Sous-doués/The Dimwits* (1979) and *Les Sous-doués en vacances/The Dimwits on Holiday* (1982). In 1984, *Les Ripoux/Le Cop* – starring Thierry Lhermitte and Philippe Noiret* – was a major hit, abroad as well as domestically, attracting a more favourable critical reception. The film scathingly sends up corruption in the police, always a favourite subject in France; its slang title ('ripoux' is the reverse of 'pourri', rotten) is now part of the French language. There was a sequel, *Les Ripoux II/Le Cop II*, in 1989. Zidi's talent for inventive comic narratives received a dubious tribute when *La Totale* (1991, with Lhermitte and Miou-Miou*) was remade as *True Lies* (1994, US) with Arnold Schwarzenegger and rather more special effects.

FRENCH CINEMA IN EUROPE

1. Trans-European personnel
Akerman, Chantal
Borowczyk, Walerian
Brel, Jacques
Buñuel, Luis
Cavalcanti, Alberto
Ferreri, Marco
Holland, Agnieska
Huillet, Danièle and Straub, Jean-Marie
Kieślowski, Krzysztof
Litvak, Anatole
Mosjoukine [Mozzhukhin], Ivan
Ophuls, Max
Otsep, Fyodor [Ozep, Fédor]
Polanski, Roman
Ruiz, Raúl
Schneider, Romy
Siodmak, Robert

2. Key European cinema concepts, genres and institutions
Avant-garde cinema in Europe
Emigration and European cinema
European art cinema
European cinema and Hollywood
European Community [now European Union] and the cinema
European film awards [FELIX]
Festivals
Heritage cinema in Europe
Lesbian and gay cinema in Europe
Sexuality, eroticism and pornography in European cinema

1. Trans-European personnel

This section regroups entries on filmmakers and actors whose work has a strong European dimension, but who also made a substantial contribution to French cinema. Some of these entries were written in collaboration with writers who contributed to the *Encyclopedia of European Cinema*: John Caughie (Cavalcanti), Cathy Fowler (Akerman, Brel), Peter Evans (Buñuel, Ferreri), Ania Witkowska (Borowczyk, Holland, Kieślowski, Polanski), Richard Taylor (Mosjoukine, Ozep), Thomas Elsaesser (Ophuls), Sabine Gottgetreu and Andrea Lang (Schneider).

AKERMAN, Chantal — Brussels 1950

Belgian director, born of émigré Polish Jewish parents. Akerman's early aspirations to be a writer were swiftly exchanged, on viewing Jean-Luc Godard's* *Pierrot le fou* (1965), for a career as a film-maker. After spending a year at the Brussels film school INSAS, Akerman travelled to Paris, then to New York after making her first short film, *Saute ma ville/Blow up My Town* (1968). Her films reflect these early years of displacement, yet despite their constant changes of form and location, evidence of a strong authorial personality remains.

Akerman's most (in)famous film, *Jeanne Dielman 23 Quai du Commerce 1080 Bruxelles* (1975), depicts roughly three days in the life of a housewife who is also a prostitute, played by Delphine Seyrig*. Rejecting both linear classical narrative and the conventional use of woman as a seductive presence, *Jeanne Dielman* offers instead a film which is shaped by Jeanne's own sense of ritual, time and space. *News from Home* (1976) extends this film's system of 'anti-seduction', replacing classical narrative's voyeuristic and fragmented gaze with an intimate and lingering look (the film consists of a series of long takes of New York with Akerman's voice-over reading letters written to her by her mother). In *Les Rendez-vous d'Anna* (1978), Aurore Clément plays a (semi-autobiographical?) Belgian film-maker who journeys from Cologne to Paris. This film won awards at festivals in Chicago and Paris. *Toute une nuit/All Night Long* (1982), a choreography around one hot night in Brussels, was followed by *Golden Eighties* (1986), a post-modern musical. The setting of this film in a shopping mall triggers an exploration of spectacle and performance, in which love becomes something to be bought and sold like a dress. Despite its charm and vitality, the film was not a success, and with her next film, *Histoires d'Amérique: Food, Family and Philosophy/American Stories* (1989), Akerman returned to a more intimate mode of production.

Akerman has moved from the avant-garde to art cinema, from feminist experiment to European *auteur* film, from Brussels via New York to Paris, the setting of *Nuit et jour/Night and Day* (1991), and back to

New York for *Un divan à New York* (1996, Fr./Bel.), starring Juliette Binoche* and the American actor William Hurt. Triply displaced as Belgian, Jewish and female, Akerman's cinema remains marginal, yet it should not be marginalised since its fundamental project is to challenge our preconceptions of what cinema can or should be.

Bib: Angela Martin, 'Chantal Akerman's Films, A Dossier', in Charlotte Brunsdon (ed.), *Films for Women* (London, 1986).

Other Films: *Je joue à être une femme mariée/Playing at Being Married* [short] (1971); *La Chambre/The Bedroom, Hotel Monterey* (1972); *Hanging out – Yonkers, Le 15/8* [co-dir. Samy Szlingerbaum] (1973); *Dis-moi/Tell Me* [short] (1980); *Les Années 80/The Eighties, Un Jour Pina a demandé/One Day Pina Asked* [doc] (1983); *L'Homme à la valise/The Man with the Suitcase* [TV], *J'ai faim, J'ai froid/I'm Hungry, I'm Cold* [short for *Paris vu par ... vingt ans après*], *A Family Business* [short for Channel 4] (1984); *Le Marteau/The Hammer* [short video], *Mallet Stevens* (1986); *Letters Home* [video], *Sloth* [short for *Seven Women, Seven Sins*] (1987); *Trois strophes sur le nom de Sacher* [short video] (1988); *Le Déménagement/Moving* [short for *Monologues*] (1992); *D'Est* [doc]; *Portrait d'une jeune fille de la fin des années 60, à Bruxelles* (1993).

BOROWCZYK, Walerian — Kwilcz 1923

Polish director. Borowczyk studied fine art and worked in lithography and poster design before turning to animation. His first films, made with Jan Lenica, revealed a bizarre and dark vision with a satirical edge influenced by surrealism. The success of *Dom/House* (1958) launched his European career and in 1959 Borowczyk moved to France. Here his macabre wit came to the fore in films like *Renaissance* (1963). Switching to live action, Borowczyk made impressively original features, especially *Goto, l'île d'amour/Goto, Isle of Love* (1969) and *Blanche* (1971). Films such as *Contes immoraux/ Immoral Tales* (1974) and *La Bête/The Beast* (1975) established Borowczyk as something of an 'eroticist', but subsequent features moved to sexploitation, using material largely unworthy of his talents.

Other Films Include: *Les Jeux des anges* (1964, anim.); *Le Théâtre de Monsieur et Madame Kabal* (1967, anim.); *Dzieje Grzechu/Story of a Sin* (1975); *La Marge* (1976).

BREL, Jacques

Brussels 1929 – Bobigny, France 1978

Belgian singer, actor and director. Known internationally for his singing and, later, his acting, Brel also directed two films in his native Belgium.

Brel's poetic songs expressed his revolt against the bourgeois world, or paid homage to Belgium. When he gave up singing for acting in 1966, he brought the same sense of intensity and tragedy to films by such directors as Marcel Carné* and André Cayatte (in the latter's *Les Risques du métier/The Risks of the Job*, 1967, he was a schoolteacher accused of raping a pupil), though he also played a comic part in Edouard Molinaro's successful *L'Emmerdeur* (1973), remade in Hollywood as *Buddy, Buddy* (1981). In 1972 Brel directed (and starred in) his first film, *Franz*, a tragi-comic love story. Despite good reviews, *Franz* failed at the box office. Brel's next film, *Le Far West* (1973), was a comedy about two men who play at being cowboys at weekends. Although it represented Belgium at Cannes in 1973 and starred Lino Ventura* and Michel Piccoli*, *Le Far West* was criticised for its portrayal of American Indians. Brel retired from film-making after these two discouraging attempts.

BUÑUEL, Luis

Luis Buñuel Portolés; Calanda, Teruel 1900 – Mexico City, Mexico 1983

Spanish director of international standing who worked in Spain, France and Mexico. Buñuel's first films, *Un chien andalou* (1929) and *L'Âge d'or* (1930), were made in Paris with Salvador Dalí (though the latter's input on *L'Âge d'or* was minimal). Both masterpieces of Surrealist cinema, they established Buñuel as a key figure of the European avant-garde. They revealed his taste for shocking images (such as an eye being slit by a razor blade), as well as anti-clerical and anti-bourgeois provocations which would reverberate throughout his entire *oeuvre*. His first Spanish film, *Las Hurdes/Land Without Bread* (1932), however, was a grim documentary on poverty in rural Extremadura. In the last years of the Republic, Buñuel produced and partially directed a handful of films for one of Spain's more liberal production companies, Filmófono.

Following the Nationalists' victory in the Civil War (1939), Buñuel left for America but moved to Mexico in 1947 after failing to make headway in Hollywood. His Mexican films included popular melodramas such as *Susana* (1950) and *El bruto/The Brute* (1952) and more personal works like *Los Olvidados/The Dispossessed/The Young and the Damned* (1950), *El/This Strange Passion* (1952) and *Nazarín* (1958), which re-established his international reputation. Buñuel went back to Spain for *Viridiana* (1961, Palme d'or at Cannes), but the film was banned there as blasphemous. Though he would later return to Spain to film *Tristana* (1970) and parts of *Cet obscur objet du désir/ That Obscure Object of Desire* (1977), Buñuel spent the postwar years in Mexico and France where, in the 1960s and 1970s, he made a series of caustic, witty and elegant films in collaboration with scriptwriter Jean-Claude Carrière and producer Serge Silberman. *Le Journal d'une femme de chambre/Diary of a Chambermaid* (1963), *Belle de jour* (1966) and *Le Charme discret de la bourgeoisie/The Discreet Charm of the Bourgeoisie* (1972), starring the likes of Jeanne Moreau*, Catherine Deneuve*, Stéphane Audran* and Fernando Rey, represent both the best of Buñuel's second French career and an important strand of the European art cinema* of the time.

Despite Buñuel's geographically split career, strong continuities appear: all his films are marked by a fascination with Surrealism, especially in its exploration of the poetry of dreams, desire and *amour fou*, and imbued with a desire for release from childhood repression. The Surrealists, the Marquis de Sade – his 'master' – along with major figures from Spanish culture (above all, the picaresque writers, Goya, Galdós and Valle-Inclán) were his key inspirations. At the same time, an early interest in Marxism prompted his repeated exposures of social injustice. Although in a sense *sui generis*, Buñuel's films are indebted to German Expressionism and Italian neo-realism as well as to popular Mexican and Spanish melodrama. His obsessions (religion, the bourgeoisie, marginalised individuals, sexual desire) are expressed in ways that explore the limits of experience without sacrificing tolerant understanding of human folly, though they are not always free from misogyny. Buñuel films, however, are graced with a distinctive brand of corrosive wit and sardonic humour.

Bib: Peter William Evans, *The Films of Luis Buñuel: Subjectivity and Desire* (1994).

Other Films Include: *Subida al Cielo/Mexican Bus Ride* (1951, Mex.); *Ensayo de un crimen/The Criminal Life of Archibaldo de la Cruz (1955, Mex.); La Mort en ce jardin/La muerte en este jardín/Death in the Garden* (1956, Fr./Mex.); *El angel exterminador/The Exterminating Angel* (1962, Mex.); *Simón del desierto/Simon of the Desert* (1965, Mex.); *La Voie lactée/The Milky Way* (1969, Fr./It.); *Le Fantôme de la liberté/The Phantom of Liberty* (1974, Fr.).

CAVALCANTI, Alberto

Rio de Janeiro, Brazil 1897 – Paris, France 1982

British/Brazilian director. Educated in law in Brazil, and in art in Geneva, Cavalcanti became an art director in Paris in the 1920s, associating himself with the avant-garde art movement, and particularly with Surrealism. His first major film was *Rien que les heures* (1926), a 'city film' which anticipated Walther Ruttmann's *Berlin: Symphony of a Great City* (1927). In 1934 he was invited by John Grierson to join the GPO Film Unit, to which he brought a concern with technical innovation and experiment that often ran counter to Grierson's more social reformist agenda. Relations between the two were strained. Harry Watt, however, credits him with training his generation of documentary film-makers: 'I believe fundamentally,' he said, 'that the arrival of Cavalcanti in the GPO Film Unit was the turning point of British documentary.' Cavalcanti's best known directed films with the Unit, *Pett and Pott* (1934) and *Coal Face* (1935), are distinctive in their intricate editing of sound and image, and his productions (for which he also supervised sound) include *Night Mail* (1936), *North Sea* (1938) and *Spare Time* (1939).

Cavalcanti left the Grierson group when it became the Crown Film Unit and joined Ealing Studios, where he directed two of the studio's best films of the early 1940s, *Went the Day Well?* (1942) and the 'Ventriloquist's Dummy' episode of *Dead of Night* (1945). But his real importance at Ealing was in training and developing new directors like Robert Hamer, Charles Frend and Charles Crichton, and in production. Michael Balcon credits Cavalcanti with a special role in establishing the 'trademark' of Ealing: 'The whole of the Ealing output had a certain stamp on it. Whether I would have done it on my own I don't know. But most certainly I acknowledge ... that of all the help I got his is the help that was most important.' From 1949, Cavalcanti divided his time between Brazil, where he founded the Brazilian Film Institute; Europe, where he directed in Britain, France, Italy, Austria and Romania; and the US, where he taught at UCLA.

Other Films Include: *Le Train sans yeux* (1925, Fr.); *La P'tite Lilie* (1927, Fr.); *La Jalousie du barbouillé* (1928, Fr.); *Le Petit Chaperon rouge* (1929, Fr.); *Coralie et Cie* (1933, Fr.); *We Live in Two Worlds, The Line to Tschierva Hut* (1937); *The Chiltern Country* (1938); *La Cause commune* [made in UK for showing in France] (1940); *Champagne Charlie, Trois Chansons de la résistance/Soup Before Sunrise* [made in UK for Free French Army] (1944); *Nicholas Nickleby, They Made Me a Fugitive* (1947); *Simão o coalho/Simon the One-Eyed* (1952, Brazil); *Herr Puntila und sein Knecht Matti* (1955, Aus.); *La Prima notte* (1958, It.); *Thus Spake Theodor Herzl* (1967, Israel).

FERRERI, Marco Milan 1928

Italian director who also worked in Spain and France. In Italy, Ferreri began working in advertising and film production and then experimented with newsreels. While selling film equipment in Spain, he met the comedy writer Rafael Azcona, who was to contribute to many of his films. Two of his features became milestones of the Spanish cinema: *El pisito/The Little Flat* (1958) and *El cochecito/The Wheelchair* (1960). Anticipating the black humour of Luis García Berlanga's films, *El pisito* shows a young couple postponing their wedding until they find a flat. Out of desperation, the young man (José Luis López Vázquez) marries an aged woman, hoping for her early death. Marriage, however, revitalises the old woman and the young couple's plans are frustrated. *El cochecito* covers a similarly grotesque territory.

Ferreri split the rest of his career between Italy and France, producing one of the most original and disturbing bodies of work of the European art cinema* of the 1960s and 1970s, a startling blend of socio-political critique (sex, consumerism, alienation), black humour and misogyny. *Una storia moderna: l'ape regina/The Conjugal Bed* (1963) ends with Ugo Tognazzi reduced to a wheelchair by women's sexuality. Ferreri reflected on male obsessions in *Break-up* (1965, uncensored version released 1969); in *Dillinger è morto/Dillinger is Dead* (1969), he portrayed a fetishistic and alienated world. His attention focused increasingly on changing sexual roles, culminating in *L'ultima donna/The Last Woman* (1976), where Gérard Depardieu*, in a celebrated scene, emasculates himself with an electric knife (as a response to feminism). Undoubtedly, though, Ferreri's 'scandalous' reputation rests principally on *La grande abbaffuta/La Grande bouffe* (1973), an allegory of the ravages of consumerism, in which a team of European stars (Marcello Mastroianni, Tognazzi, Philippe Noiret*, Michel Piccoli*) literally eat themselves to death. His films of the 1980s reflected the intellectual weariness both of Italy and of the director himself, who seemed to be simply pandering to an audience waiting to be provoked (*La carne*, 1991). However, with *La casa del sorriso* (1992), and above all *Diario di un vizio* (1993), Ferreri seems to have returned to his most scathing vein.

Other Films Include: *Los chicos* (1960); *Le italiane e l'amore* (1961, ep.); *La donna scimmia/The Ape Woman* (1963); *Controsesso* (1964, ep.); *Marcia nuziale* (1966); *L'harem* (1967); *L'udienza* (1971); *Liza/La cagna* (1972); *Touche pas la femme blanche* (1975); *Ciao maschio/Bye Bye Monkey, Il seme dell'uomo/The Seed of Man* (1978); *Chiedo asilo* (1979); *Storie di ordinaria follia* (1981); *Storia di Piera* (1983); *Il futuro è donna* (1984); *I Love You* (1986); *Come sono buoni i bianchi* (1987).

HOLLAND, Agnieszka

Warsaw 1948

Polish director and scriptwriter. Holland graduated from FAMU in Prague in 1971 and began her career as assistant to Krzysztof Zanussi on *Iluminacja/Illumination* (1973). A member of Andrzej Wajda's 'X' film unit, she was a prominent exponent of the 'cinema of moral unrest'. Her distinctive personal style, influenced by the Czech New Wave and reflecting strong political views, was evident from her first feature, *Aktorzy Prowincjonalni/Provincial Actors* (1979), which received the FIPRESCI (international film critics) award at Cannes. While Holland was not popularly perceived as a feminist in Poland, her *Kobieta Samotna/A Woman Alone* (1981), the story of a middle-aged postwoman, was critically acclaimed for its perceptive portrayal of women in Poland. She scripted several of Wajda's films, including *Człowiek z Żelaza/Man of Iron* (1981) and *Korczak/Korczak* (1990). Holland's international reputation failed to shield her from adverse repercussions for her pro-Solidarity stance, and she was forced to emigrate when martial law was imposed. Based in Paris since 1981, she is one of the few Polish directors to have forged a successful European career, with the commercial and critical successes of *Bittere Ernte/Angry Harvest* (1984, nominated for an Academy Award for Best Foreign Film) and *Europa, Europa* (1990). Her first wholly 'French' film, the intense *Olivier Olivier* (1991), is based on the true story of a young boy who disappears from home and is 'found' six years later wandering the streets of Paris, his true identity in question. For her first Hollywood production, *The Secret Garden* (1993), Holland joined forces with scriptwriter Caroline Thompson to adapt the popular British children's novel by Frances Hodgson Burnett.

Other Films Include: *Gorączka/Fever* (1980); *To Kill a Priest* (1988, US/Fr.); *Total Eclipse* [Fr./UK/Bel.], *Les Faux-monnayeurs* [Fr.] (1995).

HUILLET, Danièle
Born 1936

and

STRAUB, Jean-Marie
Metz 1933

French-born directors working in Germany. Huillet and Straub work as a co-scripting and co-directing team, their equal collaboration so close that it is scarcely meaningful to separate the roles (Huillet has, however, indicated that she tends to be in charge of sound and editing, while Straub does most of the camerawork). Huillet and Straub's work is modernist, oppositional, demanding – and rarely seen outside the film festival circuit. Their films have their roots in European (mostly German) high culture: literature (Brecht, Böll, Kafka) and music (Bach, Schoenberg) and are concerned with an exploration of history.

They are politically committed, sometimes explicitly, as in *Fortini/Cani* (1976), which reworks material about the Israeli-Palestinian conflict, but more often in the approach to their material. It is a cinema which is, in Maureen Turim's terms, 'theoretical, elliptical, innovative, and challenging'.

Feature Films: *Nicht versöhnt, oder Es hilft nur Gewalt, wo Gewalt herrscht/Not Reconciled* (1965); *Chronik der Anna Magdalena Bach/The Chronicle of Anna Magdalena Bach* (1968); *Othon (Les Yeux ne veulent pas en tout temps se fermer, ou Peut-être qu'un jour Rome se permettra de choisir à son tour)/Othon* (1969); *Geschichtsunterricht/History Lessons* (1972); *Moses und Aron/Moses and Aaron* (1975); *Dalla nube alla Resistenza/From the Cloud to the Resistance* (1979, It./Fr./Ger./UK); *Zu früh/Zu spät/Too Early Too Late* (1981, It.); *Klassenverhältnisse/Class Relations* (1984).

KIEŚLOWSKI, Krzysztof Warsaw 1941–1996

Polish director. A distinctive voice in Polish cinema, known for his uncompromising moral stance, Kieślowski first came to attention in the early 1970s for his incisive (often shelved) documentaries and shorts on the political reality of life in Poland. His features of the late 1970s explored the relationship between the personal and the political with style, directness and a raw edge of realism, making him a key figure in the 'cinema of moral unrest'. Although the authorities banned *Przypadek/Blind Chance* (1981), Kieślowski was undeterred and made *Bez Końca/No End* in 1984. In the late 1980s he turned to television, directing *Dekalog*, a series of ten films thematically inspired by the Ten Commandments. The international release of one of these, *Krótki Film o Zabijaniu/A Short Film About Killing* (1988), and the subsequent massive success of the whole series, was greeted with surprise by Polish critics, who compared *Dekalog* unfavourably with Kieślowski's earlier work. His next feature, *Podwójne Życie Weroniki/The Double Life of Véronique* (1992), was a co-production between the Tor Film Unit and French producers; it enjoyed critical and commercial success, especially in France. Kieślowski's latest (and according to him, last) work is a trilogy based on the French flag: 'liberty' (*Trois couleurs Bleu/Three Colours: Blue*, 1993), 'equality' (*Trois couleurs Blanc/ Three Colours: White*, 1993) and 'fraternity' (*Trois couleurs: Rouge/ Three Colours: Red*, 1994). They have secured for Kieślowski – hailed as 'the most truly European director' – a place in the pantheon of European art cinema*.

Bib: Danusia Stok, *Kieślowski on Kieślowski* (1993).

LITVAK, Anatole

Kiev, Russia 1902 – Neuilly-sur-Seine, France 1974

Russian-born director, whose international career took him to Germany, the UK, the US (he became an American citizen) and France. Litvak's French films show his remarkable ability to adapt to indigenous genres. His *Coeur de Lilas* (1931) is an atmospheric populist tale set in the Parisian 'lower depths' (with Jean Gabin*), which prefigures Poetic Realism*. With *L'Equipage* (1935) and *Mayerling* (1936), both 'women's melodramas', he made two of the most successful French films of the 1930s. Among his many Hollywood credits are remakes of his own *L'Equipage* as *The Woman I Love* (1937) and of Marcel Carné's* *Le Jour se lève* (1939) as *The Long Night* (1947), as well as the *noir* thriller *Sorry, Wrong Number* (1948). He made large-scale international productions such as *The Night of the Generals* (1967, UK); his last film was a French thriller, *La Dame dans l'auto avec des lunettes et un fusil/The Lady in the Car with Glasses and a Gun* (1970).

MOSJOUKINE [MOZZHUKHIN], Ivan I.

Penza, Russia 1890 – Neuilly-sur-Seine, France 1939

Russian actor. After studying law Mosjoukine began acting, first in theatre and then from 1911 in comic roles in films such as *Domik v Kolomne/The House at Kolomna* (1913). He began playing lead roles in Yevgeni Bauer's films for Alexander Khanzhonkov, such as *Zhizn' v smerti/Life in Death* (1914), in which he first shed the 'Mosjoukine tears' that became his hallmark. After a disagreement with Bauer over casting, Mosjoukine left to make films for the rival Yermolev company under the direction of Yakov Protazanov, frequently playing distraught demonic characters caught between duty and (usually) secret passion: *Nikolai Stavrogin*, *Chaika/The Seagull* and *Ya i moya sovest'/I and My Conscience* (all 1915), *Vo vlasti grekha/In the Realm of Sin*, *Pikovaya dama/The Queen of Spades* (one of his greatest popular successes), *Plyaska smerti/The Dance of Death* and *Sud Bozhii/Divine Judgment* (all 1916), *Prokuror/The State Prosecutor*, *Satana likuyushchii/Satan Triumphant* and *Malyutka Elli/Little Ellie* (all 1917), and *Otets Sergii/Father Sergius* (1918). The effectiveness of Mosjoukine's performances depended on his ability to communicate psychological states through expression and gesture, and this gave rise to the term the 'Mosjoukine style of screen acting', whose elements he himself attempted to define. He left Russia for France with Protazanov in 1920, starring in *Justice d'abord/Justice First* (1921, released in the USSR in 1923 as *Sluga slepogo dolga/The Servant of Blind Duty*), *L'Angoissante aventure/The Agonising Adventure* (1923, which he co-scripted) and *Le Brasier ardent*, which he directed himself and which is supposed to have persuaded Jean Renoir* to 'forget ceramics and try his hand at cinema'. He attempted to relaunch his career in Hollywood, then in Germany and again in France, but his later films never achieved the success that he had enjoyed earlier in Russia.

OPHULS, Max

Max Oppenheimer; Saarbrucken 1902 – Hamburg 1957

German director (sometimes spelt Ophüls; in the US occasionally Opuls). After a ten-year career in the theatre and in radio Ophuls joined Ufa in 1931. His breakthrough came with the international success of *Liebelei* (1933; also French version, *Liebelei une Histoire d'amour*), based on a play by Arthur Schnitzler. Identified with Viennese charm and bitter-sweet world-weariness, Ophuls tried to extend his range after emigrating to Paris in 1933. Proving extremely versatile in putting together unlikely projects, between 1934 and 1940 he directed French, Italian, Dutch and English-language films, most of them exquisite evocations of a world of lost illusions, such as *La signora di tutti* (1934, It.) and *La Tendre ennemie* (1936, Fr.). Ophuls became a French citizen in 1938; nevertheless, he fled to America in 1941, but was unable to realise a film project until 1947. His first Hollywood film starred Douglas Fairbanks Jr. (*The Exile*, 1947), but he has become especially known for his three classic 'women's pictures', *Letter from an Unknown Woman* (1948), *Caught* (1949) and *The Reckless Moment* (1949), produced respectively for Universal, MGM and Columbia.

At the end of the 1940s Ophuls returned to Paris where he enjoyed a *succès de scandale* with *La Ronde* (1950), his second Schnitzler adaptation. Following *Madame de …/The Earrings of Madame de …* (1953), featuring Danielle Darrieux*, he was commissioned to direct the French-German co-production *Lola Montès* (1955, with Martine Carol*), thought a failure at the time but now considered his masterpiece. Ophuls' stylistic trademarks are his intricate and extensive camera movements, functionally relating decor and music to the protagonists, and his films combine wit and an undaunted romanticism. His son Marcel Ophuls (born Frankfurt 1927) was his assistant on *Lola Montès* and himself became an international film-maker; he is especially noted for his remarkable *Le Chagrin et la pitié/The Sorrow and the Pity* (1971), a ground-breaking documentary on the complex, compromised and ambivalent attitudes of French people in a provincial town during the German occupation. He pursued the German occupation theme in *Hôtel Terminus/The Life and Times of Klaus Barbie* (1988, Fr.), on the Nazi war criminal Klaus Barbie.

Bib: Max Ophuls, *Spiel im Dasein* (1963); Paul Willemen (ed.), *Ophuls* (1978).

Other Films Include: *Dann schon lieber Lebertran* (1931, Ger.); *Die verliebte Firma, Die verkaufte Braut/The Bartered Bride* (1932, Ger.); *Lachenden Erben* (1933, Ger.); *On a volé un homme* (1934, Fr.); *Divine* (1935, Fr.); *Komedie om geld/A Comedy About Money* (1936, Neth.); *Yoshiwara* (1937, Fr.); *Le Roman de Werther/Werther* (1938, Fr.); *Sans lendemain* (1940, Fr.); *De Mayerling à Sarajévo* (1940, Fr.); *Le Plaisir* (1952, Fr.).

OTSEP, Fyodor A. [OZEP, Fédor] Moscow 1895 – Ottawa, Canada 1949

Russian director and scriptwriter. Coming to the cinema in 1916, Otsep jointly wrote scripts for a number of films, including *Polikushka* (1919), *Papirosnitsa iz Mosselproma/The Cigarette Girl from Mosselprom* and Yakov Protazanov's *Aelita* (both 1924), *Kollezhskii registrator/The Station Master* (1925) and *Kukla s millionami/The Girl with the Millions* (1928). He directed the serial thriller *Miss Mend* (1926), *Zemlya v plenu/Earth in Captivity* (1928) and the Russo-German co-production of Tolstoy's *Zhivoi trup/The Living Corpse* (1929), after which he stayed in Germany, making *Der Mörder Dimitri Karamasoff/The Brothers Karamazov* (1931) as well as its French version *Les Frères Karamazoff* (also 1931). After the Nazis came to power he moved to France, where, under the name of Fédor Ozep, he contributed to the popular genre of exotic melodrama, making the French and German versions of *Mirages de Paris/Großtadtnacht/Mirages of Paris* (1932), the Zweig adaptation *Amok* (1934), *La Dame de pique/The Queen of Spades* (1937), *Gibraltar/It Happened in Gibraltar*, and *Tarakanova/Betrayal* and its Italian version *La principessa Tarakanova* (all 1938). Interned as a displaced person, he was freed after the fall of France and fled to North America. He made his last film, *La Forteresse/Whispering City*, in Canada in 1947.

POLANSKI, Roman Raymond Polanski; Paris, France 1933

Polish director. Perhaps the most famous expatriate Polish film-maker. Polanski's international success, as well as his tragic and infamous private life, have been well documented. Polanski first made shorts, including the much noticed *Dwaj Ludzie z Szafą/Two Men and a Wardrobe* (1958). He shot to fame with his feature debut *Nóż w Wodzie/Knife in the Water* (1962), making the cover of *Time* magazine as the face of new foreign cinema. Subsequently moving to the West, he consolidated his promise with *Repulsion* (1965) and *Cul-de-Sac* (1966), both made in Britain, before moving on to Hollywood. Polanski nonetheless maintained his connection to Poland; his association with composer Krzysztof Komeda continued up to his first Hollywood success, *Rosemary's Baby* (1968), and he often uses Polish cinematographers. Versatile and idiosyncratic, his best work is characterised by his ability to look at the dark side of human nature with a sharp irony and a sense of the absurd. His Hollywood success continued with *Chinatown* (1974), starring Jack Nicholson and Faye Dunaway, but was then cut short when Polanski's private life was brought under legal scrutiny; he moved to France in 1977 to avoid prosecution by US courts. Polanski's European films have ranged from a successful adaptation of Thomas Hardy's classic novel *Tess of the d'Urbervilles* (*Tess*, 1979), through the Hitchcockian overtones of *Frantic* (1988), to the commercial failure of his comedy romp on the high seas, *Pirates* (1986). *Lunes de fiel/Bitter Moon* (1992) refers back to Polanski's earlier work, with echoes of *Nóz w Wodzie* in a tale of sexual obsession. In 1994, he directed *Death and the Maiden*, starring Sigourney Weaver and Ben Kingsley. Polanski continues to make acting contributions in his own films and others, including, recently, *Grosse fatigue* and *Une pure formalité*, the latter co-starring Gérard Depardieu* (both 1994, Fr.).

RUIZ, Raúl — Puerto Montt, Chile 1941

Chilean director working in Europe, based in France since 1973. Ruiz briefly studied theology and tried playwriting before composing scripts for Mexican and Chilean television. His first feature, *Los tres tristes tigres/Three Sad Tigers* (1968), won the Grand Prix at the Locarno film festival, immediately establishing his reputation. His European work, ranging from Portugal to Sicily and the Netherlands, has promoted him to the status of a cult art-film director. His eclectic, ironic films display great imagination, combining realism with fantasy and narratives of exile with popular entertainment; they have elicited from critics terms such as 'baroque', 'surrealist' and 'postmodern', their *mise-en-scène* drawing on non-naturalistic techniques, with frequent use of filters, mirrors and disorienting camera angles. Among his prolific output, better-known titles include *L'Hypothèse du tableau volé/The Hypothesis of the Stolen Painting* (1978), *Território/Le Territoire/The Territory* (1981), *Le Tôit de la baleine/On Top of the Whale* (1982), *La Ville des pirates/City of Pirates* (1983), *L'Île au trésor/Treasure Island* (1986–90), *L'Oeil qui ment/Dark at Noon* (1992), and *Fado Majeur et Mineur* (1994). Ruiz also made a five-minute film in defence of Salman Rushdie, *The Dark Night of the Inquisitor* (1994). Confusingly but typically, he defines himself as 'a monomaniac with several manias'.

SCHNEIDER, Romy

Rosemarie Albach-Retty; Vienna 1938 – Paris 1982

Austrian-born actress. The daughter of actors Wolf Albach-Retty and Magda Schneider, the beautiful Romy Schneider played her first role as her real mother's daughter in *Wenn der weiße Flieder wieder blüht* (1953, Ger.), the duo becoming the most popular film couple of 1950s German-speaking cinema. Schneider also enjoyed popular success as Queen Victoria in *Mädchenjahre einer Königin* (1954), but Ernst Marischka's 'Sissi' trilogy – *Sissi* (1955), *Sissi – die junge Kaiserin* (1956) and *Sissi –Schicksalsjahre einer Kaiserin* (1957) – in which she played the romanticised Empress Elizabeth of Austria, turned her into a mass icon. Disparaged by critics, the movies enjoyed huge popular acclaim throughout Europe, and helped consolidate a particular Austrian image by quoting the country's myths (the scenery, the Habsburg dynasty, Viennese waltzes ...). After appearing in two successful remakes – *Mädchen in Uniform* and *Christine* – in 1958, she moved to France. Against the wishes of producers and audiences, she distanced herself from the Sissi image and embarked on a career as a serious character actress (successfully, except in Germany). In the 1960s and 1970s she worked in international art cinema, with Luchino Visconti, Orson Welles (*Le Procès/The Trial*, 1962), Joseph Losey (*L'Assassinat de Trotsky/The Assassination of Trotsky*, 1972), but especially in France, mostly with Claude Sautet*. In Sautet's *Les Choses de la vie/The Things of Life* (1970), *César et Rosalie* (1972) and *Mado* (1976) among other films, she portrayed, alongside actors like Michel Piccoli* and Yves Montand*, 'modern' women, though her characters' emancipation was limited to sexuality and usually ended in compromise. She reached the height of her international career in Visconti's *Ludwig* (1972), portraying a mature, hard Elizabeth who had nothing in common with the Sissi of the earlier films. Her relationship with her native country and its history was ambivalent and she appeared in several films critical of fascism, including *La Passante du Sans-Souci/Die Spaziergängerin von Sans-Souci* (1982, Fr./Ger.), her last film. Schneider was for long an object of gossip press speculation, especially at the time of her liaison with Alain Delon* (with whom she appeared in, among other films, *La Piscine/The Swimming Pool*, 1968), but she became a much-liked actress in France, eliciting popular sympathy especially for the tragic death of her son.

Bib: Michael Jürgs, *Der Fall Romy Schneider: Eine Biographie* (1991).

Other Films Include: *Robinson soll nicht sterben* (1957); *Katia* (1959); *The Cardinal* (1963, US); *What's New Pussycat* (1965); *Le Train* (1973, Fr./It.); *Le Trio infernal* [Fr./It./Ger.], *L'Important c'est d'aimer* (1974, Fr.); *Le Vieux fusil* (1975. Fr.); *Gruppenbild mit Dame* (1977, Ger.); *La Mort en direct/Deathwatch* (1979, Fr.); *La Banquière* (1980, Fr.).

SIODMAK, Robert

Dresden 1900 – Locarno, Switzerland 1973

German director, who first made his mark as co-director of the feature documentary *Menschen am Sonntag/People on Sunday* (1930) with Edgar G. Ulmer. Siodmak went on to direct feature films at Ufa, among them one of the earliest German sound films, *Abschied* (1930). After the completion of *Brennendes Geheimnis/The Burning Secret* (1933), adapted from a novella by Stefan Zweig, Siodmak was forced into exile, first to France, where he had the most prolific career of all the German émigrés, making a number of seminal *noir* movies, especially *Le Chemin de Rio* (1937), *Mollenard* (1938) and *Pièges* (1939), as well as outstanding musicals like *La Crise est finie* (1934) and *La Vie parisienne* (1935).

Late in 1938, Siodmak moved to Hollywood, and directed a succession of B-pictures and atmospherically charged psychological thrillers for Universal, which count among the key examples of American *film noir*: *Phantom Lady* (1944), *The Spiral Staircase* (1945), *The Killers* (1946). Siodmak returned to Europe, directing various and variable films in France, Britain and, from 1954, Germany, but in 1957 he once more conjured up, with *Nachts, wenn der Teufel kam/The Devil Strikes at Night*, about a mentally disturbed mass-murderer, his skill as the 'master of *film noir*'.

Bib: Hervé Dumont, *Robert Siodmak: Le Maître du film noir* (1981).

Other Films Include: *Der Kampf mit dem Drachen oder: Die Tragödie des Untermieters* (1930); *Der Mann, der seinen Mörder sucht* (1931); *Voruntersuchung* (1931); *Stürme der Leidenschaft/The Tempest* (1932); *Quick, König der Clowns* (1932); *West Point Widow* (1941, US); *Son of Dracula* (1943, US); *The Suspect* (1944, US); *The Dark Mirror* (1946, US); *Time out of Mind* (1947, US); *Cry of the City* (1948, US); *Criss Cross, The Great Sinner* (1949, both US); *Die Ratten* (1955).

2. Key European cinema concepts, genres and institutions

This section gathers entries which I commissioned for the *Encyclopedia of European Cinema* on pan-European concepts, genres and institutions. They are included here as a useful and relevant background to the information contained in all the preceding sections. The authors of these entries are named at the end of each one of them.

AVANT-GARDE CINEMA IN EUROPE

From our present postmodern vantage point, the concept of the avant-garde might appear as simultaneously archaic and elitist, now that it is behind us historically and seemingly beyond us politically. Two factors recur: the relationship of film to the other arts, and of aesthetics to politics, with the term 'avant-garde' breaking into the following registers of aspiration – experimentation and abstraction, independence and opposition.

Soviet montage, German expressionism, French impressionism [> FRENCH AVANT-GARDE] and surrealism are traditionally considered the 'historical avant-gardes' of European cinema and the overlap of film with fine arts is characteristic of each of these founding moments. At its most militantly innovative and highly theorised in the work of Sergei Eisenstein and Dziga Vertov, Soviet montage was wrought from the combination of a modernist consciousness of the revolutionary moment – 1917, Bolshevism – and a fertile cross-pollination of film with Constructivist design, Futurist sound poetry and Suprematist experimentation with form. In France, impressionism and surrealism lacked the political impetus of the Soviets, but endorsed cinema as the manifestation of the Wagnerian idea of the *Gesamtkunstwerk*, the means of synthesising all the arts in the new, unique art of film, termed by Ricciotto Canudo* 'the seventh art'.

The encounter between film and the fine arts has persistently characterised the abstract tendency of the European avant-garde. And while recent work in video-art can be seen as maintaining this tradition, it might equally be seen in the Structuralist/Materialist films of the 1970s. Malcolm Le Grice, one of the leading British exponents of such work, has identified abstract work as taking place as early as 1910–12 in the experiments of Bruno Corra and Arnaldo Ginna. Corra's theoretical text, *Abstract Cinema – Chromatic Music*, serves as an early indication of the enduring tendency in abstract film to seek aesthetic alliances with painting and music. This example predates the work of abstract animators Walther Ruttmann, Viking Eggeling, Hans Richter and Oskar Fischinger, often seen as inaugurating this aesthetic tendency. Richter gave perhaps the best summary of the abstract film position when he wrote: 'Problems in modern art lead directly into the film. The connection to theatre and literature was completely severed. Cubism, Expressionism, Dadaism, Abstract Art, Surrealism found not only their expression in film, but a new fulfilment on a new level.'

Two words serve to encapsulate the motivation of this first, historical phase of the European avant-garde: silence and 'specificity'. It is noticeable that this experimental phase ended with the coming of sound. While for the Soviet directors this can in part be attributed to Stalin's cultural policies of the late 1920s and early 1930s, the termination was also informed by the anti-realist agendas common to all the avant-gardes, with sound representing a decisively realist 'supplement' to the image. The change in the mode of production from the artisanal/patronage-based one enjoyed by the avant-garde to the labour and capital intensive base demanded by the new sound cinema also had a part to play in the end of the silent avant-gardes. The search for cinematic 'specificity' was polemical and separatist on the one hand – against theatrical and narrative models – synthesising and hybridising on the other, with models from painting and music.

The notion of the avant-garde in film was constructed around the idea of its oppositional status vis-à-vis the established cinematic order both generally and specifically in European cinema. This tendency can be defined in terms either of opposition or of independence, the former being predicated along militant political lines, the latter a means of constructing an alternative space for independent production, distribution and exhibition. This taxonomy works usefully in respect of the works of the 1960s and 1970s that best illustrate the bifurcation of European avant-garde practice into what Peter Wollen christened in 1975 'the Two Avant-Gardes', one concerned with a politically oriented 'politics of form', the other with a formalist 'politics of perception'. The strand of European practice that came to be known as Counter-Cinema, while having its immediate origins in the political revolt of May 1968 in France, nevertheless took its conceptual and asthetic leads from a longer European tradition of radical, oppositional aesthetic practices, drawing on ideas from Brechtian dramaturgy – distanciation, the *Verfremdungseffekt* – and lauding Vertov over Eisenstein in the 'second discovery' of Soviet cinema of the mid- to late 1960s. While Jean-Luc Godard* is most commonly associated with the counter-cinematic turning away from what he dubbed 'the Hollywood-Mosfilm' and towards a didactic cinema of '*films tableaux noirs*' (blackboard films), he was by no means alone in opting for this radical strategy. Chris Marker* in France, Rainer Werner Fassbinder and Werner Schroeter in Germany, Věra Chytilová in Czechoslovakia and Dušan Makavejev in Yugoslavia experimented with a Brechtian challenge to narrative transparency against the perceived stylistic – hence ideological – hegemony of Hollywood cinema.

The other more Formalist/Structuralist-Materialist strand of avant-garde film-making rooted itself in an opposition to conventional narrative that owed much to the abstract cinema of the 1920s, although it might be said that the master-text of both the Structuralist-Materialist and counter-cinematic movements of the 1960s and 1970s remains Vertov's remarkable *Chelovek s kinoapparatom/The Man with the Movie Camera* (1929). The Co-op movements of the 1970s, particularly the London Film-makers Co-op, represented the pursuit of a radical, independent practice both aesthetically and institutionally. Film-makers such as Malcolm Le Grice and Peter Gidal participated in a cinema of minimal effects concerned with the material properties of film – grain, emulsion, flicker, qualities of light – and in the spectatorial experience, experimenting with duration and performance-art styled interventions during projection. This strand arguably had more in common with the North American and Canadian avant-garde of Brakhage, Sharits and Snow than with the militancy of European counter-cinema. Godard himself attempted, in *Tout va bien* (1972), a Brechtian cinema-with-stars (Jane Fonda and Yves Montand*), while other art cinema directors such as Yvonne Rainer and Chantal Akerman* employed avant-garde strategies to question the sexual politics of cinematic representation, notably in Akerman's *Jeanne Dielman 23 Quai du Commerce 1080 Bruxelles* (1975), with its experimentation with duration.

With the advent of video technologies in the mid-1960s one would have imagined a revival of the European avant-gardes. However, in the hands of Godard and Marker, video has been used as a means of thinking cinema and of expressing an analytic relationship with the image. Marker's *Sans soleil/Sunless* (1983) and Godard's *Scénario du film Passion* (1982) are most representative of this application of video, the Marker film also being an eloquent piece of mourning-work for the lost illusions of 1960s political radicalism and so-called 'guerrilla film-making', while fully and euphorically exploiting the possibilities of video. European video-art *per se* has yet to achieve the international visibility of North American and Canadian video-artists such as Bill Viola, Gary Hill and Nam June Paik. However, the avant-garde has been – and, in the example of video-art, remains – an international, exportable phenomenon that cuts across both national, cultural and artistic boundaries, addressing a wide set of disparate art/film constituencies, in contrast to European popular cinemas that remain more firmly embedded in specific national traditions and hence export less effectively. (Chris Darke)

Bib: Peter Wollen, 'The Two Avant-Gardes', in *Readings and Writings: Semiotic Counter-Strategies* (1982).

EMIGRATION AND EUROPEAN CINEMA

The phenomenon of emigration both within Europe and from Europe greatly affected the cinema throughout its first century. Social factors (poverty and racism, especially anti-semitism) and historical events such as wars, revolutions and totalitarian regimes drove people from their home countries, usually west, towards Germany and the Netherlands, then France and the UK, and massively to the US. Economic and cultural factors specific to the film industry have also repeatedly drawn European film personnel to North America. There has been a small movement in the opposite direction, with American directors such as Joseph Losey and Jules Dassin, and stars like Eddie Constantine* and Paul Robeson making a career in Europe.

Many Hollywood pioneers and movie moguls came from central Europe. Subsequently, Hollywood attracted film people who went either of their own volition or as a result of the studios' systematic policies of talent-scouting. Some made a first or second career there (Charlie Chaplin, Mihály Kertész [Michael Curtiz], Jean Negulescu [Negulesco], Ernst Lubitsch, Greta Garbo, Ingrid Bergman, Douglas Sirk [Detlef Sierck*]) while for others Hollywood was a – more or less extended and more or less successful – episode: Victor Sjöström, Mauritz Stiller, Max Ophuls*, Fritz Lang, René Clair*, Julien Duvivier*, Jean Renoir*, S. M. Eisenstein, Louis Malle*, Nestor Almendros* and many others. The country most affected has been Germany. While directors, actors, scriptwriters, art directors and cameramen were forced to leave Germany when the Nazis came to power in 1933, others had already left. Those tempted, apart from Lubitsch, Sirk and Lang, included F. W. Murnau, William Dieterle, E. A. Dupont, Paul Leni, Ludwig Berger, Emil Jannings, Marlene Dietrich, Robert Siodmak*, Pola Negri, Lya de Putti, Erich Pommer, Carl Mayer, Karl Freund, Joe May, Richard Oswald, Otto Preminger, Billy Wilder and Reinhold Schünzel. From 1 April 1933, Jews were systematically excluded from public life in Germany and consequently almost a third of Germany's film industry personnel fled to neighbouring countries and the US. France and Britain were especially important for émigré film-makers, since their film industries were then experiencing a period of dramatic growth. Consequently, producers like Pommer, Seymour Nebenzal and Alexander Korda set up new production companies which provided work for fellow émigrés. Between 1933 and 1940, Lang, Siodmak, Ophuls, Kurt Bernhardt, G. W. Pabst, Anatole Litvak* and others made nearly fifty films in France, including box-office hits such as *Mayerling* (1936), *Carrefour* (1938) and *Pièges* (1939), while in Britain Korda and Max Schach produced highly successful costume films for the international market.

Most émigrés resettled in the US, though few of those who arrived in Hollywood between 1933 and 1938 had a studio contract. After 1938–39, the number of refugees to the US increased dramatically. Altogether, about 500 German film-makers lived in Hollywood. In the 1920s–30s the German émigrés in Hollywood worked on films with a 'European flavour' and from the early 1940s film-makers such as Wilder, Siodmak and Lang contributed greatly to the development of *film noir* with such films as *Double Indemnity* (1944), *Phantom Lady* (1944), *Scarlet Street* (1945) and many others. German émigrés are also known for the sub-genre of the anti-Nazi film, of which about 180 were produced between 1939 and 1945 in the US, transmitting an anti-fascist message in traditional genre films such as spy thrillers (*Confessions of a Nazi Spy*, 1939), melodramas (*The Mortal Storm*, 1940) and comedies (*To Be or Not to Be*, 1942). In addition, German actors and their accents were much sought-after, ironically often to play Nazis (or their victims) in anti-Nazi films; Schünzel, Peter Lorre* and Conrad Veidt were particularly successful in this respect. Only a handful of film-makers returned to Germany after World War II; most had settled permanently in the US and, furthermore, the German film industry was still run by those who had been successful in the Third Reich. Though it is impossible to speculate on what might have happened otherwise, there is no doubt that German film production suffered incalculably from this drain of talented film personnel.

Less visible because of the shared language has been the drain from the British film industry. Among the most famous British émigrés (or British personnel who worked substantially in Hollywood), apart from Chaplin, are: Julie Andrews, Cecil Beaton, Ronald Colman, Alfred Hitchcock, James Mason and David Niven. The important migrations mentioned above slowed down somewhat in the postwar period, as Hollywood itself went through a crisis and started investing in European productions [> EUROPEAN CINEMA AND HOLLYWOOD]. Since the 1980s, however, a renewed migration has taken place, with European film-makers seeking work abroad as their own national cinemas weaken; examples include Andrei Mikhalkov-Konchalovsky, Miloš Forman, George Sluizer, Wolfgang Petersen, Paul Verhoeven, Roman Polanski* and Bernardo Bertolucci, as well as actors such as Rutger Hauer.

During the same period many other film-makers have turned to France, following another long tradition. In the 1920s, the French cinematic avant-garde was international, with film-makers such as Alberto Cavalcanti*, Carl Theodor Dreyer and Luis Buñuel* among others [> FRENCH AVANT-GARDE; AVANT-GARDE CINEMA IN EUROPE]. A significant group of émigrés had already arrived from Russia in the wake of the October revolution. The old Pathé* studios in Montreuil became the centre of an active community. Iosif Yermolev [Joseph Ermolieff in France], an ex-Pathé employee, founded Ermolieff-film in 1920, with a team of prestigious directors including Yakov Protazanov [Jacob Protazanoff], Alexandre Volkov [Volkoff], Vjačelav Turžanskij [Victor Tourjansky], actor Ivan Mozzhukhin [Mosjoukine*], set designers and cinematographers. Yermolev produced a dozen films before leaving for Berlin in 1922, and Ermolieff-film became Les Films Albatros, specialising in literary adaptations of French and Russian classics, with emphasis on nostalgia and exoticism, and producing prestigious films by Marcel L'Herbier*, Jacques Feyder*, René Clair*, and others. Other firms, such as Ciné-France-Film, had a strong Russian contingent and produced French films, including Abel Gance's* *Napoléon* (1926) and Volkov's *Casanova* (1927, starring Mosjoukine). The Russian influence continued in the 1930s when personnel included directors Fyodor Otsep* [Fédor Ozep], Nicolas Farkas and Tourjansky and many others, as well as gifted cinematographers and set designers, generating the popular French genre of the 'Slav melodrama'. Lazare Meerson* revolutionised set design and taught other designers such as Alexander Trauner* and Georges Wakhevitch. New directors from Russia emerged, such as Litvak, and Władysław Starewicz [Ladislav Starevitch]. There were, during the same period, significant exchanges between France and Italy. Franco-Italian bilingual films were made, and several Italian directors worked in France: Mario Bonnard, Carmine Gallone and Augusto Genina.

Meanwhile, despite the threatening political climate, the attraction of better conditions in German studios remained strong, and French stars and directors became frequent travellers between Paris, Berlin and Munich. The coming of sound also contributed to the acceleration of cross-European journeys, with the making of multi-language versions by Ufa in Germany, Paramount in Paris and British International in London, between 1929 and 1932. Films were made in sometimes as many as a dozen versions (especially at Paramount) but more often in two or three, with German, French and English the most common languages, usually using the same decor but native stars (it was also at that time that Hollywood initiated the practice of remaking European films, especially French films, a phenomenon renewed with particular vigour in the 1980s and 1990s). As mentioned above, Paris in the 1930s also saw a major influx of German and central European personnel, the result of both economic and political emigration. During World War II, while some French film personnel left for Hollywood (Renoir, Duvivier, Jean Gabin*, Michèle Morgan* and others), French cinema lived in virtual autarchy.

In the postwar period, emigration to France took an individual character, with a wide range of personnel (Buñuel, Luis Mariano*, Roman Polanski*, Walerian Borowczyck*, Eddie Constantine*) working in Paris, though two strands can be detected. First, the intense programme of co-productions (especially with Italy) in the 1940s and 1950s brought many actors to France: Antonella Lualdi, Lea Massari, Gina Lollobrigida, Raf Vallone, Romy Schneider* and Maria Schell among others. Secondly, the combination of generous French aid and of the break-up of the Eastern block, has produced another wave of eastern Europeans in France, among them Andrzej Wajda, Krzysztof Kieślowski* and Otar Iosseliani, and, from other countries, directors such as Pedro Almodóvar and Manoel de Oliveira. No doubt the increasing 'Europeanisation' of European cinema, through co-productions and EU-backed projects, will further increase this transnational movement of personnel [> EUROPEAN COMMUNITY AND THE CINEMA]. (Ginette Vincendeau and Joseph Garncarz)

EUROPEAN ART CINEMA

We think we know what we mean by 'art cinema'. Yet in the European cinema of the 1990s, when directors as diverse in their preoccupations and styles as Krzysztof Kieślowski*, Leos Carax* and Pedro Almodóvar can be united by the same term, it would be more accurate to talk of 'art cinemas' to indicate the national and historical plurality concealed by the term. While being a means of defining and marketing a certain kind of European film, art cinema is also the institutional and aesthetic space into which the work of directors from beyond Europe has been integrated: for example, Kenji Mizoguchi from Japan, Satyajit Ray from India and, more recently, Zhang Yimou from China. Art cinema operates as a means of merging aesthetic and national 'difference', and of encouraging both.

Two moments can be loosely identified as having contributed to the formation of what Peter Lev calls 'a continuing impulse in film history', and to its association with Europe: the European avant-gardes of the 1920s and the New Waves that flourished from the late 1950s to the early 1970s [> NEW WAVE, AVANT-GARDE CINEMA IN EUROPE]. The first of these moments includes the schools of Soviet montage, surrealism, French impressionism [> FRENCH AVANT-GARDE] and German expressionism, all sharing a common search for creative and conceptual liaisons between the then silent medium and painting, music and poetry. In its earliest incarnation, then, art cinema implied an aesthetic project based in formal experimentation and innovation. Equally, as Steve Neale has observed, the concept of art cinema as an institutional space was developed by the national cinemas of Europe from the 1920s as 'attempts to counter both American domination of their indigenous markets in film and to foster a film industry and a film culture of their own'. The second, postwar, flourishing of art cinema can thus be seen as a consolidation of characteristics established in the 1920s.

The crucial role of Italian neo-realism in the development of postwar European art cinema is, as David Bordwell notes, in its being 'a transitional phenomenon' between the prewar and wartime national cinemas and those that were to develop after the war. The demise of the American studio system and the Paramount anti-trust decrees of 1948 created a shortage of films for international distribution. Equally, television was emerging both as a competitor for audiences and as a new market for films. This combination of factors meant that, from the mid-1950s onwards, films were increasingly made for international distribution. Italian neo-realism, then, can be seen as the forerunner of the art cinemas of the 1950s and 1960s, wherein the themes, styles and authorial address specific to a national cinema would find international audiences. 'The fullest flower of the art cinema paradigm', as Bordwell has called the postwar New Waves, 'occurred at the moment that the combination of novelty and nationalism became the marketing device it has been ever since'. The late 1950s/early 1960s thus brought the cinematic 'shocks' of the French New Wave, of Michelangelo Antonioni's *L'avventura* (1960), Federico Fellini's* *La dolce vita* (1960) and the international discovery of Ingmar Bergman*, for many the archetypal European art cinema director.

The stylistic modes of art cinema – as opposed to Hollywood popular genres – traditionally privilege realism and ambiguity, two registers generally unified through the appeal to authorial expressivity. The notion of the *auteur* director as developed in *Cahiers du cinéma** in the 1950s, and then modified by Andrew Sarris in the US during the 1960s, speaks both of the critical support system that comes into being around art cinema and of the complexity of art cinema's internationalism. After all, the French New Wave defined itself positively in relation to American cinema and negatively in relation to the French cinema of the 1950s. Similarly, the New German Cinema of the late 1960s and 1970s established the *auteur* as 'public institution' in order to mark out a space for a national cinema founded on a combination of art cinema precepts: an aesthetics of personal expressivity supported by state funding. This tendency to 'institutionalise' the idea of the *auteur*, and with it an idea of a national art cinema, reached its apogee in the cultural policies of the French Minister for Culture, Jack Lang, in the 1980s when French *auteur* cinema was regarded as a significant part of the national cinematic patrimony. Perhaps the most high-profile example of this particular strategy is the French co-production of the French/Swiss/Polish *Trois couleurs/Three Colours* trilogy: *Bleu/Blue*, *Blanc/White* (both 1993) and *Rouge/Red* (1994) directed by Kieślowski, who represents the paradigm of the European *auteur*.

While Kieślowski, Carax and Almodóvar serve as significantly different versions of contemporary European art cinema directors, the specificity of European art cinema is increasingly unclear. Since the 'New American Cinema' of De Palma, Scorsese and Cimino took part of its inspiration from the European cinema of the 1960s, the idea of the *auteur* has become a critical/industrial commonplace. Yet since its heyday in the 1960s, art cinema has been understood, in some European film industries at least, as both a generic and an institutional option that, if no longer guaranteeing international visibility, at least preserves some of the cultural cachet associated with its past. (Chris Darke)

Bib: David Bordwell, *Narration in the Fiction Film* (1985).

EUROPEAN CINEMA AND HOLLYWOOD

Before 1914, France and Italy were the two main exporters of film. Between 1913 and 1925, however, American exports of film to Europe increased fivefold. If Hollywood secured its position as the world leader in film exports at the expense of a war-ravaged Europe, there was little American production involvement in Europe until 1945. European concern over the extent of the influx of American films began to take shape in the 1920s, with Germany the first major industry to take action against American films in the form of the Film Europe initiative spearheaded by Erich Pommer. Following the German example – whereby distributors were issued a permit to release a foreign film each time they financed and distributed a German one – France and Italy began to impose import restrictions, quotas, tariffs and quid pro quo conditions that sought to secure screen time for domestic production. In the UK, the 1927 Cinematograph Films Act instituted a quota on foreign film imports, which resulted in a flurry of British 'quota quickies' to satisfy quota demands. The Motion Picture Producers and Distributors of America (MPPDA; renamed the Motion Picture Association of America, MPAA, in 1945) gave what was to become the conventional American response to attempts by European countries to protect their industries, claiming that 'This government had adopted no restrictive regulations similar in any way to those enforced in certain foreign countries.' Nearly seventy years later, the same disingenuous free-trade rhetoric would be repeated in the 1993 Uruguay Round of the General Agreement on Tariffs and Trade (GATT).

American production involvement in Europe increased dramatically after World War II, the devistated continent now reliant on American aid and having little capacity or will to dictate strict import quotas. Equally, there were hundreds of American films, unreleased in Europe during the war, with which Hollywood could saturate European markets. At the same time, as Peter Lev has pointed out, 'European markets became a necessity, not a luxury, to American film companies in the 1950s, because the American audience for motion pictures was rapidly shrinking.' The Paramount decrees of 1948 which signalled the end of the vertical integration of Hollywood led to a drop in the number of films produced, and thus the increasing importance of the export market. In the face of the American strategy of market saturation, European countries returned either to quota systems or to a system of 'blocked funds' to try to counter American domination of domestic markets. The 1948 Anglo-American Film Agreement allowed US companies to withdraw only $17 million of their earnings, leaving over $40 million each year to accumulate in blocked accounts, the proviso being unlimited American access to the British market. The 1948 Franco-American Film Agreement allowed US firms to withdraw up to $3.6 million of their funds annually, leaving around $10 million blocked to be used for joint production with French companies and the construction of new studios, among other things. This latter agreement replaced the 1946 Blum-Byrnes trade agreement that had given America generous terms to export their films to France. Both 1948 agreements laid the ground for what became known as 'runaway productions', one of the three sorts of production that came to characterise the postwar relationship between Hollywood and Europe, the others being co-productions and what Peter Lev calls 'the Euro-American art film'.

With high unemployment in Hollywood in the 1950s and 1960s, and with lower production costs and more flexible labour regulations in Europe – especially Italy and Spain – the two immediate postwar decades saw a spate of European-American film production. 'Runaway productions' relied on a combination of European and American personnel and stars, were financed through blocked funds and tended towards the spectacular epic, films like *Alexander the Great* (1955), *Ben-Hur* (1959), *Lawrence of Arabia* (1962) or *55 Days at Peking* (1964); the ground-breaking Italian (so-called) 'Spaghetti' Westerns of the mid-1960s should also be included here. Co-production agreements were increasingly part of the production structure of such films; although they had been tried in the 1920s, they became common practice only after World War II. Jean-Luc Godard's* *Le Mépris/Contempt* (1963) is both a satire on the exigencies of co-production – Georgia Moll as the harassed interpreter caught between Jack Palance's overbearing American producer, Fritz Lang's urbane European director, Michel Piccoli's* French screenwriter and Brigitte Bardot's* alienated sex goddess – and the very incarnation of the Euro-American art film. Such a film, according to Lev, 'attempts a synthesis of the American entertainment film (large budget, good production values, internationally known stars) and the European art film (auteur director, artistic subject and/or style) with the aim of reaching a much larger audience than the art film normally commands'. While the 1960s can be seen as the high point of such ventures, a nominal list of some of the more celebrated examples of the Euro-American art film indicates the longevity of this production style: *Blowup* (1967), *Ultimo tango a Parigi/Last Tango in Paris* (1972), *Paris, Texas* (1984), *The Last Emperor* (1987).

The 1993 GATT talks illustrated the extent to which the relationship between Europe and Hollywood remains 'a two-way fascination and a one-way exploitation', to use Godard's phrase. American objections to European film subsidies and 'protectionist' measures resulted in a piece of concerted brinkmanship by the French government – supported by a prestigious group of film-makers and stars – over the issue of 'cultural exception', which threatened to scupper the entire GATT agreement, of which film and audiovisual issues constituted only a small part. 'Cultural exception' was the idea that films and audiovisual material – because of their 'cultural specificity' to a particular nation – should not be governed by the same terms applied to foodstuffs, minerals, cars, etc. At the eleventh hour this principle was effectively acknowledged in a piece of EU/US political legerdemain: in order to save the GATT treaty, it was agreed simply to exclude film and audiovisual material from its terms. That the French government was so active in facing down American *laissez-faire* petitioning was accounted for by the French film critic Michel Ciment in December 1993 as follows: 'If French cinema has survived it is because of two measures that an American interpretation of GATT could decide were illegal. The first is the quota imposed on films shown on televison (60 per cent of them must be European). The second is a 13 per cent tax on all tickets sold at the box-office, which is used to subsidise innovative films, art-house cinemas, independent distributors, film festivals, film schools and East European and African production.' In retrospect, this aspect of GATT looks less resolved than simply put on hold, and the proliferation of cable and satellite channels promises to pose questions of broadcasting territory and intellectual property rights as well as to challenge definitions of the 'national' that underwrite positions such as those adopted by the French over their film industry.

Aesthetically speaking, the relay between Europe and Hollywood has had complex and diverse consequences, from the fascination and support evinced in the 1920s by American studios for German directors such as F. W. Murnau, Ernst Lubitsch and Paul Leni, to the sometimes uncomfortable exile that Hollywood offered to émigré European directors such as Lang, Jean Renoir*, Douglas Sirk (Sierck) and Robert Siodmak* in the 1930s and 1940s. A prime example of this international cross-pollination of film style can be seen in critical approaches to *film noir* as a hybridisation of American generic structures, German Expressionism and French Poetic Realism*. The European New Waves and art cinemas of the 1950s and 1960s were often fascinated by Hollywood, a fascination epitomised by Godard's films, and in turn can be seen to have fed into the stylistics of American directors such as Martin Scorsese, Francis Ford Coppola and Brian De Palma of the 'New American Cinema' of the 1970s. This traffic of influence and mutual acknowledgment has been evident more recently in the American vogue for remaking successful European, and particularly French, films, for example Coline Serreau's* *Trois hommes et un couffin/Three Men and a Cradle.* (1985) as *Three Men and a Baby* (1988), Luc Besson's* *Nikita* (1990) as *The Assassin* (1993) and Daniel Vigne's *Le Retour de Martin Guerre* (1981) as *Sommersby* (1993). (Chris Darke)

Bib: Peter Lev, *The Euro-American Cinema* (1993).

EUROPEAN COMMUNITY [NOW EUROPEAN UNION] AND THE CINEMA

While European cinema production had previously fallen under general EC legislation and directives on trade and industry, it was not until the 1980s that the Brussels authorities developed a coherent policy specifically concerning film and other European media. The issue had been brought to a head by a 1984 proposal from French president François Mitterand to establish a pan-European co-production fund for work in cinema and television. Mitterand's plan was rejected but it had started the ball rolling.

In 1986 the Commission's Directorate for Information, Communication and Culture put forward its *Mesures pour Encourager le Développement de l'Industrie de Production Audio-Visuelle* (or MEDIA for short). Once accepted by the Council, MEDIA began a pilot phase in 1987, to last until 1990, under the control of the EC Ministers for Cultural Affairs. As a symbol of the EC's commitment to its MEDIA programme, 1988 was designated European Cinema and Television Year. Events included the first ever European Film Awards*, although somewhat ironically the Berlin ceremony garnered very little media attention. During the same year, in an attempt to emphasise the economic implications of MEDIA, the suffix '92' was added to the programme's acronym. MEDIA 92 was to be a high-profile test case for the new EC internal market, encouraging collaboration between the twelve member states.

The full MEDIA programme was adopted by the Council of Ministers of the EC in December 1990 and was retitled MEDIA 95. From 1991 to 1995, MEDIA was awarded a budget of 200 million ECU (roughly £340 million). Most of this money was designated as 'seed' funding, a system of repayable advances with the programme's initiatives sharing in any profit they had helped to create. Thus it was hoped that the MEDIA budget would largely become self-perpetuating in years to come. In an attempt to broaden the scope of MEDIA (and its funding), European states from outside the EC have been encouraged to join the programme's activities. In 1992 MEDIA initiatives were opened to five members of the European Free Trade Association (EFTA) – Austria, Finland, Iceland, Norway and Sweden – as well as to Poland, Hungary and Czechoslovakia.

MEDIA is made up of an ever-increasing programme of initiatives which support the development, production and distribution of European audiovisual culture. Of these, nineteen are partly or wholly concerned with film. The remit of the respective initiatives can usually be gleaned from their catchword titles. CARTOON, for example, comprises a package of measures to support European animation production, including a database of contacts and incentives to encourage cooperation between studios. The most important MEDIA initiative with regard to development is the European Script Fund (SCRIPT). Recognising that securing finance for the development of projects is often the biggest hurdle faced by European film-makers, SCRIPT provides loans and advice to help get proposals up and running. The loans, averaging 50 per cent of a project's pre-production budget, become reimbursable if the project goes into production. Completed films which have benefited from assistance by SCRIPT include *Acción Mutante* (1992, Spain), *Daens* (1992, Belgium/France/Netherlands) and *Naked* (1993, UK). For projects that have made it to the production stage, Euro Media Garanties (EMG) provides film-makers with a measure of financial security. Supporting ventures that involve producers from at least three Council of Europe members, EMG will guarantee up to 70 per cent of the loan finance taken out on the project.

Perhaps the biggest success story of the MEDIA programme, the European Film Distribution Office (EFDO) has helped many films reach wider markets, both within the continent and around the world. EFDO's main remit is to support distribution between EU member states, but through 'EFDO Abroad', which presents films at festivals outside Europe, it now also promotes European cinema to countries worldwide. With the vast majority of European cinema consisting of low-budget projects which are only ever distributed in their country of origin, EFDO has been particularly beneficial to smaller productions. In fact 80 per cent of EFDO's available funds are set aside for films costing no more than 2.25 million ECU (£3.825 million). Covering up to 50 per cent of distributors' pre-costs, EFDO offers interest-free loans to films which have secured a distribution deal for no less than three EU countries. Moreover, the loan is only repayable if the release is successful. Conversely, if a supported film does especially well at the box-office, EFDO becomes entitled to a small share of the profits, or 'success dividend', which can then be reinvested. Among the well-known films to have received support from EFDO are *Babettes gaestebud/Babette's Feast* (1987, Denmark), *Spoorloos/The Vanishing* (1987, Netherlands/France) and *Volere volare* (1991, Italy).

Another film to have benefited from EFDO money, *Toto le héros/Toto the Hero* (1991, Belgium/France/Germany), serves as a testament to the package of MEDIA initiatives and the spirit of cooperation they have fostered within European cinema. A co-production of three member states, *Toto* was aided at every stage by European funding, beginning with support from SCRIPT and ending with the promotion of the video release by Espace Vidéo Européen (EVE). Yet one of the film's major sources of funding came from outside the MEDIA programme, via an initiative of the Council of Europe, EURIMAGES.

Set up in 1988, EURIMAGES is a co-production fund in the mould of that proposed by François Mitterand four years earlier. Providing financial support for films made by production partners from at least three member countries, the fund initially comprised twelve Council countries. A notable absentee from the final agreement, though, was the UK. Displaying the all too prevalent combination of ignorance about what is happening in Europe and a belief that the British still lead the way, the UK government soon established its own European Co-Production Fund (ECF). In the meantime EURIMAGES has gone from strength to strength and the UK finally joined in 1993.

European government initiatives aimed at the media industries are completed by the Audiovisual EUREKA programme (AVE). Again proposed by Europe's prime mover in this field, François Mitterand, AVE's remit is somewhat less specific than those of MEDIA or EURIMAGES. AVE exists primarily to encourage the development and application of advanced audiovisual technology. It also differs from the other major programmes in that it has a wider membership base of nearly thirty countries and responds to specific proposals from the industry rather than attempting to initiate projects itself.

At the time of writing (early 1995), the MEDIA programme is preparing to enter a new phase, MEDIA 2. Although details are still to be confirmed, MEDIA 2 looks quite different from its predecessor, reducing the nineteen initiatives to three strands: training, development and distribution. MEDIA 2 should also have a considerably larger budget for its next five-year programme, but the decision not to provide any specific measure in favour of exhibition has already proved controversial.

Each EU country now has a Mediadesk to provide information and answer queries about the MEDIA programme. (Simon Horrocks)

EUROPEAN FILM AWARDS (FELIX)

Established in 1988 as part of the European Community's Cinema and Television Year, the FELIX awards were intended as a European rival to the Oscars. Yet their initial impact can be measured from the challenge made by Sean Day-Lewis after the first ceremony in Berlin went almost unnoticed: 'Hands up anybody who can name one of the winners or, come to that, anybody who knows whether the epoch-making occasion happened at all.'

FELIX largely follows the format of its Hollywood counterpart, awarding its major prizes in the categories of Best Film, Best Actor/Actress and so on. One innovation is the prise for Best Young Film, recognising the achievements of up-and-coming talents in European cinema. Suitably, the first recipient of this award was the *enfant terrible* of Spanish film, Pedro Almodóvar, for his *Mujeres al borde de un ataque de nervios/Women on the Verge of a Nervous Breakdown* (1988). As if to emphasise the 'European-ness' of the awards, the annual FELIX ceremony does not have a permanent home, visiting Berlin, Paris and Glasgow in its first three years. Reinforcing FELIX's identity, the prefix 'European' was added to the award categories from 1990, Best Film becoming European Film of the Year, etc. In 1991 responsibility for FELIX was assumed by the newly founded European Film Academy (EFA), bringing with it the respected name of the Academy's president, Ingmar Bergman. But perhaps the most significant change was made to the awards in 1993. While the European Film of the Year continues to be judged on artistic merit, potential winners now have to achieve a designated amount of box-office revenue before qualifying for nomination. FELIX thus recognises that commercial viability is as important as critical acclaim if European cinema is to resist Hollywood's continued domination of the market.

Although the European Film Awards have undoubtedly made significant progress since their inception, FELIX has a long way to go before it can hope to compete with the Oscars in the popular imagination. In the words of EFA chairman Wim Wenders, 'our handicap is that the awards should have started at least twenty years ago'. (Simon Horrocks)

The winners in the major FELIX categories so far are as follows:

Best Film (European Film of the Year from 1990)
1988 *Krótki Film o Zabijaniu/A Short Film About Killing* (Krzysztof Kieślowski; Poland)
1989 *Topio stin Omichli/Landscape in the Mist* (Thodoros Angelopoulos; Greece/France/Italy)
1990 *Porte aperte/Open Doors* (Gianni Amelio; Italy)
1991 *Riff-Raff* (Ken Loach; UK)
1992 *Il ladro di bambini/Stolen Children* (Gianni Amelio; Italy/France)
1993 *Urga. Territoriya lyubvi/Urga. Territory of Love* (Nikita Mikhalkov; Russia/France)
1994 *Lamerica* (Gianni Amelio; Italy)
1995 *Land and Freedom* (Ken Loach; UK/Spain/Germany)

Best Young Film (Young European Film of the Year from 1990)
1988 *Mujeres al borde de un ataque de nervios/Women on the Verge of a Nervous Breakdown* (Pedro Almodóvar; Spain)
1989 *300 Mil do Nieba/300 Miles to Heaven* (Maciej Dejczer; Poland/Denmark)
1990 *Henry V* (Kenneth Branagh; UK)
1991 *Toto le héros/Toto the Hero* (Jaco van Dormael; Belgium/France/Germany)
1992 *De Noorderlingen/The Northerners* (Alan van Warmerdam; Netherlands)
1993 *Orlando* (Sally Potter; UK/Russia/France/Italy/Netherlands)
1994 *Le Fils du requin* (Agnès Merlet; France) and *Woyzeck* (Janos Szasz; Hungary)
1995 *La Haine/Hate* (Mathieu Kassovitz; France)

Best Actor (European Actor of the Year from 1990)
1988 Max von Sydow for *Pelle Erobreren/Pelle the Conquerer* (Denmark)
1989 Philippe Noiret for *La Vie et rien d'autre/Life and Nothing But* (France) and *Nuovo Cinema Paradiso/Cinema Paradiso* (Italy)
1990 Kenneth Branagh for *Henry V* (UK)
1991 Michel Bouquet for *Toto le héros/Toto the Hero* (Belgium/France/Germany)
1992 Matti Pellonpää for *La Vie de bohème/Bohemian Life* (Finland/France/Sweden)
1993 Daniel Auteuil for *Un Cœur en hiver/A Heart in Winter* (France)
[from 1994: no award]

Madeleine Renaud and children in *La Maternelle* (Marie Epstein and Jean Benoît-Lévy, 1933).

Jack Palance (left), Brigitte Bardot and Michel Piccoli in *Le Mépris/Contempt* (Jean-Luc Godard, 1963).

Jacques Tati (left) in his own *Mon Oncle* (1958).

Anne Parillaud in *Nikita* (Luc Besson, 1990).

Edwige Feuillère (left) and Simone Simon in *Olivia/Pit of Loneliness* (Jacqueline Audry, 1951).

Catherine Deneuve in *Les Parapluies de Cherbourg/ The Umbrellas of Cherbourg* (Jacques Demy, 1964).

Jean Gabin as 'Pépé' in *Pépé le Moko* (Julien Duvivier, 1936).

Fernandel, as the priest in *Le Petit monde de Don Camillo/ The Little World of Don Camillo* (Julien Duvivier, 1952).

Martin Lasalle and Marika Green in *Pickpocket* (Robert Bresson, 1959).

Marie Déa and Maurice Chevalier in *Pièges* (Robert Siodmak, 1939).

Suzy Delair and Bernard Blier in *Quai des orfèvres* (Henri-Georges Clouzot, 1947).

Annabella and Georges Rigaud in *Quartorze juillet* (René Clair, 1932).

Alain Delon in *Le Samouraï* (Jean-Pierre Melville, 1967).

Sandrine Bonnaire in
Sans toit ni loi/Vagabonde
(Agnès Varda, 1985).

Anna Karina in
Vivre sa vie/My Life to Live
(Jean-Luc Godard, 1962).

Lino Ventura (left) and Jean Gabin in *Touchez pas au grisbi/ Honour Among Thieves* (Jacques Becker, 1954).

Two of the men (Michel Boujenah, left, and Roland Giraud) and the baby in *Trois hommes et un couffin/Three Men and a Cradle* (Coline Serreau, 1985).

Best Actress (European Actress of the Year from 1990)

1988 Carmen Maura for *Mujeres al borde de un ataque de nervios/ Women on the Verge of a Nervous Breakdown* (Spain)
1989 Ruth Sheen for *High Hopes* (UK)
1990 Carmen Maura for *¡Ay, Carmela!* (Spain)
1991 Clothilde Coreau for *Le Petit Criminel* (France)
1992 Juliette Binoche for *Les Amants du Pont-Neuf* (France)
1993 Maia Morgenstern for *Balanta/Le Chêne/The Oak* (Romania/ France)
[from 1994: no award]

FESTIVALS

Film festivals gather films (as well as film-makers and stars) in one venue for the purpose of promotion and information. Although such events have taken place since the 1910s, the first festival in the modern sense of the term was Venice, opened in 1932, followed by Cannes* in 1946 and Berlin in 1951. These three constitute the major league of European film festivals, joined by Karlovy Vary and Locarno in 1946, Edinburgh in 1947, London in 1957, and a host of others. Festivals' *raison d'être*, apart from media and tourist appeal, is to be a market place for new product and, incidentally (and often controversially), a forum for critical evaluation. Many award prizes and a Cannes, Venice or Berlin prize carries promotional value. Since the early 1980s, as the theatrical market for film has shrunk, festivals in Europe have taken on a vital role, as the *only* place of exhibition for an increasing number of films, at worst creating the ghetto of the 'festival circuit', but at best a springboard for media exposure and occasional release: the films of Emir Kusturica and Kira Muratova are two examples of the latter. Concurrently a veritable explosion of smaller festivals has taken place, especially in western Europe, where they are substantially supported by central and local state funds, catering for a wide variety of specialisms (animation, horror, shorts, thrillers, women's films, gay and lesbian films, children's films, silent cinema, realist cinema, national cinemas, etc.). While the market value of the smaller events is negligible, they perform a crucial cultural function, continuing and to some extent replacing the work of film clubs as a forum for discovery and debate, and providing an opportunity to circulate other European and non-American films. (Ginette Vincendeau)

Below is a *selective* list of film festivals. Information is from British Council and British Film Institute documentation. For further details, see: *Directory of International Film Festivals*, published by the British Council, and the *BFI Handbook* (both yearly).

Albania hosts a biennial national film festival in Tirana. **Austria** has three main annual film festivals. The Viennale – Internationale

Filmfestwochen Wien (Vienna international film festival, every autumn) is subsidised by the Vienna City Council and a private sponsor, and includes symposia and publications. The other two festivals are dedicated to Austrian cinema: the Österreichische Film Tage Wels (Austrian Film Days, in Wels) since 1984, and the Diagonale – Festival des Österreichischen Films (festival of Austrian cinema) held in Salzburg since 1993 and organised by the Austrian Film Commission. **Belgium**'s most famous, though short-lived, festival was Exprmntl (experimental films) at Knokke-le-Zoute which ran in 1949, 1958, 1963, 1967, 1971 and 1974, and remains legendary for both its films and its passionate climate of debates and 'happenings'. Out of the country's large number of festivals should be mentioned the Brussels international film festival (January), the Brussels international festival of fantasy and science-fiction film and thrillers (March), and, also in Brussels, Cinédécouvertes (cine-discoveries) in July and Filmer à tout prix ('To film no matter what') in October. In November, a festival of European film is held in Virton. Ghent holds the Internationaal Filmgebeuren (international film festival) in October and an art film festival in February. **Bulgaria**'s main festival is the international festival of comedy films in Gabrovo in May (odd years). There is also an animation festival in Varna in October (odd years). **Czechoslovakia**. First held in 1946 and established permanently in 1950, Karlovy Vary (now in the Czech Republic) has been the main festival. Until 1992 it alternated bi-ennially with Moscow and functioned as the Communist block alternative to Cannes* and Venice, showcasing Eastern European cinema, but also 'Third World' cinema. Bratislava (now Slovakia) holds several festivals, including the Forum (festival of first feature films, November–December). **Denmark**. The main festival is the Odense international film festival (August, odd years). There are also a film and video festival in Copenhagen (June, even years) and the Copenhagen gay and lesbian film festival (September, annually).

Finland. The Midnight Sun festival takes place every June (since 1986) in Sodankylä, a small Lapland community, focusing on new Finnish cinema and silent films. Espoo ciné, in southern Finland, started in 1990. Kettupäivät ('The Fox-days') in Helsinki in early November is a forum for new Finnish shorts, documentaries and videos. The international children's film festival (launched in 1982) takes place in Oulu in late November. The Tampere short film festival in early March (since 1970) is an important forum for new Finnish film-makers. MuuMedia in early March in Helsinki (since 1991) concentrates on video and the new media. **France**. Founded in 1938 to counter the fascist influences thought to contaminate Venice, Cannes* opening was delayed by World War II. Since 1946, it has been the international film industry's most prominent meeting place. The festival takes place in May. The most important specialist events are: the Annecy festival (January), the Clermont-Ferrand short film festival, the Cognac festival of thrillers, the Créteil* international women's film festival (March–April), the Cinéma du réel (documentary) festival in Paris (March) and the Deauville festival of American cinema in September (notoriously boycotted in the early 1980s by French Minister of Culture Jack Lang). The Institut Lumière in Lyons and the Cinémathèque Française* organise regular retrospective festivals, the latter in particular with Cinémémoire (Paris, November), which shows newly restored prints. **Germany**. The most important German Festival is in Berlin, founded in 1951. The Internationale Kurzfilmtage Oberhausen (Oberhausen international short film festival), held annually since 1955 (in April), exhibits a wide variety of short films. The Internationales Film-Festival Mannheim (November), established in 1952, emphasises debut features and documentaries. The Internationale Hofer Filmtage (Hof International Film Days) has since 1967 been a meeting place for younger German film-makers, especially film school graduates. The Leipzig festival (November–December), launched in 1957, is a forum for politically committed documentary film-making. Although its political focus has shifted since the end of the GDR to Third World film, it still functions as a window for central and eastern Europe. Germany has two major women's film festivals, Feminale (Cologne, May, since 1984) and Femme totale (Dortmund, since 1987). The Stuttgart animation festival has been running since 1982. **Greece**. The major cinematic event in Greece is the Thessaloniki festival, founded in September 1960. **Hungary**. The main festival is the Hungarian Film Week, which provides a survey of Hungarian cinema, including documentary, experimental and student films. It is usually held in February, a week before Berlin. **Ireland**. Established in 1956, the Cork festival was the first in Ireland. It was joined in 1986 by the Dublin festival as well as festivals in Galway, Derry and Belfast.

Italy. For many years Venice was Italy's sole major film festival. Since the early 1960s many smaller festivals have emerged. A pioneering role was played, from 1960, by the Festival del Cinema Libero at the Apennine resort of Porretta Terme, for films made outside or on the fringes of the system. This was followed in 1965 by the Mostra del Nuovo Cinema at Pesaro (June). Founded by critic Lino Micciché, Pesaro has devoted itself to the discovery or rediscovery of *auteurs*, movements and national cinemas, promoted conferences, and produced a steady stream of important publications. Throughout the 1970s and early 1980s numerous local initiatives followed. Among the most important were the Salso Film and TV Festival at Salsomaggiore, devoted (until its demise in the 1990s) to research and experiment; Filmmaker in Milan, dedicated to independent production; the Festival Cinema Giovani in Turin, with retrospectives of the 'New Waves' of the 1960s; and the Bergamo Film Meeting, a festival-market for quality films awaiting distribution. Among specialist festivals the most noteworthy are Mystfest at Cattolica, near Rimini, for thrillers, and the Pordenone festival of early cinema (October). **Netherlands**. The three main festivals are the Netherlands Film Festival (formerly Dutch Film Days), in Utrecht (September), where an independent film festival (Cinemanifestatie) ran 1966–71; the documentary festival in Amsterdam (December); and the Rotterdam festival (January–February). **Norway**. The main Norwegian film festival is held in Haugesund annually (August–September). In addition, a festival takes place in Oslo in November, and a short films festival in Trondheim in June. **Poland** has four annual festivals. The festival of Polish feature films in Gdansk/Gdynia (September) presents Poland's latest productions, and holds the annual meeting of the Association of Polish Film-makers. The Cracow festival of short films (late May) celebrated its thirty years as the major Polish short film festival in 1993. The Warsaw International Film Festival has grown in recent years from a student film club event to a well organised festival of recent international releases (modelled on London). The Lubuskie Lato Filmowe, run by the Association of Film Societies (Dyskysyjne Kluby Filmowe) at Lagow in western Poland, presents the latest films produced in Poland and eastern and central Europe.

Portugal. Among Portugal's numerous festivals are the Espinho festival (November) for animation, the Encontros Internacionais de Cinema Documental (documentaries) in Odivelas, the Fantasporto (fantasy films) in Oporto in February, the Figueira da Foz festival (September) and the Troia festival (June–July). **Romania**. There is a biennial animation festival in Mamaia; the national film festival has taken place at Costinesti since 1976, but its future is in doubt. **(Former) Soviet Union**. The major film festival of the Soviet Union has been Moscow, in July (odd years, alternating with Karlovy Vary), traditionally the showcase for Soviet and eastern European socialist cinema; other festivals are held in St Petersburg (June), Sochi (May–June) and Tashkent (May–June). Among other festivals in the ex-Soviet states are the International Film Forum 'Arsenal' in Riga (Latvia) in September, for experimental film, the 'Golden Taurus' festival in Kaunas (Lithuania) in June and the 'Molodost' international film festival in Kiev (Ukraine) in October. **Spain**. The San Sebastián Film Festival (annually in September, since 1953) initially contributed glamour and an indirect legitimacy to Franco's regime, showcasing films which were then further cut or prohibited in Spain. After the transition to democracy, it is still Spain's premier film event; under Pérez Estremera, San Sebastián presents a competitive section built around the pick of Spanish autumn releases and the best new Latin American films, plus major international titles. Under Fernando Lara, festival director since 1983, the Valladolid International Film Festival (October) premieres major art films, complemented by tributes and retrospectives. Spain's other large festivals are Sitges (October) for fantasy and horror, and Valencia for Mediterranean cinema.

Sweden's main festivals are in Stockholm (November) and Uppsala (October, specialising in short films); there is also a festival in Gothenburg (February). **Switzerland**. Apart from Locarno, founded in 1946 as a showcase for the international film market, the main festivals in Switzerland are Nyon and Solothurn. Emerging from the 'Festival du film amateur' (Rolle 1963–64, Nyon 1965–68), Nyon is concerned with documentary. Its director was Moritz de Hadeln (also Locarno's director 1972–77) until 1980, when Erika de Hadeln took over, pursuing the festival's remit of showing politically and socially committed films. Solothurn, or the Solothurner Filmtage (Solothurn Film Days), held annually in the last week of January since 1966, is the most important venue for domestic productions, together with theme-specific films by foreign directors, exhibitions and round-tables on issues of national film policy. Solothurn has since the early 1990s opened up towards video, television and co-productions. Video art finds a place at the Internationale Film- und Videotage in Lucerne, the International Video Week in Geneva and the Video Festival at Locarno. **UK**. Apart from Edinburgh, established in 1947 as the first British film festival, the major event is the London Film Festival (November), held at the National Film Theatre and other London cinemas, created as a non-competitive 'festival of festivals' to present material shown at other festivals earlier in the year, as well as films released in their own country but not in Britain. The National Film Theatre also hosts the London lesbian and gay film festival (March) and the Jewish film festival (October). Smaller film festivals in the UK include Aberystwyth (November), Birmingham (October), Brighton (May), Cambridge (July), Leeds (October), the Norwich Women's Film Weekend (May), Nottingham ('Shots in the Dark', a thriller film festival, May–June) and Southampton (September). **(Former) Yugoslavia**. There is an international festival of animated films in Zagreb (Croatia) in June (even years). The Pula (Croatia) festival was first held in 1954, as the national film festival of Yugoslavia. In 1993 it was remodelled the national Croatian film festival. Fest was established in Belgrade in 1970 as a 'festival of festivals' and it became a major gathering point for international filmmakers. It collapsed under the economic and cultural embargo of Serbia in 1993.

GAY CINEMA IN EUROPE – see LESBIAN AND GAY CINEMA IN EUROPE

HERITAGE CINEMA IN EUROPE

The term describes period films made since the mid-1970s. Characteristic, successful examples include *Jean de Florette* (1986, France), *A Room with a View* (1985, UK), *Babettes gæstebud/Babette's Feast* (1987, Denmark) and *Belle Epoque* (1992, Spain). The term suggests an affinity with what has been called the heritage industry, notably retro fashion and the popularisation of museums and historical sites through the use of simulacra, lighting and sound effects and actors in period costume. Films may be characterised by use of a canonical source from the national literature, generally set within the past 150 years; conventional filmic narrative style, with the pace and tone of '(European) art cinema'* but without its symbolisms and personal directorial voices; a museum aesthetic, period costumes, decor and locations carefully recreated, presented in pristine condition, brightly or artfully lit; a performance style based on nuance and social observation.

It is arguable whether this is a distinct phenomenon. There are precedents (for example, the French costume dramas of the 1950s such as *Les Misérables*, 1958), but heritage films may be distinguished from many period films in a number of ways. While displaying high production values, they are generally small-scale and intimate, not spectacular; they do not (on the whole) deal with the great events of history, as conventionally understood, or even, like *Senso* (1954, Italy) or *Angi Vera* (1978, Hungary), treat such events through their impact on personal lives; much less do they address the construction of historical representation, like *Ludwig – Requiem für einen jungfräulichen König/ Ludwig – Requiem for a Virgin King* (1972, Germany) or *Amarcord* (1974, Italy). However, it is not a uniquely European genre, except perhaps in the sense of Eurocentric, since it has been important to the cinema of most white settler nations, notably Australia, Argentina and Canada.

The focus of the films is, typically, on attractively presented everyday bourgeois life. Critically they are an interesting case study. Often hugely popular in their country of origin, they tend to be sold as art cinema outside it. Though the market research is not available, it seems likely that they are especially popular with middle-class audiences, in a period when this class has become the majority or at least a significant minority in many European countries. They are thus embraced by the same class from which the critical establishment is drawn, yet the latter has generally viewed them negatively. Often characteristics such as nostalgia or attention to fixtures and fittings are criticised without considering the potential of the former to be a critique of the present or the sensuousness of the latter and its iconographic expressivity (typically requiring the skilled reading of a female spectator). Equally, the genre has provided a space for marginalised social groups, a sense of putting such people back into history, for instance women: *Rouge Baiser* (1985, France), *Rosa Luxemburg* (1986, Germany), *Howards End* (1991, UK); lesbians and gay men: *El diputado/Congressman* (1978, Spain), *Ernesto* (1979, Italy), *Avskedet/The Farewell* (1980, Finland); even ethnic minorities (*Cheb*, 1990, France) and the disabled (*My Left Foot,* 1989, Ireland). None of this argues for the merit of the genre, but suggests a critical issue of some complexity that warrants exploration. (Richard Dyer)

Bib: Andrew Higson, 'Re-presenting the National Past: Nostalgia and Pastiche in the Heritage Film', in Lester Friedman (ed.), *British Cinema and Thatcherism* (1993).

LESBIAN AND GAY CINEMA IN EUROPE

It is generally assumed that European cinemas have a good track record on homosexuality: more images, sooner, less prejudiced, more often produced by openly lesbian/gay people. This account needs qualification and explanation, and more research.

Lesbian/gay representation has been all but entirely absent from East European cinemas. In Western Europe, lesbian/gay stereotypes are widely used, not only in popular comedies and thrillers but in canonical *auteur* works: *Die Büchse der Pandora/Pandora's Box* (1929, Germany); *Roma città aperta/Rome Open City* (1945, Italy), *La Fiancée du pirate/Dirty Mary* (1969, France). They are not necessarily the same as in Hollywood, nor are stereotypes unambiguously negative, something radical gay/lesbian films have often taken up, as in *Un hombre llamado Flor de Otoño/A Man Called Autumn Flower* (1977, Spain), or *Madame X – eine absolute Herrscherin/Madame X – an Absolute Ruler* (1978, Germany). The greater number of lesbian/gay representations in Western European cinemas has much to do with identifying markets with which Hollywood did not compete: pornography and the educational film, not always firmly distinct genres. Soft-core heterosexual pornography has been a mainstay of many European industries and invariably includes lesbian sequences. Sex education films have treated male and female homosexuality and have often been enlightened as texts even when marketed as titillation, for instance *Anders als die Anderen/Different from the Others* (1919, Germany) or *Der Sittlichkeitsverbrecher/The Sex Criminal* (1962, Switzerland).

At the same time, European cinemas dealt with homosexuality in a serious manner much earlier than others. This did not only occur in films of blatant high seriousness: among the most cherishable early images of homosexuality are the male relationship in the highly strung melodrama *Geschlecht in Fesseln/Sex in Shackles* (1928, Germany) and the lesbian character in the French thriller *Quai des Orfèvres* (1947). The earliest known representation is in *Vingarne/The Wings* (1916, Sweden), with the earliest lesbian representation perhaps *Die Büchse der Pandora*. *Anders als die anderen* and *Mädchen in Uniform/Girls in Uniform* (1931, Germany) represent the earliest explicitly progressive treatments, a tradition taken up in the postwar years by *Victim* (1960, UK): the presence of contemporaneous, relatively strong homosexual rights movements in these countries is significant in accounting for these breakthroughs.

Government policies in many countries have facilitated *auteur* cinema, in which many more or less openly lesbian/gay directors have worked (Chantal Akerman*, Pedro Almodóvar, Jean Cocteau*, Rainer Werner Fassbinder, Marleen Gorris, Derek Jarman, Ulrike Ottinger, Pier Paolo Pasolini, Luchino Visconti), as have (straight) women directors who treated homosexuality in a sympathetic, even at times envious, manner – among others, Mai Zetterling's *Älskande* *par/Loving Couples* (1964, Sweden), Margarethe von Trotta's* *Das zweite Erwachen des Krista Klages/The Second Awakening of Krista Klage* (1977, Germany) or Diane Kurys'* *Coup de foudre/Entre Nous/At First Sight* (1983, France). In recent years, the European heritage* film has been remarkably hospitable to lesbian/gay themes, as for instance in *Novembermond/November Moon* (1984, Germany), *Maurice* (1987, UK), *Meteoro ke skia/Meteor and Shadow* (1962, Greece); one might consider Jacqueline Audry's* *Olivia* (1950, France) an important early example. *Auteur* and heritage cinema do not treat homosexuality as an issue or problem, but are not always lacking in anguish, as for instance in *Tystnaden/The Silence* (1962, Sweden), or melancholy, as in *Gli occhiali d'oro/The Gold-rimmed Spectacles* (1988, Italy), and few European films have had the (often bland) affirmative impulse of post-gay liberation cinema in the USA. (Richard Dyer)

Bib: Richard Dyer, *Now You See It: Studies on Lesbian and Gay Film* (1990).

SEXUALITY, EROTICISM AND PORNOGRAPHY IN EUROPEAN CINEMA

Representations of sexuality and eroticism are as old as the cinema in Europe. While 'actualities' and little comic scenes entertained audiences in fairgrounds, short pornographic movies drew a few of them into brothels. A wide underground network of porn or 'stag' films flourished, usually unknown to mainstream audiences and film history alike, except when they surfaced in 'scandalous' manifestations, as with the Romanian-born French entrepreneur Bernard Natan [> PATHÉ] who directed, and starred in, a large number of them. In the 'legitimate' cinema, eroticism quickly became a feature too, in early French movies for instance and, notoriously, in the pre-World War I Danish erotic melodrama, credited with the 'invention' of the on-screen passionate kiss.

In 1935, the American authorities burned a print of the Czech film *Extase/Ecstasy* (1932, dir. Gustav Machatý), in which Hedy Lamarr appeared naked. This took place five years after the introduction of the notoriously censorious Hays Code in the US and, for a good thirty years afterwards, the cinema of Europe was regarded as comparatively free in its depiction of sexuality. Of course, such 'freedom' was, as it would be later, within the confines of dominant (and often misogynistic) representations of women as sexual icons. It was also subject to censorship laws in the European countries themselves. Germany, for example, banned *Extase*, but that was on the grounds of Lamarr being Jewish. And if, in Arletty*, the French cinema of the 1930s and 1940s had an icon of 'independent' female sexuality, her brief 'nude' shower scene in *Le Jour se lève* (1939) was nevertheless excised.

The national cinemas of postwar Europe, particularly those of

France and Italy, began to redefine the permissible limits of cinema's depiction of on-screen sexuality. The Italian neo-realist cinema achieved an immense international visibility based on the perceived 'realism' of its depiction of specific social milieux. Such success might equally be said to have been achieved by its depiction of female sexuality. The 'earthiness' of Silvana Mangano in *Riso amaro/Bitter Rice* (1949) and the revealing filming of Anna Magnani*, not to mention the barely concealed lesbian subplot in *Roma città aperta/Rome Open City* (Roberto Rossellini*, 1945), prepared international audiences for the appearances in the 1950s and 1960s of Italian stars such as Gina Lollobrigida, Sophia Loren and Claudia Cardinale.

In France, in a string of films starting with *Caroline Chérie* (1950), Martine Carol* continued the line of French female stars whose presence guaranteed that their vehicles would be, as Claude Beylie wrote, 'lightly spiced with a pleasant eroticism'. If Carol and others, such as Françoise Arnoul, gave international currency to certain ideas of French cinema and French femininity, the advent of Brigitte Bardot* in *Et Dieu … créa la femme/And God Created Woman* (1956) promoted different, modern versions both of this femininity and this cinema. The same might be said, forty years on, of Béatrice Dalle*, whose explosive performance in *37°2 le Matin/Betty Blue* (1985) can be read as a reprise of the Bardot sex-kitten persona, treated with *Emmanuelle*-like explicitness.

In François Truffaut's *Les Quatre cents coups* (1959), Jean-Pierre Léaud* steals a publicity still of an Ingmar Bergman* film showing Harriet Andersson* in a revealingly off-the-shoulder outfit. It is a moment in which one European art cinema*, the French New Wave*, addresses the important figure of Bergman, the most celebrated European *auteur* of the period, via the concern common to both: the 'realistic', 'adult' and hence 'explicit' treatment of sexual themes. These three terms, often interchangeable, became associated with the European art cinemas of the 1960s. It was equally the case that the 'adult' treatment of sexuality by these cinemas was accompanied by the *frisson* of the well-publicised relationships between male *auteurs* and their leading actresses, Roberto Rossellini and Ingrid Bergman, Jean-Luc Godard* and Anna Karina*, Michelangelo Antonioni and Monica Vitti, Ingmar Bergman and Liv Ullmann. Interestingly, the postwar rise in European art cinema was also paralleled by the burgeoning genre of pornography.

If the difference between pornography and eroticism is that between display and suggestion, the late 1960s and the 1970s saw a short-lived convergence of the two. While the sex industry in Europe had formerly restricted itself in the 1950s to low-tech 'stag films' and 'loop movies' for peep shows, and with cinema encroaching progressively upon its territory either in pseudo-documentaries on naturism, so-called 'nudie cuties' and American B-movie exploitation, the late 1960s saw a major increase in the profile of films normally associated with the sex industry.

Two moments are worth isolating in the growing explicitness of sexually oriented material – the first production of hardcore pornography in colour magazines in Scandinavia in 1967, and the international *succès de scandale* of the Swedish film *Jag är nyfiken – gul/I am Curious – Yellow* (1967), which dispensed with any documentary alibis in its straightforwardly explicit depiction of (simulated) sexual action. These two events presaged the increasing commercial importance of explicit sexual content in European cinema of the 1970s. The first half of the decade saw the great commercial success of Bernardo Bertolucci's *Ultimo Tango a Parigi/Last Tango in Paris* (1972), whose superbly performed confection of stellar cast, hack psychoanalysis and chic sodomy set a model that many *auteurs* would follow throughout the decade. Most notable among examples of this increasing hybridisation of art cinema and pornography were Dušan Makavejev's Brechtian disquisition on sexual theorist Wilhelm Reich, *W. R. Misterije organizma/ W. R. Mysteries of the Organism* (1971), Bertrand Blier's* anarchic, misogynistic *Les Valseuses/Going Places* (1973); Alain Robbe-Grillet's vacuous exercise in softcore imagery and narrative origami, *Le Jeu avec le feu/Giochi di fuoco* (1975, Fr./It.); Pier Paolo Pasolini's punishing Sadian parable of Italian fascism, *Salò o le 120 giornate di Sodoma/Salò* (1975); Nagisa Oshima's brilliant, French co-produced excursion into hardcore, *Ai no corrida* (1976); and Jean-Luc Godard's highly mediated take on sexuality and domesticity, *Numéro deux* (1975).

The 'sexual revolution' of the 1960s created a climate in which the explicit depiction of sex was more acceptable to a mainstream audience. For a while, softcore and hardcore pornography flourished on European screens, especially in France where censorship began to be phased out from 1967. The most spectacular example of mainstream softcore success was *Emmanuelle* (1974), the top-grossing film of its year, making an international star of its lead actress, Sylvia Kristel. A year later, French hardcore took to similarly mainstream screens with *Exhibition* (1975). The response of the French government was not so much one of outright censorship as a fiscal and institutional one that created, in the law of 31 October 1975, the 'X' certificate to designate pornographic films, the creation of a specialised distribution circuit and the imposition of taxes on domestic pornography and a heavier tax on imported porn. While this approach kept the domestic pornography industry marginalised but financially healthy for a short period, it equally serviced the conventional film industry through the siphoning off of porn-tax income into the 'avances sur recette' funding of art cinema. However, the bubble soon burst and by the 1980s the porn cinema accounted for only 5 per cent of the national audience.

The brief foray into mainstream public consciousness that the 1970s bought to the genre of pornography, particularly in France, also saw, towards the end of that decade, the beginnings of the video boom. The European porn industries latched onto video as a means of bypassing cinematic censorship but also as a way of producing low-budget porn.

While the genre of 'amateur porn' began inauspiciously in Germany in the 1970s with the so-called *Hausfrauenporn* (housewife porn), by the 1990s video had become hugely lucrative and the standard means of distribution, so that in France an organisation such as 'Nanou Contact' can organise casual sexual encounters, tape them and market them as product. Equally, the European porn industry has its own stars, many of them celebrities beyond their particular fan-base: Brigitte Lahaie and Tabatha Cash in France, Teresa Orlovski in Germany and La Cicciolina (Ilona Staller) in Italy.

If censorious worries with on-screen sexual explicitness have recently been replaced with a concern over levels of violence, it is clear that, as screens themselves have multiplied, the concern is now as much over access to such images as over their contents. The French pay-channel Canal Plus, for example, programmes soft and hardcore pornography regularly. The extension and multiplication of the audio-visual media throughout Europe with cable and satellite will doubtless revivefy the old debates. (Chris Darke)

Bib: Nick Anning and David Hebditch, *Porn Gold: Inside the Pornography Business* (1988).

APPENDIX I

European Production and Audience Statistics*

* Sources from *Encyclopedia of European Cinema*

FILM PRODUCTION FIGURES

Dates

	1945	1946	1947	1948	1949	1950	1951	1952	1953	1954	1955	1956	1957	1958	1959	1960	1961
Albania	–	–	–	–	–	–	–	–	–	–	–	–	1	–	1	1	1
Austria	1	3	13	25	25	15+2	23+5	16+3	18+10	16+6	22+6	28+9	24+2	19+4	17+2	18+2	21+2
Belgium	9	3	1	2	1	0	1	1/0	0	0	0/5	8	3	4+1	3+2	2/0	6+0
Bulgaria	2	3	4	–	1	1	3	3	1	2	4	6+1	6+4	7+2	12	11	7
Czechoslovakia	3	12	22	20	–	20	8	17	18	15	17	21+1	24+3	29	33+2	35+1	44+1
Denmark	10	13	8	8	8	14	15	16	13	14	13	17	17	14	16	17	24
Finland	21	12	14	16	16	12	18	26	23	29	29	17	20	18	17	15	20
France	72	94	72	91	99+8	99+18	94+18	88+21	64+47	52+46	76+34	90+39	81+61	75+51	68+65	79+79	69+98
Germany (East)	–	–	–	–	–	10	–	–	–	–	13	18	21	25	28	29	27
Germany (West)	–	1	9	23	61+1	73+9	57+3	78+4	89+15	94+15	120+8	115+8	96+11	98+17	85+21	85+10	69+11
Greece	5	4	5	8	13	13	15	22	21	14	24	30	31	51	52	58	68
Hungary	3	–	–	6+0	–	4	8	5	8	7	11+0	9	16	13	18	15	19
Iceland	–	–	–	–	–	–	–	–	–	–	–	–	–	–	–	–	–
Ireland	0	–	–	–	–	0	0	2	–	–	1	–	4	3	3	2	2
Italy	–	62	60	54	76	92+0	104+0	119+13	125+21	144+46	74+52	68+23	66+71	76+65	83+81	94+66	117+88
Luxemburg	–	–	–	–	–	0	0	0	0	0	0	0	0	0	0	0	0
Netherlands	2	0	1	2	2	1	0	1	1	–	3	2	2	4	2	5	1
Norway	4	6	2	5	5	4	11	10	7	10	11	9	10	12	8	8	8
Poland	0	1	2	4	4	4	4	1	9	6	9	13	10	23	15	19+2	24
Portugal	4	9	10	4	7	2	4	8	4	–	0	4	1	4	5	2	2
Romania	1	–	–	–	1	1	2	2	2	3	5	3	4	4	5	8	10
ex-Soviet Union	19	23	23	17	18	13	9	24	45	51	81+3	104	108	121	137	119	133
Spain	33	38	49	45	36	47+2	37+5	33+7	37+7	56+13	49+7	53+22	50+22	51+24	50+17	55+18	72+19
Sweden	44	42	45	32	38	36	32	33	32	37	37	34	32	29	21	24	18
Switzerland	1	0	1	1	1	0	1	2	–	–	3	3	4	3	5	4	7
UK	51	66	73	120	125	99	102	132	142	148	115	130	164	135	140	157	151
ex-Yugoslavia	0	–	2	4	3	4	6	5	9	4+3	12+2	11+1	14+2	14+2	13+2	15+1	32+0

	1962	1963	1964	1965	1966	1967	1968	1969	1970	1971	1972	1973	1974	1975	1976	1977	1978
Albania	1	1	1	1	–	–	–	–	–	3	–	–	6	10	14	–	10
Austria	16+4	13+2	11+8	11+5	7+11	7+5	2+5	1+2	3+4	2+3	4+5	3+3	4+4	2+4	3+2	4+4	1+2
Belgium	5+0	0/1	1+1	1/1	1/1	3/1	5/1	10/0	3/1	3/4	11/3	9/4	4/2	–	8/0	3/2	3/3
Bulgaria	9	11	13	11+1	12+2	12+2	13+2	13+2	14+2	17+1	22	19+1	19	22+3	26+2	19+2	30
Czechoslovakia	35+4	39	41	42+3	40	49	44+1	42+8	52+2	57+2	45+4	65+3	63+3	54+8	65+3	61+2	48
Denmark	19	21	17	18	21	20	20	20	20	28	18	20+0	22+0	16+2	20+0	16+0	17+0
Finland	19	11	9	9	6	3	12	11	9	8	8	7	2	7	9	7	10
France	43+82	36+105	45+103	34+108	45+85	47+73	49+68	70+84	66+72	67+60	71+98	97+103	137+97	160+62	170+44	190+32	116+44
Germany (East)	27	20	15	15	–	–	–	–	–	–	10+7	14+2	14+1	15+1	17+1	16	–
Germany (West)	43+18	44+22	35+42	25+47	27+33	56+40	61+46	82+39	86+27	68+31	57+28	80+18	58+22	47+26	42+18	38+14	50+7
Greece	82	92	93	101	117	99	108	98	87	90	64	44	42	38	17	17	15
Hungary	16	18+1	19+1	23	21	21+1	36+1	22+1	21+2	15+4	21	21	19+1	19	19	24+1	28
Iceland	–	–	–	–	–	–	–	–	–	–	–	–	–	0	–	1	–
Ireland	3	2	3	1	3	1	1	0	5	2	6	4	2	2	0	0	1
Italy	139+106	135+95	135+155	94+109	89+143	130+117	130+116	146+103	132+99	128+88	169+111	171+81	176+55	177+53	203+34	142+23	119+24
Luxemburg	0	0	0	0	0	0	0	0	1	1	0	0	0	0	0	0	1
Netherlands	6	5	3	1	5	–	–	–	4	4+1	6+1	8+3	8	16	8+2	7+2	–
Norway	6	6	7	9	6+1	4	7	5+1	11	7+1	8	9+2	12	13+1	14	9	7
Poland	23	27	23	20+0	25	–	–	–	24+0	27	19	19	27	20+1	–	27	31
Portugal	4+1	7+1	5+3	6	5	5+2	4	4	4	7	6	3	–	6	10	9	21
Romania	12	14	14	14+1	11+4	16	6+2	12+2	9+2	15	19	22	22	24	19+3	23	24
ex–Soviet Union	121	133	–	167	159	175	161+2	194+2	215+3	208+6	230+4	166	162+7	176+8	150+6	146+2	–
Spain	64+24	59+55	67+63	53+98	67+97	55+70	49+68	55+70	42+63	48+43	52+51	73+45	71+41	89+21	90+18	83+19	77+30
Sweden	17	21	19	25	29	23	36	28	23	17	19	15	21	25	18	26	15
Switzerland	4	2	4	10	5	2	3	5	5	6	6+2	17+3	13+4	28+2	19+1	16+4	–
UK	171	150	126	97	99	140	107	112	122	67	131	98	89	91	92	73	77
ex-Yugoslavia	22+0	14+4	17+1	18+2	17+3	33+3	32+1	27+4	23+0	21+3	20+2	20+3	14+1	17+2	14+0	20+0	20+1

Figures are for feature film production by country. 47+2 indicates films + co-productions. 5/1 indicates division of French language/Dutch and Flemish language films produced. Zero (0) indicates no films produced. A dash (–) indicates no figure available.

FILM PRODUCTION FIGURES (continued)

Dates

	1979	1980	1981	1982	1983	1984	1985	1986	1987	1988	1989	1990	1991	1992	1993
Albania	12	–	–	–	7	14	12	–	–	–	11	5	0	1	–
Austria	5+1	5+2	3+2	12+1	8+3	16+1	9+3	11+2	8+2	8+1	10+1	10+5	11	10+0	–
Belgium	8/2	4+2	1/2	4/1	4/3	3/2	6+1	4+1	7+5	4+11	10+0	9+11	3+3	3+9	4+4
Bulgaria	29	31	42	–	32	–	40	23	35	15	20	19	22	3	5+3
Czechoslovakia	47	52	48	–	66	–	50	63	55	58	70	62	17	15	20
Denmark	9+0	13+0	12+0	7+0	11+0	10+1	7+2	10+0	9+2	14+2	16+2	12+1	9+2	10+5	11+3
Finland	9	7+3	12	17	16	17	13	23+1	12	10	7+3	14	11	20	20
France	126+48	144+45	186+45	134+31	101+30	120+41	106+45	97+37	96+37	93+44	66+70	81+65	73+83	72+83	67+85
Germany (East)	–	17	–	–	16	–	16	16	5	–	–	–	–	–	–
Germany (West)	53+12	37+12	60+16	57+13	69+8	62+13	46+18	45+15	47+18	49+8	53+15	38+10	53+19	53+10	50+17
Greece	27	25	46	48	37	40	30	27	26	13	14	10	15+0	6+4	15+3
Hungary	21+5	26	25	–	25	11+6	21	26	26	14+6	37	23	15+4	17+5	9+7
Iceland	–	2	3	3	4	5	4	2+0	1+0	2+0	2+0	2+0	4	1+2	0+2
Ireland	1	5	2	1	3	2	2+0	3+1	1+3	2+3	2+1	3	1	3+1	3+3
Italy	122+24	128+32	79+24	99+15	101+9	86+17	81+8	94+15	106+10	103+21	102+15	98+21	111+18	114+13	86+20
Luxemburg	0	0	3	0	0	1	1	1	1	1	3	1	1+1	1+2	0+4
Netherlands	–	7	11	10	10	12	10+1	13+0	15+3	8+2	13	13	14	13+0	16+0
Norway	13	10	10	10	8	6	10	13	7+2	10	11	9	10	8	9
Poland	32	33+6	17+2	23+3	31+5	35	37	34	35	34	22	27	–	8+13	11+10
Portugal	6	9	6	8	4	8	8	6	9+2	16	4+3	2+7	6+3	2+6	10+6
Romania	28	32	31	32	32	–	26	30	26	23	23	4+5	15+4	12+6	10+5
ex-Soviet Union	–	156	–	–	–	–	158	142	158	153	160	300	400	65	137
Spain	56+33	82+36	92+45	118+22	81+18	63+12	65+12	49+11	62+7	54+9	43+5	37+10	46+18	38+14	41+15
Sweden	20	23+3	22+3	14+4	17+6	16+2	12	17+3	26+1	13+8	15+6	20+5	10+17	9+11	13+14
Switzerland	–	13	11	–	–	20	15	3+19	6+15	6+12	8+8	8+11	5+12	3+6	0+16
UK	77	61	66	46	56	51	53	29+6	42+6	38+2	22+5	39+8	24+22	29+13	31+29
ex-Yugoslavia	27+1	24+2	23+3	32+2	23+2	30+3	30+2	21+4	23+4	28+7	26+7	21+4	–	3	–

Figures are for feature film production by country. 47+2 indicates films + co-production. 5/1 indicates division of French language/Dutch and Flemish language films produced. Zero (0) indicates no films produced. A dash (–) indicates no figures available.

AUDIENCE FIGURES (Millions)

Dates

	1945	1946	1947	1948	1949	1950	1951	1952	1953	1954	1955	1956	1957	1958	1959	1960	1961
Albania	–	–	–	–	–	–	–	–	4.6	–	5.9	–	5.9	6.6	8.0	–	7.6
Austria	–	–	–	–	–	92.5	93.9	94.1	107.9	110.0	114.0	116.1	119.9	122.0	114.9	106.5	100.5
Belgium	–	–	–	–	–	116.4	114.1	110.4	112.2	111.4	106.0	109.7	106.7	99.9	88.7	80.0	71.7
Bulgaria	–	–	–	–	–	–	37.0	39.0	42.0	55.2	60.0	69.0	77.9	89.4	101.2	112.1	118.0
Czechoslovakia	–	–	–	–	–	–	128.0	135.0	144.0	152.0	162.6	185.5	186.2	183.3	178.0	176.5	166.0
Denmark	47.0	53.8	54.4	–	–	52.2	56.6	57.3	59.0	58.7	55.0	52.1	51.3	50.0	46.7	44.0	42.0
Finland	36.3	30.0	29.6	29.1	26.2	25.7	26.8	26.8	29.4	30.3	33.5	31.2	31.3	28.8	25.5	24.6	23.8
France	402.0	419.0	424.0	–	–	370.7	372.8	359.6	370.6	382.8	394.9	398.9	411.7	371.0	353.7	354.7	328.4
Germany (East)	–	–	–	–	–	184.0	–	–	–	–	310.0	–	–	273.1	258.6	237.9	–
Germany (West)	–	–	–	–	–	487.4	554.8	614.5	680.2	735.6	766.1	817.5	801.0	749.7	670.8	604.8	516.9
Greece	–	–	–	10.0	35.6	37.5	38.8	41.3	42.6	45.3	49.5	56.9	62.2	66.8	74.8	84.2	86.3
Hungary	–	–	–	–	–	47.1	63.0	69.0	73.0	98.0	115.8	113.6	133.4	131.0	135.0	140.1	135.4
Iceland	–	–	–	–	–	–	–	–	–	–	–	–	–	–	–	–	–
Ireland	–	–	–	–	–	46.1	47.8	49.1	50.7	54.1	50.9	52.1	49.8	45.6	43.8	41.2	38.0
Italy	–	411.0	525.0	580.0	600.0	661.5	705.7	748.1	779.9	800.7	819.4	790.2	758.4	730.4	747.9	744.8	741.0
Luxemburg	–	–	–	–	–	–	–	–	–	–	4.0	5.0	5.0	5.0	5.0	4.5	5.0
Netherlands	–	–	–	–	–	63.9	63.5	63.1	63.7	65.1	66.0	69.9	65.6	64.2	55.5	55.4	51.0
Norway	–	30.1	–	–	–	30.0	32.0	34.0	33.0	34.0	33.0	35.0	35.0	35.0	35.0	35.0	33.9
Poland	–	–	–	–	–	–	121.0	136.0	152.0	166.0	208.3	198.0	231.4	205.3	195.5	196.0	186.0
Portugal	–	17.7	20.9	20.7	19.9	20.6	20.9	23.0	22.1	24.1	25.9	27.0	27.9	26.5	26.6	26.6	26.1
Romania	–	–	–	–	–	52.4	66.0	67.0	83.0	84.0	85.4	113.0	119.0	113.5	134.1	150.3	164.3
ex-Soviet Union	–	–	–	–	–	–	–	–	–	–	2506.0	–	3063.0	3392.0	3519.9	3610.0	3849.0
Spain	–	–	–	–	–	–	315.0	310.0	314.0	320.0	310.0	324.0	360.0	362.0	365.0	370.0	370.0
Sweden	–	–	–	–	–	–	60.0	67.0	70.0	65.0	60.0	67.0	65.0	70.0	60.0	55.0	54.0
Switzerland	–	–	–	–	–	–	–	33.0	–	–	34.0	37.0	40.0	42.0	44.0	40.0	40.0
UK	1585.0	1635.0	1462.0	1514.0	1430.0	1395.8	1365.0	1312.1	1284.5	1275.8	1181.8	1100.8	915.2	754.7	581.0	515.0	449.1
ex-Yugoslavia	–	–	–	–	–	–	64.0	60.0	68.0	85.0	97.0	101.4	108.0	114.3	125.0	130.1	129.0

AUDIENCE FIGURES (Millions) (continued)

Dates

	1962	1963	1964	1965	1966	1967	1968	1969	1970	1971	1972	1973	1974	1975	1976	1977	1978
Albania	–	–	–	7.8	–	–	–	8.4	–	8.4	–	8.4	–	–	–	–	–
Austria	90.8	84.9	76.0	72.1	65.8	57.7	50.6	39.5	32.9	28.5	26.7	23.9	23.4	20.8	17.5	17.9	17.4
Belgium	63.9	52.7	46.6	40.9	39.5	36.7	33.9	31.5	30.5	29.8	29.4	26.3	26.5	24.9	23.2	22.3	21.7
Bulgaria	122.8	124.0	125.0	126.4	124.1	119.9	114.0	110.2	109.6	111.1	112.3	114.0	112.3	114.3	114.7	113.4	111.3
Czechoslovakia	152.0	140.7	134.2	128.4	127.0	118.8	118.7	120.6	114.8	110.7	98.4	89.3	87.7	85.9	85.3	86.4	84.7
Denmark	39.3	34.5	33.2	33.9	33.5	29.7	26.8	25.6	24.3	22.1	20.7	18.9	19.2	18.9	18.6	16.7	17.4
Finland	17.8	13.2	10.6	14.0	15.1	14.5	10.1	10.5	11.7	13.0	10.1	10.9	9.6	9.6	8.9	9.0	9.8
France	311.7	292.1	275.8	257.2	234.7	211.4	203.2	182.1	184.4	177.0	184.4	176.0	179.4	180.7	177.3	170.3	178.5
Germany (East)	191.2	–	140.6	119.0	–	99.2	100.6	93.3	91.4	83.4	81.5	84.5	79.5	76.9	79.7	84.1	–
Germany (West)	442.9	366.0	320.4	294.0	257.1	215.6	180.4	180.6	160.1	152.1	149.8	144.3	136.2	128.1	115.1	124.2	135.5
Greece	96.1	100.5	109.5	121.1	131.8	137.1	137.4	135.3	128.6	118.0	92.6	62.2	57.1	47.9	39.9	39.0	39.2
Hungary	122.0	115.7	111.1	106.0	104.6	96.8	84.5	82.2	79.6	79.7	74.7	74.4	77.9	74.4	73.6	76.0	71.7
Iceland	–	–	–	–	2.3	–	–	–	1.7	1.8	2.0	2.0	2.3	2.6	2.5	–	–
Ireland	35.0	–	–	30.0	–	–	–	–	20.0	–	–	–	18.0	15.0	–	–	–
Italy	728.6	697.5	683.0	663.1	632.0	568.9	559.9	550.9	525.0	535.7	553.7	544.8	544.4	513.7	454.5	373.8	318.6
Luxemburg	4.0	4.0	3.5	3.0	–	2.1	1.9	1.5	1.3	1.1	1.1	1.0	1.0	1.1	0.8	0.7	–
Netherlands	47.9	43.1	38.7	36.4	34.3	31.6	27.4	24.8	24.1	25.7	25.0	26.5	28.1	28.3	26.5	26.2	28.4
Norway	32.8	26.5	24.5	23.0	21.8	21.0	19.2	19.2	18.6	18.9	18.3	17.5	17.9	18.5	16.8	16.8	16.8
Poland	194.0	164.8	177.0	168.0	164.7	163.1	–	141.3	137.8	130.4	136.2	140.6	142.8	143.4	144.2	131.6	116.0
Portugal	25.6	24.8	24.5	25.7	26.1	27.7	26.6	26.4	28.0	27.2	28.1	28.9	35.7	41.6	42.8	39.1	34.0
Romania	181.0	191.0	181.7	204.7	216.1	209.2	203.7	200.4	198.8	189.2	179.7	177.4	182.3	185.7	191.2	183.5	187.9
ex-Soviet Union	3900.0	3900.0	–	4280.0	4200.0	4502.8	4715.0	4655.9	4651.8	4656.3	4569.0	4583.3	4566.9	4497.3	4211.0	4080.0	–
Spain	–	320.0	–	435.2	403.1	393.1	376.6	364.6	330.9	295.3	295.2	278.3	262.9	255.8	249.0	211.0	220.0
Sweden	50.0	39.5	40.0	38.2	37.3	35.4	32.6	30.4	28.2	26.0	26.7	22.9	22.1	23.7	23.7	22.5	23.5
Switzerland	40.0	39.0	37.0	45.0	34.0	32.0	35.0	33.0	32.0	30.0	28.0	27.0	25.5	23.7	20.4	21.2	20.0
UK	395.0	357.2	342.8	326.6	288.8	264.8	237.3	214.9	193.0	176.0	156.6	134.2	138.5	116.3	103.9	103.5	126.1
ex-Yugoslavia	121.8	117.0	123.0	121.2	114.6	104.9	100.2	90.3	86.3	81.5	84.2	86.3	83.3	81.7	79.7	75.8	75.4

	1979	1980	1981	1982	1983	1984	1985	1986	1987	1988	1989	1990	1991	1992	1993
Albania	–	–	–	–	–	–	–	–	–	–	3.8	–	–	–	–
Austria	17.5	17.5	18.2	16.6	17.9	16.1	17.0	12.6	11.5	10.0	11.8	10.2	10.5	9.3	12.0
Belgium	19.8	21.6	20.1	20.5	21.3	19.0	17.9	17.7	15.7	15.2	15.0	16.2	16.9	16.6	18.3
Bulgaria	109.4	100.0	91.4	92.5	93.5	–	95.5	93.2	84.2	81.0	79.0	65.0	25.7	30.0	11.0
Czechoslovakia	82.5	82.3	81.0	78.6	–	–	76.7	76.6	73.8	73.8	70.6	65.0	40.6	43.0	31.0
Denmark	17.2	15.9	16.2	14.3	13.7	12.0	11.3	11.3	11.4	10.0	10.3	9.6	9.2	8.6	10.2
Finland	10.1	9.9	9.4	9.1	9.1	7.6	6.7	6.3	6.5	6.7	7.2	6.2	6.0	5.4	5.8
France	178.1	174.8	189.2	201.9	198.8	190.8	172.2	163.4	136.7	124.7	120.9	121.8	117.0	115.9	133.3
Germany (East)	–	79.5	–	72.4	–	73.4	70.0	70.2	69.2	69.3	64.0	30.0	13.0	11.2	–
Germany (West)	142.0	143.8	141.3	124.5	125.2	112.1	104.2	105.2	108.1	108.9	101.6	102.5	106.9	94.7	57.7
Greece	34.1	43.0	40.5	35.3	35.0	22.0	23.0	22.0	22.5	17.0	17.5	16.5	6.2	6.7	7.0
Hungary	69.0	60.7	67.1	70.0	68.9	71.0	70.2	68.0	55.9	50.7	45.8	36.2	22.3	15.6	15.2
Iceland	–	2.6	–	2.2	–	–	1.4	1.2	1.3	–	1.2	1.2	1.2	1.2	1.2
Ireland	–	9.5	–	11.4	12.7	14.0	11.6	11.0	5.2	6.0	7.0	7.4	8.1	8.2	9.3
Italy	276.3	241.9	215.2	195.4	162.0	131.6	123.1	124.8	112.5	93.0	95.2	90.5	88.6	83.6	92.2
Luxemburg	–	0.8	–	0.7	0.7	0.7	0.7	0.7	0.7	0.5	0.5	0.5	0.6	0.6	0.7
Netherlands	25.8	27.9	24.7	20.5	20.2	17.4	15.3	14.9	15.5	14.8	15.6	14.6	14.9	13.7	15.9
Norway	17.8	17.5	16.4	15.1	14.8	12.8	12.9	11.1	12.4	11.5	12.6	11.4	10.8	9.6	10.9
Poland	96.2	96.9	91.1	89.4	99.7	127.6	107.0	100.0	94.0	95.3	86.4	38.0	18.0	12.0	13.7
Portugal	32.6	30.8	28.8	26.0	22.9	21.0	19.0	18.4	16.9	13.0	13.8	11.0	11.8	12.0	12.7
Romania	185.7	193.6	198.3	143.7	209.4	217.0	191.5	204.7	208.3	–	170.0	130.0	76.0	41.0	30.0
ex-Soviet Union	–	4260.0	–	4220.0	–	–	4100.0	–	3775.0	3920.2	3640.0	3500.0	2000.0	1000.0	–
Spain	200.0	176.0	173.7	156.0	141.0	118.6	101.1	87.3	85.7	69.6	78.1	78.5	79.1	83.3	87.7
Sweden	25.1	24.9	23.2	21.3	19.0	17.1	17.9	16.4	17.4	17.5	19.2	15.3	15.1	15.7	16.0
Switzerland	21.3	20.9	20.4	20.1	19.7	17.9	16.4	16.3	16.2	14.9	15.2	14.3	15.4	15.0	15.9
UK	111.9	101.0	83.0	64.0	65.7	58.4	70.2	72.6	74.8	84.0	96.0	98.2	101.6	103.6	114.4
ex-Yugoslavia	–	80.0	76.5	80.0	85.0	87.0	81.0	80.8	78.1	70.8	65.0	58.0	25.7	20.9	–

APPENDIX II

Select Bibliography for European and French Cinema

BIBLIOGRAPHY

Europe

Roy Armes, *The Ambiguous Image: Narrative Style in Modern European Cinema* (London: Secker and Warburg, 1976).

Grzegorz Balski, *Directory of Eastern European Film-makers and Films, 1945–1991* (Trowbridge, Wilts: Flicks Books, 1992).

Peter Cowie, *International Film Guide* (now *Variety International Film Guide*) (London: Andre Deutsch, annual from 1964).

Peter Cowie, *Scandinavian Cinema: a survey of film and film-makers in Denmark, Finland, Iceland, Norway and Sweden* (London: Tantivy Press, 1992).

Richard Dyer and Ginette Vincendeau (eds.), *Popular European Cinema* (London and New York: Routledge, 1992).

The European Film in the World Market (Vienna: The Austrian Film Commission, 1988).

David W. Ellwood and Rob Kroes, *Hollywood in Europe, Expressions of a Cultural Hegemony* (Amsterdam: Amsterdam University Press, 1994).

Daniel J. Goulding (ed.), *Five Filmmakers: Tarkovsky, Forman, Polanski, Szabó, Makavejev* (Bloomington: Indiana University Press, 1994).

Daniel J. Goulding (ed.), *Post New Wave Cinema in the Soviet Union and Eastern Europe* (Bloomington: Indiana University Press, 1989).

Thomas H. Guback, *The International Film Industry: Western Europe and America since 1945* (Bloomington: Indiana University Press, 1969).

Thomas H. Guback, 'Cultural Identity and Film in the European Economic Community', in *Cinema Journal*, vol. 14, no. 1, 1974.

Nicholas Hewitt (ed.), *The Culture of Reconstruction. European Literature, Thought and Film, 1945–1950* (Basingstoke and London: Macmillan, 1989).

Andrew S. Horton and Joan Magretta (eds.), *Modern European Film-makers and the Art of Adaptation* (New York: Frederick Ungar, 1981).

Mira and Antonín J. Liehm, *The Most Important Art: East European Film After 1945* (Berkeley and London: University of California Press, 1977).

David W. Paul (ed.), *Politics, Art, and Commitment in the East European Cinema* (New York: St. Martin's Press, 1983).

Duncan Petrie (ed.), *Screening Europe: Image and Identity in Contemporary European Cinema* (London: BFI, 1992).

James Quinn, *The Film and Television as an Aspect of European Culture* (Leyden: A. W. Sijthoff, 1968).

Pierre Sorlin, *European Cinemas, European Societies 1939– 1990* (London and New York: Routledge, 1991).

France

Richard Abel, *The Ciné Goes to Town. French Cinema 1896–1914* (Berkeley, Los Angeles, London: University of California Press, 1994).

Richard Abel, *French Cinema: The First Wave, 1915–1929* (Princeton: Princeton University Press, 1984).

Dudley J. Andrew, *Mists of Regret, Culture and Sensibility in Classic French Film* (Princeton: Princeton University Press, 1995).

Roy Armes, *French Cinema* (London: Secker and Warburg, 1985).

Francoise Audé, *Ciné-modèles, Cinéma d'elles: situation des femmes dans le cinéma français 1956–1979* (Lausanne: L'Age d'Homme, 1981).

Mary Lea Bandy (ed.), *Rediscovering French Film* (New York: Museum of Modern Art, 1983).

André Bazin, *Le Cinéma français de la libération à la Nouvelle Vague (1945–1958)* (Paris: Cahiers du Cinéma, Editions de l'Etoile, 1983).

Stéphane Brisset, *Le Cinéma des années 80* (Paris: M.A. Editions, 1990).

Freddy Buache, *Le Cinéma français des années 60* (Paris: Hatier, 1987).

Freddy Buache, *Le Cinéma français des années 70* (Renens: 5 Continents/Hatier, 1990).

Raymond Chirat, *Le Cinéma français des années 30* (Renens: 5 Continents, Hatier, 1983).

Raymond Chirat, *Le Cinéma français des années de guerre* (Renens: 5 Continents, Hatier, 1983).

Raymond Chirat, *La IVe République et ses films* (Paris: Hatier, 1985).

Raymond Chirat and Olivier Barrot, *Les Excentriques du cinéma français (1929–1958)* (Paris: Henri Veyrier, 1983).

Francis Courtade, *Les Malédictions du cinéma français* (Paris: Alain Moreau, 1978).

Colin Crisp, *The Classic French Cinema, 1930–1960* (Bloomington and Indianapolis: Indiana University Press, 1993).

Jacques Deslandes and Jacques Richard, *Histoire comparée du cinéma, I: 1826–1896* (Paris: Casterman, 1966); *Histoire comparée du cinéma, II: 1896–1906* (Paris: Casterman, 1968).

Evelyn Ehrlich, *Cinema of Paradox, French Filmmaking Under the German Occupation* (New York, Columbia University Press, 1985).

Sandy Flitterman-Lewis, *To Desire Differently: Feminism and the French Cinema* (Urbana and Chicago: University of Illinois Press, 1990).

Jill Forbes, *The Cinema in France After the New Wave* (London: BFI/Macmillan, 1992).

Peter Graham (ed.), *The New Wave* (London: Secker and Warburg, 1968).

Susan Hayward, *French National Cinema* (London and New York: Routledge, 1993).

Susan Hayward and Ginette Vincendeau (eds.), *French Film, Texts and Contexts* (London and New York: Routledge, 1990).

Jean-Pierre Jeancolas, *Le Cinéma des Français – La Ve République, 1958–78* (Paris: Stock, 1979).
Jean-Pierre Jeancolas, *15 ans d'années trente, le cinéma des Français 1929–44* (Paris: Stock, 1983).
Jean Mitry, *Histoire du cinéma, art et industrie* [5 vols] (Paris: Editions Universitaires, 1967–80).
René Prédal, *Le Cinéma français depuis 1945* (Paris: Nathan, 1991).
Keith Reader and Ginette Vincendeau (eds), *La Vie est à nous! French Cinema of the Popular Front, 1935–38* (London: BFI, 1986).
Georges Sadoul, *French Film* (London: Falcon Press, 1953).
Jacques Siclier, *Le Cinéma français 1: de la Bataille du rail à La Chinoise 1945–1968* (Paris: Ramsay, 1990).
Jacques Siclier, *Le Cinéma français 2: de Baisers volés à Cyrano de Bergerac 1968–1990* (Paris: Ramsay, 1991).
Alan Thiher, *The Cinematic Muse: Critical Studies in the History of French Cinema* (Columbia and London: University of Missouri Press, 1979).
Alan Williams, *Republic of Images. A History of French Filmmaking* (Cambridge, Mass. and London: Harvard University Press, 1992).